The Gates of Janus

The Gates of Janus

Serial Killing and its Analysis,
by the 'Moors Murderer,'
Ian Brady

Foreword by Dr Alan Keightley
Introduction by Colin Wilson
Afterword by Peter Sotos

Feral
House

The Gates of Janus©2001 Ian Stewart-Brady and Feral House

ISBN: 0-922915-73-3

Feral House
P.O. Box 13067
Los Angeles, CA 90013

www.feralhouse.com

info@feralhouse.com

Design by Linda Hayashi

10 9 8 7 6 5 4 3 2 1

Author's Note

This book was originally intended to be published under a pseudonym, which explains the style adopted throughout to conceal my identity. Unfortunately, when I decided to publish under my own name, I was unable to revise or incorporate additional information in conditions of captivity where all items of interest are sold to the tabloids by officials. The book is not ghostwritten. The polemic is not designed to justify criminal conduct, but rather to exemplify its common legal and socially acceptable usage in respectable society.

Ian Brady
Ashworth Hospital
August, 2001

Publisher's Note

After Ian Brady agreed to publish this book under his own name, the text was slightly altered to make all third-person references to the 'Moors Murderer' in first person.

The Gates of Janus is not consonant with a time in which language is degraded, and meaning is less. Ian Brady's words seethe with menace, despair and possibility, a throwback to Schopenhauer and de Sade. And when he drifts into memory, Brady's power of description becomes quite powerful. The sights and smells of times past are no doubt far more real to Brady than the banal cesspool he sees today. His book is infused with a feeling of acute memory and acute loss — and apparently very little regret.

Then there are the paragraphs when Ian Brady, the chess player, becomes an Iago whispering comments and questions that gnaw away at the reader's most cherished presumptions. Loss of comfort and belief? Checkmate.

Before I ever saw this book, Peter Sotos informed me of a rumor regarding its existence. I wish to thank Peter for stimulating my interest in Ian Brady and publishing his book.

Without the kind assistance of Colin Wilson, this book would not have been published. Colin's insistence that Ian Brady possesses a human dimension far beyond the extremes promoted by the yellow press has become a welcome antidote to the depressing reductions of capitalist sensationalism. Benedict Birnberg, Ian Brady's solicitor, deserves appreciation for his concern and help.

And most of all, I wish to thank Ian Brady, for allowing us to print his remarkable book.

Adam Parfrey
Feral House
July, 2001

Contents

Foreword by Dr Alan Keightley

As soon as I received and began to read this manuscript I knew that I had a remarkable document in my hands.

The author, who did not reveal his name to me, and who I assumed to be a man, seemed to be offering a hunting manual for the tracking down of the serial killer by the use of psychological profiling and a study of his after-image at the scene of the murder. Doing this successfully would be an achievement in itself. I leave others at the knife-edge of forensic investigation to judge its efficacy in the pursuit of what the author calls the greatest and most dangerous game in existence: man.

Expert profilers have, of course, already produced studies of serial killers. FBI detective Robert Ressler wrote the substantial *Whoever Fights Monsters*. His associate at Quantico, John Douglas, produced *Mindhunters*. So, what's new here?

The Gates of Janus is a book written by a serial killer about other serial killers, or, as the author himself says, a dissection of what murder is really all about from the point of view of a murderer, for a change. Criminals have written books before — and classically, Dostoevsky and *The House of the Dead*, but the present study has a uniqueness of its own.

This leads me on to the second reason for its special character — the sheer quality and intelligence of the writing and its acute observation of human behaviour. The author investigates the psychology of the serial killer by discussing a number of notorious cases, which fleshes out the bare bones of his general conclusions about profiling. Again, it's true that lay authors have written high-grade books on murder. Joseph Wambaugh, Stephen Michaud and Ann Rule come to mind. They themselves were not killers, although Ann Rule knew Ted Bundy quite well according to her book, *The Stranger Beside Me*. But Bundy remained the *stranger* beside her. A murderer writing on murder possesses a perspective denied crime writers and detectives. As the author of *Gates of Janus* sees it — we are all beyond one another's experience, but, hauntingly, not so far beyond.

Most books, particularly in the true crime genre, are simply books about books. This one is an exception. It is mercifully free of footnotes — or, should we say, footprints? In his own field of disturbing expertise, the author speaks with great authority and originality.

The third reason for the uniqueness of this study is, for me, the most fascinating. Although I have read a great deal in the areas of true crime and criminal psychology, my own field is philosophy and religious studies. I am impressed by the philosophical and spiritual light it sheds on the dark corners of homicide and its occult dimensions. It's apparent that the author has spent a great deal of time reading and reflecting on the world he once knew prior to years monastically shuttered within a prison cell. The result reaches a rare level of philosophical maturity, a 'spiritual' perspective of existential relativism, questioning vital issues in psychology, philosophy and theology.

The author shrewdly observes that psychiatrists rarely stray into the field of philosophy. Psychology, like every other discipline, has hidden metaphysical assumptions regarding human identity and the nature of reality. The poverty of Western academia in the fields of psychology, philosophy and theology is highlighted by their failure to respond radically and passionately to the idea, the assumption, that life is meaningless. Academic philosophy is a nine-to-five job in which its professionals spend their lives repeating the assumption that life has no ultimate meaning.

Perhaps it requires the aptitude of a highly sensitive and perceptive serial killer to spell out the consequences of this belief. Dostoevsky, whose psychological perceptions are highly valued by the author of this book, observed that without God, everything is permitted.

Since the time of St. Augustine, theologians have addressed the problem of evil with an inherent naïvete. It's a naïvete which this book indirectly but mercilessly exposes to the point of mockery and even of pity. In this universe, everything comes in two's, everything. Wherever there is the light of consciousness there is a shadow. There is a dark force in this universe that will have its way.

Western ethical monotheism still speaks touchingly of the eventual advent of the kingdom of God, in which all things shall be well, either in this world or in the bright blue yonder. The writings of Carl Jung were an exception to this monotheism in its recognition of the shadow archetype. Oriental philosophy and religion also share a realism about this world's polarities. Humans think in categories and divide in thought what remains undivided by nature. Western culture, by and large, is a celebration of the illusion that light may exist without darkness, good without evil and pleasure without pain. This book will have none of it. It leaves the challenge on the table: is there really a great gulf between the instincts of a serial killer and the public at large? Wittgenstein said, 'Man can regard all the evil within himself as delusion.' But is there what Kierkegaard would call a 'fatal defect' in everybody? One hopes that the present study goads the philosopher, psychologist and theologian into talking turkey and addressing the real issues.

The author asks us to look through the lace curtain of the conventional world, to wake up from the ontological sleep and see the world in its terrifying grandeur. Most people live and dream enchanted by the social trance of mediocrity, blind to what the Zen teacher Sokei-an Sasaki called the 'shining trance.'

Imprisoned for years with psychopaths, psychotics and schizoids, the author has seen things the rest of us can scarcely dream of. Here we have human nature in all its fascinating devious guises. As Dostoevsky darkly observed, 'If the devil doesn't exist, that man has created him, he has surely created him in his own image and likeness.' In this book we are in a short time introduced to the extremes of behaviour, the psychospiritual quagmire: 'The horrors of hell can be experienced within a single day; that's plenty of time' (Wittgenstein). We are offered observations from personal acquaintance of the likes of the poisoner Graham Young and the ripper Peter Sutcliffe. All of this is done with verve, wit and arresting imagery in a manuscript studded with literary, philosophical and religious allusions.

The author surveys the scene in which he once participated. He laconically admits that he is genuinely glad his life is as good as over already, that he is a ghost on the human stage. He feels no sense of betrayed fellowship or breach of loyalty in giving the game away. The murderer knows the dangers anyway. Perhaps it will require another serial killer to recognize the paradoxical wisdom of these pages, as written by an authority situated in the shadows.

Dr Alan Keightley
King Edward VI College
Stourbridge
West Midlands
England

Publisher's note: Dr Keightley wrote the Foreword when Ian Brady wanted to publish *The Gates of Janus* under the pseudonym, François Villon.

Introduction
The Moors Murders by Colin Wilson

One Saturday morning, soon after Easter 1990, my wife Joy told me that we had had a visitor after I had gone to bed the previous evening. A young lady had knocked at the door asking to see me. She claimed to be a friend of the Moors Murderer Ian Brady, and wanted to ask my advice about a book she intended to write. To prove that she knew Brady, she had left behind one of his letters. It was written in a neat, very readable handwriting, and signed 'Ian' — it certainly looked genuine. Moreover, Brady talked about 'outsiders,' and it was obvious that he knew my work.

Her name was Christine Hart, and she told Joy that she and Brady had concocted a hoax suggesting that she was his illegitimate daughter. This rang a bell. I had been going through my press cuttings the day before, and had seen a popular tabloid with a headline: AM I IAN BRADY'S DAUGHTER? I showed my wife the picture of a pretty blonde girl on the front page.

'Yes, that's her.'

The girl was apparently staying at a local hotel, and I rang and arranged to meet her. After explaining why she wanted to write a book, she moved to our house for the rest of the weekend.

She had spent the first six years of her life in a Manchester orphanage, then been fostered by a couple from London. But they had found her so difficult that they had returned her to the orphanage when she was ten. And life ever since then had been miserable and insecure.

That was why she decided to write to Ian Brady. Brady, one of the most notorious murderers in jail in Britain, had been committing his crimes in Manchester at about the time Christine was born. She fantasised that he might be her father. So she wrote to him; he replied, and she went to visit him in jail. A journalist got wind of the story that he was being visited by an attractive blonde, and came to interview her. And as a joke, she told him that she believed she was Brady's daughter. Hence the tabloid story, for which she was well paid.

Now she wanted to write an autobiography in which he would feature largely — she was shrewd enough to realise that if his name sold newspapers it would also help sell her book — and she proposed quoting some of his letters. That was what she wanted to ask my advice about.

I told her that Brady's letters remained his copyright, and that she could only quote them with his permission. But this, she explained, was unlikely, for he had recently decided that she was trying to exploit him, and they were now no longer on the best of terms.

In due course, she sent me some of her book, and I was impressed — she was a born writer. I encouraged her, and she found herself an agent who believed he might sell the book for a huge advance, and for months she dreamed of overnight celebrity. Unfortunately, this failed to materialise, and the book was finally accepted by a small publisher for a miniscule advance. I wrote an Introduction. And in 1993, *The Devil's Daughter* appeared, and after a minor flurry of publicity, was soon remaindered. The publisher had given it this title to perpetuate the myth that Ian Brady was her father, and I regarded the whole business as exploitative and dishonest.

By that time I had already been corresponding with Ian Brady for more than a year. He had written to me in November 1991, asking me if it was true that Christine intended to write a book about him quoting his letters. I wrote back explaining just what was happening, and that I had told her she was not allowed to use his letters.

We have been corresponding ever since. By this time, I alone have written enough letters to fill twenty-seven disks of files — about the length of a 500-page book, and Ian has probably written about the same.

The Moors case had always interested me. Brady was the first British example of a type I had noted several years earlier: what I called 'the self-esteem killer.' The American psychologist Abraham Maslow, about whom I was later to write a book, had made me aware that the psychological evolution of human beings tends to follow a definite pattern, like a flight of steps. If you are poor and starving, the only thing you care about is food, and you imagine that if you could just have one square meal a day, you would be ideally happy. But if you achieve this — let us say, by moving into a hostel — the next step is to want your own home — every tramp dreams of a country cottage with roses round the door. And if you achieve this, the next stage is the desire for sexual fulfillment — not just sex, but to be loved and wanted. And if you achieve this, then the next step emerges — the self-esteem level. You want the liking and respect of your fellow men. (This is the stage when men join rotary clubs and women give coffee mornings.) And, according to Maslow, if you have achieved all these things, there is a fifth possible stage, which he calls self-actualisation. This basically means some kind of creative fulfillment, although not necessarily writing poetry or symphonies. It is just doing something you are good at for the sheer fun of it — and it might be as simple as putting ships in bottles.

I had noted that, historically speaking, crime follows the same stages. In the late 18th and early 19th centuries, when most people were poor, crime tended to be motivated simply by the need to stay alive — highway robbery, burglary and so on. Then came the Victorian phase of domestic murder, where the motivation was home and security.

Towards the end of the 19th-century, a new type of crime emerged — sex crime. In the previous century, sex was so easy to obtain, with working girls selling themselves for the price of a glass of gin, that rape would have been absurd. But 19th century respectability made sex morbidly desirable. The murders of Jack the Ripper are the most notorious sex crimes of the period, and it is significant that most people did not even recognise them as sex crimes; the most popular theory was that he was a religious maniac who hated prostitutes.

In the late 1950s, a jazz musician named Melvin Rees committed a number of sex murders in Maryland, including a family of four, whom he forced off the road with his car. He killed the husband and baby, then took the mother and five-year-old girl to a remote location where they were murdered and raped. Rees was finally arrested in Arkansas and sentenced to death. But he had told a friend: 'You can't say it's wrong to kill — only individual standards make it right or wrong' — an argument also advanced by the Marquis de Sade.

It struck me immediately that these were, to some extent, crimes of intellectual rebellion, and therefore could not be classified simply as sex crimes. He was justifying his sex crimes with his intellect, and felt, like Sade, that he had seen through the sham of morality. He saw himself as being above normal morality, and in that sense, could be classified as a self-esteem killer.

This was even more clear in the case of eighteen-year-old Robert Smith, who went into a hairdressing parlour in Arizona, made three women and a child lie on the floor, then shot them all in the back of the head. Asked why he did it, he replied: 'I wanted to get known — to get myself a name.'

During the Moors trial, extracts were read aloud in court from the journals of Brady's friend and disciple David Smith. 'Murder is a hobby and a supreme pleasure,' 'People are like maggots, small, blind, worthless fish bait,' 'God is a disease, a plague, a weight around man's neck,' And when Smith admitted he had absorbed these views from Brady, it was clear once again that the Moors Murders could not be classified simply as sex crimes; they involved Maslow's fourth level, self-esteem.

The Moors Murders always seemed a typical case of *'folie à deux,'* yet there were certain anomalies. I entered into correspondence with Ian Brady hoping to solve some of these riddles, such as why a quiet, normal girl who loved animals and children should take part in child-murder; from this point of view, it proved as intriguing and rewarding as I had hoped.

Even a bare outline of the case is electrifying. A girl of eighteen takes a job in an office in Manchester, and becomes wildly infatuated with a tall, good-looking Scottish clerk in his early twenties, who at first ignores her. Eventually they become lovers, and she is not too shocked to learn that he has been in prison, nor alarmed when he proposes that they embark on a criminal career, robbing banks and building societies. In fact, this Bonnie and Clyde collaboration never comes about; instead, they decide on a more sinister agenda — killing children; she lures them into the car, and later helps in the disposal of the violated bodies on Saddleworth Moor.

It was this young girl's involvement in child murder that so shocked the British public, and led to a morbid fascination with the case that is still as strong after forty years. As I write this, in May 2001, the chain-smoking Myra Hindley is known to be in poor health, possibly with only a matter of months to live, and there is still a furious public outcry every time a newspaper even hints that the Home Secretary may be thinking of granting her parole. For some odd reason, she is hated even more than Brady, who was, after all, the instigator of the murders.

Who is Ian Brady? He was born Ian Duncan Stewart on January 2, 1938 in Glasgow. His mother, Margaret Stewart, was a twenty-eight-year-old waitress in a hotel tea room; his father was a journalist, who died three months before Ian's birth.

Margaret Stewart did her best to support the child, farming him out to babysitters when she had to work in the evening, but finally advertised for a full-time 'childminder.' Mary and John Sloan took him into 'their warm and friendly home' (to quote Jean Ritchie's book on Myra Hindley), where his mother, who now called herself Peggy, came to visit him every Sunday, bringing him clothes and presents. So it hardly seems that Ian Brady can be regarded as someone who was subjected to childhood neglect and brutality.

Jean Ritchie has one highly significant story to tell: how, at the age of nine, he was taken on a picnic to the shores of Loch Lomond.

'For Ian it was a day of discovery. He discovered in himself a deep affinity with the wild, rugged and empty scenery around the lake. He was moved by the grandeur of the hills, awed by the vastness of the sky. When it was time to go home, the family found him halfway up one of the hills, standing still absorbing something — who knows what? — from the strange, open, inspiring scenery around him. It was an unusual Ian who came down the hill, one who babbled happily about his day out to his foster sisters . . .'

This story, which epitomises the Ian Brady I have come to know, sounds as if it was told to Jean Ritchie by the Sloan family, and it is supported by other comments from those who knew him: for example, Lord Longford, who visited him in prison. The latter is also on record as saying that Brady knew his Tolstoy and Dostoevsky better than anyone he had met.

What most writers on the case seem agreed upon is that Brady was — as Jean Ritchie puts it — 'a loner, an outsider.' He was also a highly dominant child at school, a born leader, who seems to have embarked on burglary at an early age (nine has been quoted) — not, as in the case of Panzram, out of envy of contemporaries from wealthier backgrounds, but simply out of devilment. He tells me that on his first burglary — the house of a naval man — he did not take anything, but simply looked around.

When he was ten, the family were moved from the Gorbals to a new council estate at Pollock, with 'indoor bathroom and lavatory, a garden and nearby fields.' At the age of eleven he started attending Shawlands Academy, a school for above-average pupils, but seems to have taken a certain pleasure in misbehaving, perhaps in reaction against richer schoolmates. But he received high marks for his English essays, and was a natural leader.

At the age of thirteen he came before a juvenile court for burglary, but was bound over; nine months later, he was again bound over for the same thing. He left school at sixteen, and worked as a butcher's boy, and then as a tea boy in a Glasgow shipyard. He tells me that it was the feeling of frustration, of being in a dead-end job, that made him feel that he needed to start accumulating 'working capital.'

In that same year he appeared again before a Glasgow court with nine charges against him. This time he was put on probation on condition that he joined his mother in Manchester. Margaret Stewart had moved there when her son was twelve, and had married a meat porter named Patrick Brady, whose name Ian was to take.

His stepfather found him a job in the fruit market. He was still a loner, spending hours in his room reading — including Dostoevsky's *Crime and Punishment* and *The Possessed*. But in November 1955, he was again in court, this time on a charge of aiding and abetting. A driver asked him to load some stolen lead on to his lorry. On being caught, the scrap dealer gave the driver away to the police, and he in turn implicated Brady. In court, Brady pleaded guilty, expecting a fine for such a trivial offense — after all, everybody in the market was 'on the fiddle.' But because he was on probation, the judge decided that severity was called for. To his bewilderment — and rage — Brady was remanded to Strangeways jail to await his sentence. Here, I suspect, was the beginning of that resentment that led to the Moors Murders.

In jail he spent three months among professional criminals, and deliberately cultivated fences, cracksmen, even killers. He had made up his mind that society was going to get what it deserved. This reaction is typical of the high-dominance male faced with what he considers outrageous injustice. The two-year Borstal sentence that followed only confirmed the decision — particularly when, in an open Borstal at Hatfield, he found himself in further trouble. He had been selling home-distilled liquor and running a book on horses and dogs. One day, after getting drunk and having a fight with a warder, he was transferred to an altogether tougher Borstal housed in Hull prison. This, says Jean Ritchie, 'was where he prepared himself to become a big-time criminal.' The aim was to become wealthy as quickly as possible, so he could enjoy the freedom he dreamed about. This was why he studied bookkeeping in prison — to learn to handle money.

Three months in Strangeways and two years in Borstal had turned a youth with a minor criminal record and a tendency to bookishness into an anti-social rebel. Even taking into account the fact that he had been on probation, the ineptitude of the law seems incredible.

He was released at the end of two years, but remained on probation for another three. When he was released, he returned home to Manchester, under the terms of the probation. Fred Harrison, the journalist who interviewed Brady in prison, and who wrote a book on the case (*Brady and Hindley, The Genesis of the Moors Murders*, 1986) has an interesting passage that makes it clear that Brady soon became actively involved in crime. He speaks of a Borstal friend named Deare, who delivered a stolen Jaguar to Manchester — not to Brady but to another man. The car was to be used in a 'job.' The other man, says Harrison, made the mistake of not getting rid of the Jaguar after the 'job,' and was arrested. He gave Deare's name to the police. Deare subsequently vanished, and Harrison suggests that Brady might have killed him. But Brady pointed out to me that Gilbert Deare was still around at the time of Brady's arrest for the Moors Murders, and died some time later in a drowning accident. On this matter, Harrison is inaccurate. But he is correct in saying that Brady was involved in crimes that required a getaway car soon after he returned to Manchester, and that he had at least two accomplices. What is also clear is that Brady spent a great deal of time 'casing' banks and building societies, watching the transportation of money.

Apart from one brush with the law for being drunk and disorderly, Brady managed to stay out of trouble. His probation officer obliged him to take a labouring job in a brewery, which he understandably detested. In 1959, at the age of twenty-one, he succeeded in changing this for something less disagreeable; the bookkeeping training led to a job as a stock clerk with Millwards Ltd, a small chemical firm. He was a careful and neat worker, although inclined to be unpunctual, and to slip out of the office to place bets with a local bookmaker.

But he remained a loner, spending the lunch hour alone in the office, reading books, including *Mein Kampf* and other volumes on Nazism. By the time Myra Hindley came to work at Millwards, Brady was a fervent admirer of Hitler and Nazism.

There was another element in Brady that Fred Harrison was the first to point out: a curious black romanticism associated with death. Harrison describes how Brady became an atheist at the age of twelve, when he prayed that his pet dog would not die, and his prayers remained unanswered. Two years later, cycling to a job interview, he felt giddy and halted in the doorway of a newsagent's shop. There he saw 'a green, warm radiation, not unattractive to the young man who tried to steady himself. The features were unformed but still recognisable. Ian knew that he was looking at The Face of Death . . . he instantly knew that his salvation was irrevocably bound to its demands. "I'll do it a favour, and . . . it will do me favours." The bond with death was fused by the green radiation.'

On the day Myra Hindley came to work at Millwards as a shorthand typist — Monday, January 16, 1961 — Ian Brady dictated her first letter. She was four and a half years his junior, a completely normal working-class girl, not bad looking, with a blonde hair-do and bright lipstick, interested in boys and dancing. She had been born (January 23, 1942) a Catholic, brought up a Protestant, and returned to Catholicism when she was sixteen. When she was four, the birth of a sister made the home too cramped, and she went to live with her grandmother nearby. This was not particularly traumatic since she could spend as much time as she liked at her home around the corner. In fact, since her father was a heavy drinker and inclined to violence when drunk, she preferred her grandmother's house.

At school she received good marks and wrote poetry and excellent English essays. She played the mouth organ and was known as a high-spirited tomboy.

Myra had been engaged but had broken it off, finding the boy 'immaturé.' This was one of the problems for working-class girls at that time, whose notions of male attractiveness were formed by cinema and television — hard-bitten heroes with strong jaws, or charismatic rebels like James Dean and Elvis Presley. By contrast, the youths they met at dance halls seemed commonplace and boring.

Ian Brady was certainly not that. He had slightly sulky good looks reminiscent of Elvis Presley, and a dry and forceful manner. His self-possession was intriguing. So was his total lack of interest in her. Myra's infatuation blossomed, and she confided it to her red diary. 'Ian looked at me today.' 'Wonder if Ian is courting. Still feel the same.' 'Haven't spoken to him yet.' Then: 'Spoken to him. He smiles as though embarrassed.' On August 1: 'Ian's taking sly looks at me at work.' But by November: 'I've given up with Ian. He goes out of his way to annoy me . . .'

Just before Christmas 1961, there was an office party; he got drunk and danced with her, then walked her home and kissed her goodnight, saying 'I've been wanting to do this for a long time'. Myra felt she was in heaven. On December 22, she told her diary: 'Out with Ian!' They went to see the film *King of Kings*, the life story of Jesus. Just over a week later, on the divan bed in her gran's front room, Ian Brady and Myra Hindley became lovers. 'I hope Ian and I love each other all our lives and get married and are happy ever after.'

Many books on the Moors Murder case imply that Brady's attitude towards her was cold and manipulative. In fact, it seems to have been exceptionally close. Myra was over-awed and fascinated by her lover. She declared later: 'Within months he had convinced me there was no God at all: he could have told me the earth was flat, the moon was made of green cheese and the sun rose in the West, I would have believed him.' Ian told me that the relationship was so close that they were virtually telepathic.

They spent every Saturday night together, went on visits to the moors on Ian's second-hand motor bike, taking bottles of German wine, read the same books, and went to see films like *Compulsion*, based on the Leopold and Loeb murder case.

Within a fairly short time, Myra had been indoctrinated. She had become an atheist, and accepted what he called 'moral relativism,' the notion that right and wrong are creations of the human mind. She was soon as enthusiastic as he was about the Nazis. From then on, it was only a short step to accepting the ideas of the Marquis de Sade, whose basic notion is that physical pleasure is the only real value, and that all the rest of our moral values have been concocted by the ruling classes to keep the poor in their place.

According to de Sade, nature knows nothing about morality or good and evil; it inflicts pain or pleasure, happiness or misery, ecstasy or death, with utter indifference. Therefore there is no reason why the individual should not follow its example, and do whatever brings pleasure without regard to its effect on other people. In Sade's novels, pity and compassion are regarded as a form of feeble-mindedness.

It follows logically that there is no such thing as crime. Since we owe nothing to other people — in this world it is every man for himself — there is no moral reason why, if crime pays better than honesty, we should not live by crime. Which is why Brady had soon persuaded Myra Hindley that it would be sensible to make a large sum of money from crime, and then retire to somewhere with a better climate than rain-sodden Manchester.

Brady's influence on Myra's personality and outlook was immense. Her sister Maureen would later describe in court how Myra had changed completely, from being a normal girl and a regular churchgoer who loved children and animals, to someone who claimed she hated human beings, including babies and children. Maureen noted that her sister also became hostile and suspicious, keeping all her belongings — books, tape recordings and clothes — under lock and key.

There may have been another reason for this: Myra did not want anyone prying into evidence that would reveal just how much she had changed. For example, she and Brady had taken up photography, and bought a time-lapse camera so they could take 'pornographic pictures' to sell. Jean Ritchie points out that eighteen months earlier, Myra had been so prudish that she would not even allow her sister to see her undressed. Now she posed for the camera wearing black crotchless panties, and engaged in sexual intercourse. Other photographs show her tied up with whip lashes on her flesh. So her secretiveness is understandable.

What had happened to her is obvious. She had not merely fallen in love; she had experienced something like religious conversion. Brady became her whole life. She must have felt that she had been asleep before she met him, and was now finally awake. She was seeing everything with new eyes.

Given this neo-Sadeian outlook (which Brady claims he held long before reading Sade), it is easy to see that it is only one small step from planning bank robberies to murder. If what is called crime is justifiable, because the individual has the right to do whatever suits him best, without taking other people into account, then the same certainly applies to sex.

Philosophically speaking, this step is the most dangerous of all. It is natural for dominant individuals to enjoy sex, and both Ian Brady and Myra Hindley were dominant. But because nature has designed them as child-bearers, even dominant women tend to look for 'Mr Right.' Every dominant male, on the other hand, wishes he had a slave of the lamp who would use magic to enable him to have sex with every pretty girl he passed in the street. This is why the dominant male finds it difficult to engage in binding relationships.

I suspect that, even so, Brady found Myra's devotion and subservience intoxicating, and that he suddenly felt like a starving man who has been invited to a ten-course banquet. There is nothing like an adoring and uncritical girl to fill you with self-confidence. It seemed that life had ceased to treat him as an outcast, and was inviting him to help himself.

Most males, under these circumstances, would decide on sex as a priority. And since his relationship with Myra was one of total dominance, he would certainly not meet any resistance there.

The first 'Moors Murder,' that of Pauline Reade, happened on July 12, 1963, a month after Brady had moved in with Myra at her grandmother's house in Bannock Street, Gorton. The only account we have of the murder is from the confession Myra Hindley made to Detective Chief Superintendent Peter Topping in January 1987, when she finally decided to admit her guilt. According to Myra, she picked up Pauline Reade — who was sixteen, and a friend of her sister Maureen — in a newly purchased mini-van. Pauline was on her way to a dance, but agreed to go and look for an expensive glove which Myra claimed she had lost at a picnic on Saddleworth Moor — Myra offered her a pile of gramophone records in exchange. When they had been on the moor about an hour, Brady arrived on his motorbike, and was introduced as Myra's boyfriend. Brady and Pauline then went off to look for the glove, while, Myra claims, she waited in the car. Later, Brady returned to the car, and took her to Pauline's body. Her throat had been cut and her clothes were in disarray, indicating rape. They then buried the body with the spade that Myra had brought in the back of the van.

In an open letter to the newspapers in 1990, Brady claimed that Myra had been involved in the actual killing, and had also made some kind of sexual assault on Pauline Reade. He says that Myra took the necklace off Pauline, saying: 'Where you're going, you won't need this.' On the whole, his version sounds the more plausible. Myra's accounts of the murders invariably have her elsewhere at the time, and Topping indicates that Myra told the truth only insofar as it suited her.

Although I initially accepted Myra's account when I first read Topping's book, I have since come to feel that it is simply implausible. It seems to me far more likely that Myra had absorbed the Brady/de Sade philosophy to the point where she actively participated in the murders and sexual assaults.

But I can accept one comment that Myra made for the benefit of a television documentary: that Brady complained that Pauline Reade had been too hard to subdue, and that in the future he would prefer children.

In October 1963, three months after the murder of Pauline Reade, Ian Brady made the acquaintance of sixteen-year-old David Smith, the husband of

Myra's sister Maureen (who was now also working at Millwards). Smith was a big youth who had been a member of a street gang and had been in trouble with the law. Soon David and Maureen took a trip to Lake District with Ian and Myra, where they sailed on Windermere. While not homosexual, Smith experienced an emotional attraction to males; soon he was almost as completely under Brady's spell as Myra.

On Saturday, November 23, 1963, Ian Brady and Myra Hindley drove to the small market town of Ashton-under-Lyne. A twelve-year-old boy named John Kilbride had spent Saturday afternoon at the cinema, then went to earn a few pence doing odd jobs for stallholders at the market. It began to get dark and a fog came down from the Pennines. At that moment, a friendly lady approached him and asked if he wanted a lift. It seemed safe enough, so he climbed in. It was the last time he was seen alive. Later, Brady was to take a photograph of Myra kneeling on his grave on the moor.

On June 16, 1964, twelve-year-old Keith Bennett set out to spend the night at his grandmother's house in the Longsight district. When his mother called to collect him the following morning, she learned that he had failed to arrive. Like John Kilbride, Keith Bennett had accepted a lift from a kind lady. His body has never been found.

Meanwhile, David Smith's admiration for his mentor was steadily increasing. Brady took him up to Saddleworth Moor and they engaged in pistol practice — Myra had obtained a gun license by the expedient of joining the Cheadle Rifle Club. Myra was not entirely happy about this intimacy; her attitude to Smith had an undertone of hostility; in fact, both of them were getting sick of the Smiths. She was glad when her gran was rehoused in Wardle Brook Avenue, in the suburb of Hattersley, in September 1964, when she and Ian were able to move into the little house at the end of a terrace. Nevertheless, Ian continued to consolidate his influence over David. If he was going to rob banks, a partner would be needed. Soon David Smith was recording in a notebook sentences like the ones quoted at the trial: 'Rape is not a crime, it is a state of mind. God is a disease which eats away a man's instincts, murder is a hobby and a supreme pleasure.' Soon he and Brady were 'casing' banks and drawing up elaborate plans.

One day Brady asked him: 'Is there anyone you hate and want out of the way?'

Smith mentioned several names, including an old rival named Tony Latham. After some discussion, they settled on Tony Latham as the murder victim. But first, Brady explained, he would need a photograph. This was no problem. Smith had a Polaroid camera, and he knew the pub where Latham drank. The next evening, Ian and Myra drove him to the pub, then drove away. Unfortunately, Smith had forgotten to insert the film, and when he went into the toilet to develop the photograph, found the camera empty.

When he went out to Wardle Brook Avenue to confess his failure, Brady seemed to take it casually enough. In reality he did not believe Smith was telling the truth, and was alarmed. Now, suddenly, David Smith was a potential risk. If he had participated in the murder of Tony Latham, he would have been bound to Ian and Myra. Now Brady began to think seriously about removing him. Oddly enough, it was Myra who dissuaded him. 'It would hurt Mo' (Maureen).

On December 26, 1964, there was another murder. Like the others, this was planned in advance. Myra had arranged for her grandmother to stay the night with an uncle at Dukinfield. At about six o'clock that evening, she picked up ten-year-old Lesley Ann Downey at a fair in Hulme Hall Lane. In Myra's version of what happened to Topping, they took Lesley back to the house in Wardle Brook Avenue, and switched on a tape recorder. Myra claims that she was in the kitchen when she heard the child screaming. Brady was squeezng her neck and ordering her to take off her coat. Lesley was then made to undress, and to assume various 'pornographic' poses, while Brady photographed her. On the tape, Myra can be heard ordering her to 'put it in, put it in tighter,' presumably referring to the gag that appears in the photographs. Lesley screams and asks to be allowed to go home. At this point, Myra claims she was ordered to go and run a bath; she stayed in the bathroom until the water became cold. When she returned, Lesley had been strangled, and there was blood on her thighs. The following day they took the body to the moors and buried it.

In his open letter to the press, Brady declares that Myra 'insisted upon killing Lesley Ann Downey with her own hands, using a two foot length of silk cord, which she later used to enjoy toying with in public, in the secret knowledge of what it had been used for.'

Brady had killed approximately once every six months since July 1963: Pauline Reade, John Kilbride, Keith Bennett, Lesley Ann Downey. For some reason, July 1965 went by without a further murder. The reason may be found in something Brady said to Fred Harrison, in a prison interview: 'I felt old at twenty-six. Everything was ashes. I felt there was nothing of interest — nothing to hook myself onto. I had experienced everything.'

Harrison tells how Brady suggested to David Smith one evening that they should play Russian roulette. He removed all the bullets from the revolver, then replaced one, and spun the chambers. Then he fired at Smith. There was just a click. Brady laughed. 'There would have been an awful mess behind you if the bullet had hit you.'

But if the bullet hit Smith, Brady would have been arrested on a manslaughter charge. The fact that he took such a risk reveals his self-control was being eroded.

Then, in September 1965, Brady decided to kill out of sequence. The aim seems to have been to cement David Smith's membership with the 'gang.' According to Smith, during a drinking session on September 25, Brady asked him: 'Have you ever killed anybody? I have — three or four. The bodies are buried up on the moors.'

Two weeks later, on October 6, Smith turned up at Wardle Brook Avenue hoping to borrow some money, but they were all broke. Brady had already suggested that they should rob an Electricity Board showroom, and the robbery had been planned for two days later. Smith's urgent need for money to pay the rent suggested that now was the time to 'cement' him beyond all possibility of withdrawal.

Towards midnight, Myra called at her sister's flat with a message for their mother, then asked David Smith to walk her home. As he stood waiting in the kitchen — expecting to be offered a drink — there was a scream from the sitting room, and Myra called, 'Dave, help him!' As Smith ran in, Ian Brady was hacking at the head of a youth who was lying on the floor. In spite of blow after blow, the youth continued to twist and scream. Finally, when he lay still, Brady pressed a cushion over his face and tied a cord around the throat to stop the gurgling noises. Brady handed Smith the hatchet. 'Feel the weight of that.' Smith's fingers left bloodstained prints on the handle.

Gran called down to ask what the noise was about, and Myra shouted that she had dropped a tape recorder on her foot.

When the room had been cleaned up, the body was carried upstairs between them. Brady commented: 'Eddie's a dead weight,' and he and Myra laughed. The victim was seventeen-year-old Edward Evans, a homosexual who had been picked up in a pub that evening.

They all drank tea while Myra reminisced about a policeman who had stopped to talk to her while Brady was burying a body. Smith agreed to return with an old pram the next day, and help in the disposal of Edward Evans.

When he arrived home Smith was violently sick. And when he told Maureen what happened, it was she who decided to go the the police.

At eight o'clock the next morning, a man dressed as a baker's roundsman knocked on the door of 16 Wardle Brook Avenue. Myra answered the door, still rubbing the sleep out of her eyes. The man identified himself as a police officer, and said he had reason to believe there was a body in the house. Brady was on the divan bed in the living room in his undervest, writing a note to explain why he was not going to work that day. Upstairs, the police demanded to see into a locked room. When Myra said the key was at work, a policeman offered to go and fetch it. At this, Brady said: 'You'd better tell him. There was a row here last night. It's in there.' Under the window in the bedroom there was a plastic-wrapped bundle.

In a letter to me, Ian described how, when the police came in, and told him to dress, he had cautiously felt under the settee, where he kept the loaded gun — he had made up his mind to shoot the policemen, then himself. But it was not there. Then he remembered: the previous evening, as they had been carrying the body upstairs, the revolver in its shoulder holster had been banging against his ribs, and he had taken it out and left it upstairs.

Myra was not arrested at the same time as Brady. The police probably accepted that Evans had been killed in the course of a quarrel, and Brady's bad limp — due to a kick on the shin from Evans — seemed to support this. So for the next five days, Myra remained free, going to see Brady every day.

But David Smith told the police that Brady had stored two suitcases in the left luggage at Manchester Central Station, and these were recovered. (The cloakroom ticket was later found where Brady had described it — in the spine of a prayer book.) These proved to contain pornographic photographs — including nine of Lesley Ann Downey — photographs of Ian and Myra on the moors, the tape of Lesley Ann pleading to be allowed to leave, various books on sex and torture, and wigs, coshes and notes on robbing banks. The police decided to dig on the moors, using the photographs as a guide, and the bodies of Lesley Ann Downey and John Kilbride were recovered.

On May 6, 1966, Ian Brady and Myra Hindley were both sentenced to life imprisonment. (Only the abolition of the death penalty a month after their arrest saved them from the hangman.) There had been no confession — at the trial, Brady maintained that Lesley had been brought to the house by two men, who had taken her away after taking the photographs.

Myra was sent to Holloway, Brady to Durham, where he opted for solitary confinement, and studied German. He and Myra wrote constantly, and he began a campaign to try to secure her visiting rights, insisting that they were, in effect, man and wife. When this came to nothing he went on hunger strike. But although Myra had his photograph on her cell wall, she was embarking on a lesbian affair with a teenager called Rita; it was the first of many. She was gradually drawing apart from Ian, who was irritated to learn that she was in the process of returning to Catholicism — here the Catholic peer Lord Longford seems to have been instrumental.

Fred Harrison has an interesting anecdote. In 1967, a child killer named Raymond Morris was sent to Durham; he had murdered and raped three little girls, aged five, six and seven. Brady loathed him; on one occasion he threw boiling tea in his face — for which he received twenty-eight days confined to his cell — and subsequently punched him in the face as he was walking upstairs, knocking him down again. Brady told Harrison: 'Years later . . . I realised that, in a way, I was attacking myself. I could see myself in the Cannock Chase killer.' He was, in other words, beginning to feel remorse about killing children. And when Mrs Ann West, the mother of Lesley Ann Downey, tried to get permission to see him in prison in 1986, but was refused because of his 'mental condition', Brady told a correspondent: 'Re: letters from Mrs West and the mother of Keith Bennett.° Although I have been given them I have not been able to bring myself to read them. I have been afraid to read them. Understand? I have to keep mental blocks tightly shut and keep control. The authorities have refused Mrs West's requests to visit me . . . I can't say how it would have worked out if the meeting had taken place. Remorse for my part in this and other matters is axiomatic, painfully deep.'

Brady knew from the beginning that he would never be released from jail. Myra, on the other hand, felt there was a good chance of parole, and in the 1970s, newspapers began carrying reports that she now claimed that Brady was totally responsible for the murders and she was innocent. It was that point that Brady began to hate her.

In 1973, a singer named Janie Jones was sentenced to seven years for controlling prostitutes and sent to Holloway. She heard that the Moors Murderess admired her, but refused to be introduced, because she was revolted by the case. But when they finally met, she felt sorry for Myra, who looked like a bag of bones. Far from being hard-faced and brutal, as she looked in the trial photographs, she struck Janie Jones as shy and rather pathetic. Myra told her about the murders, and insisted that she had never been involved. She had helped pick up the children, but had no idea that Brady had killed them.

Janie Jones was completely taken in, and sympathy for Myra turned to pity when she saw her being attacked by a fellow prisoner. Myra stayed passive as a boot smashed her nose, and blood spurted on the floor. Janie finally intervened to prevent Myra from being thrown over the top floor balcony railing to certain death.

Janie Jones soon became convinced that Myra was suffering a great injustice, and when she was released in 1977, she joined Lord Longford in campaigning for her release.

° Whose body has never been found. His mother wrote to Brady asking for help recovering Keith's remains.

In 1979, Myra wrote a 20,000-word document for the Home Secretary, begging for release. This completed the alienation between the former lovers, for Myra insisted that Brady alone was guilty of the murders, and that she was merely his dupe. And Ian, who had made every effort at the trial to establish Myra's innocence, now took every opportunity to state that she was as guilty as he was.

In November 1986, a policeman who had been born in her area, Gorton, went to see her in Cookham Wood prison, where Myra had been transferred in 1983. Detective Chief Superintendent Peter Topping wanted her help in finding the two unrecovered bodies: Keith Bennett and Pauline Reade. Myra, undoubtedly seeing this as a step towards parole, promised to help. Besides, Brady was showing signs of mental stress, and his weight had dropped to a hundred pounds. That was why, in 1985, he was moved to the Park Lane Hospital, a mental institution (later Ashworth Hospital) in Liverpool. In that state, he might well confess to the murders, and implicate Myra. She considered that her best defense against this was to make the first move. She agreed to help in the search for missing bodies.

The search began on December 16, 1986, a freezing day, and snow was falling by lunch time. Predictably, the search failed to find anything, although it went on — without Myra — all week. David Smith came to the moor one day, but the snow was now too deep to see anything but the vague contours of the moor; he was only able to indicate the spot where he and Myra and Brady sometimes parked the car and drank German wine. Myra was not present on that occasion, which was just as well, since both she and Brady continued to regard Smith with hatred. (Paradoxically, Smith had been forced to move from Manchester because of the detestation with which he was regarded. Maureen had died of a brain hoemorrhage in 1977.)

Myra was still maintaining that she was not involved in the actual murders, but in late January 1987 she dropped this pretense, and began to confess to Topping. As she talked, she chain-smoked, and on two occasions became so tense that she had to be given tranquilisers.

Myra's version was that Brady blackmailed her into helping with the murders. One night, she claimed, he had given her wine with a gritty deposit and she lost consciousness; later he admitted that he had drugged her with sleeping tablets. When he began to talk to her about his desire to commit the perfect murder, and she was appalled, he showed her pornographic pictures he had taken of her while she was drugged, and told her he would show them to her family if she refused to help. Topping disbelieved this story — as he disbelieved much of her 'confession' — feeling that she was simply trying to excuse herself.

Myra continued to claim that she had never been present when the victims were killed — Brady sent her away. And when she returned, the victim (John Kilbride, Keith Bennett, Lesley Ann Downey) was already dead. After the first murder of Pauline Reade, Myra claimed of being so sickened that she decided to take the van and go to the police, but she was deterred because Brady had the key. From then on, she insisted, she was terrified that he would kill her too if she resisted. She even claimed that he had threatened to kill her grandmother by pushing her downstairs.

Describing the final killing, of Edward Evans, Myra told Topping that Brady and David Smith had planned it together. Clearly, she was still determined to involve Smith.

Although Myra had gone to so much trouble to emphasise that she was in the last analysis blameless, former supporters like Janie Jones and Lord Longford were upset to learn how far she had deceived them.

In March 1987, Topping went to the Park Lane Hospital to interview Brady. He had been told that he would not understand what Brady was saying, and would be incapable of answering; this proved to be untrue. In fact, Topping felt that Brady was perfectly lucid, and obsessed by a need to feel 'in control' of situations.

Brady agreed to confess if he could be given the means of killing himself. Topping explained that this was impossible. 'Talking to him was like playing chess,' said Topping, 'He was always thinking three moves ahead.' When — at a later meeting — Topping had finally made it clear that he had no power to offer 'a deal,' Brady offered to locate bodies on the moor if he could be granted what he called his 'human week' — a week of normal life, eating the food he chose, drinking Drambuie and watching old films. He felt deprived of these things after twenty years, and felt it was not much to ask; again, Topping had to refuse.

Topping was with Brady on July 1, 1987 when Pauline Reade's body was finally located. It was lying on its side, fully clothed, and the throat had been cut. The clothes had obviously been pushed up, then carelessly pulled down. The following day, Brady agreed to go on to the moor and try and find the body of Keith Bennett. On July 3, Brady was allowed back on to the moor, the first time in twenty-two years. But by mid-afternoon, he had lost his bearings; the moor had changed a great deal since the 1960s. By that time, so many reporters and news cameramen were following that Topping decided to call it a day. And although Brady offered to go back to the moor to try again, the Home Office refused to allow it.

During many visits to Park Lane, Topping and Brady talked a great deal about the topography of the moor, but Brady would not discuss the murders themselves — except to say that Myra's accounts were thoroughly untrustworthy.

During one of these conversations, Brady talked about other murders (as he had, in fact, with Fred Harrison). He claimed that, in Glasgow, he had seen a man mistreating an old woman, and had followed him and stabbed him with a sheath knife. Near Manchester station he had quarrelled with a man on a piece of waste ground and 'bricked him,' leaving him on the ground. Again, in Manchester, after getting into an argument with a woman, he picked her up and threw her over the parapet wall into the canal. He told Topping that the body of a youth he had killed was buried near one of the markers on the A635, but declined to elaborate.

I have no idea whether these 'murders' actually happened — although something Ian said in one of his letters to me inclines me to think not.

After Topping's book came out in 1989, Ian was indignant that he had, while still a serving officer, been allowed to publish his account of his Moors investigation, when the police, like the armed forces and the Civil Service, have to sign a confidentiality agreement. Brady's protests led to the book being withdrawn.

During our early exchanges of letters, Ian would put two parallel red lines across every page, with the words: 'Personal and confidential. Not for publication.' Finally, as he came to trust me, he stopped bothering to do it.

His letters often contained personal anecdotes that threw an interesting light on his personality, like the following (dated December 12, 1992):

> Another absurd insight. I always liked the best seats in the cinema. But, when there was a full house and we had to queue, and the doorman would come walking along the queue declaring that two of the best seats (also the most expensive) were available, I hated having to walk past the queue in order to accept them; I felt that I was deliberately snubbing or insulting them by my action: 'I can afford the most expensive; you can't.' Not very flattering to my 'demon' image. But I can laugh at such paradoxes.
>
> Now, to even the account, I'll give you the other side of the coin. In *Inside the Mind of a Murderer*, M [Myra] refers to a true crime incident. We had come out of a cinema and gone for a late night drink in a town-centre bar in Manchester. As we were drinking, a group of five or six men came in together and sat at right angles to us. The one nearest kept staring at M with

a stupid grin on his face. I gave him a few warning glances, but he continued. I fumed silently for some minutes, and then suddenly I took a decision, and the 'black light' began to operate. Casually I slipped my hand into my overcoat pocket and, with thumb and forefinger, opened the lock-back knife I always carried, made entirely of stainless steel, devoid of ornament and with the functional purity of scalpel. I glanced at the bottles on the table in front of me, selecting which ones to choose as additional weapons. I felt marvellous, delighted, and ready to hack the halfwits. I turned towards them. 'Who the fuck are you staring at? You looking for trouble?' Words to that effect. I waited for the first move, and intended to deal with the starer first. His grin had disappeared and his mouth hung slack in a white face. His mouth gave me the idea of sticking the knife into it and expanding the sliced grin up to his ear. During all this I hadn't said a word to M, and my hand was still in my overcoat pocket. I just sat patiently. Suddenly, apologies were coming from the men, including the starer. I felt a mixture of disappontment and relief. Afterwards I castigated myself for making such a stupid move — stupid, not from a moral viewpoint, but because of the certainty of being caught. I referred to it as 'the danger of audience potential,' of being pushed into a situation I would have avoided had I been alone. After that I never took M into the Gorbals at night; I wandered the area alone, loving the atmosphere of cobbled alleys and gaslit streets I'd known so well as a child.

Letters like this made me aware of Ian as a human being, and I could understand why he hated journalism — and books — that stereotyped the two of them as 'The Moors Murderers' or 'The Monsters of the Moors.'

Anecdotes like this also made me aware that Ian is what zoologists call a 'king rat.' It has been known for more than a century that five percent of any animal group is 'dominant' — that is, possesses drive and enterprise. Shaw once asked the explorer Stanley: 'If you were injured and unable to lead the party, how many people in the group could take over from you?,' and Stanley replied without hesitation: 'Five percent — one in twenty.' This applies to all animals, birds and fishes.

But there are in any large group a very small proportion of 'king rats,' individuals of such high dominance that they dominate even the dominant. These are the Napoleons and Hitlers. Beethoven and Wagner were 'king rats.' But they were fortunate because they were king rats who had found a way of expressing their dominance in a socially acceptable manner.

And this, of course, is the major problem for such men — in fact, for all members of the dominant five percent. For before the dominant individual has found a way of expressing this dominance, he is bound to feel irritable and frustrated — a misfit or 'outsider.' Shaw's Undershaft — the 'armament king' in *Major Barbara* — says: 'I moralised and starved until one day I swore that I would be a full-fed free man at all costs; that nothing should stop me except a bullet, neither reason nor morals nor the lives of other men. . . . I was a dangerous man until I had my will: now I am a useful, beneficent, kindly person.'

The reason that I soon came to feel a great deal of sympathy for Ian was that I felt that he was a frustrated king rat. In one letter he expresses his basic aim:

> To shed the boring, accepted realities that suffocate the majority, and embrace or confront what lies beyond. I always had the sense of seeing far and deep, and had contempt for those who couldn't. Sometimes I felt weary, as though being dragged down into a mire by others, but I always threw them off successfully, as if an inner generator was simply biding its time to save me, expanding the spirit in tune with a vast gestalt. Confronting a sea, a moor, or standing on a mountain, you can almost hear the unknown, invisible presences; you know they are there, almost within touch, speaking an arcane language, and you feel the power rise up within as you become a receiver. No religious twaddle involved, just a pantheistic and atavistic surge of ultimate energy and power, and it makes you laugh with pure delight or cry with gratitude.

What struck me about this passage — also from a letter of December 1992 — is that what he is saying would normally be called mysticism. In fact, in my reply I quoted the famous passage from Wordsworth's 'Prelude,' in which he describes finding a boat moored by Windermere in the moonlight, and climbing in and rowing into the middle of the lake, until a huge black peak towers above him like a living creature. He writes that for days afterwards:

> My brain
> Worked with a dim and undetermined sense
> Of unknown modes of being . . .

I have also noted again and again how much Ian enjoys travel. We all do, of course (although I, as a typical Cancer, easily become bored with it). But for some people, it undoubtedly means more than for others — Ernest Hemingway, for example. And the reason, I think, is that Hemingway's child-hood in Michigan was rather claustrophobic, so that travelling — first to Chicago, then to Paris, produced an almost dizzying sense of freedom, of 'escape from personality.' Ian's letters make it clear that it was the same for him. Even his latest letter, which arrived today (May 31, 2001) has a typical passage:

> Under Brooklyn Bridge, on the Brooklyn side, there's a little place called Grimaldi's among the warehouses; it still had coal-fired ovens like the shops in the Gorbals . . . and did pizzas and pies hot from the oven; so New York likes to hold on to old tra-ditions more than this country. I prefer the old to the new.

And he goes on to reminisce:

> The few times I used long-distance buses, I used to like the half-hour stopovers in little slumbering places in the middle of the night, with only a diner remaining open for the bus pas-sengers and I'd go for a stroll along the sleeping streets and dark shops, enjoying the experience of being awake and alert, living while the world slept, having confidential conversations with nocturnal cats and dogs . . .

His point is underlined by another passage in the same letter:

> We are never more truly ourselves than when we are briefly someone else — as on travels, for instance, free of the condi-tioning of our normal surroundings. . . . The theory that we only use a fraction of the power the brain commands, but have not the knowledge to access it — I've experienced times of increased conscious awareness . . . a sensation of cerebral, as opposed to physical dizziness, as though from the vibrations of an awakened dynamo slowly gathering speed . . . Switching the dynamo on seemed to be preceded by an unusually long period of sustained mental exertion and concentration, rather like the degree required to get through the initial inertia of the

sleep barrier in order to remain awake for days with little subsequent effort.

All this, I believe, has to be taken into account in order to fully understand
the Moors Murders. Here, at least, I am in a position to sympathise, since I
hated the claustrophobia of my home town Leicester — a Midlands manufacturing city, devoted (in my childhood) to hosiery and shoe factories. I hated it
and dreamed of escape, which is why I taught myself to type, then poured out
thousands of words a week — plays, stories, essays — with that same dream of
freedom that drove Ian. My frustration became so intense that at one point I
seriousy contemplated suicide. And this was not out of self-pity as much as a
desire to 'spite God,' who seemed to have condemned me to a life of futility.
And I can easily believe that if I had felt that the only chance of escape was
crime, I would have taken to crime with enthuasiasm.

But would I have committed murder? I doubt it. But that is simply a
matter of the degree of frustration. I was born into a normal family situation,
the first born among siblings and cousins, and since I was an attractive and
intelligent child, also received a great deal of admiration and affection. Now I
look at my own grandchildren, I can see how important it is to have the feeling
of being loved and admired unconditionally. I have no doubt that Ian's mother
did her best to give him the kind of affection that a child needs; but without a
husband, this must have been difficult.

What I do remember clearly is how, in my mid-teens, I had the feeling
that I had to dispense with love and understanding; there seemed no chance
that my mother and father could provide it: they already regarded me as a
cuckoo in the nest. I had the feeling that I had to face up to the reality, and
that reality was that I had to get used to living without love. At that stage,
working in factories (because my parents felt it was time I earned some
money) I first read *A Farewell to Arms*, and the pessimism of Hemingway
spoke to me. '. . . they killed you in the end. You could count on that. Stay
around and they would kill you.'

I was lucky; a period of National Service in the RAF gave me a chance to
recover my old optimism. Ian spent the same period of his life in prison. So by
the time he came out, the hardness born of innate pessimism was endemic; he
had learned to live 'without appeal.' And in that psychological state, crime
must have seemed the logical solution to the problem of making a living.

Yet here — and again I am recalling my own situation — there still
remains a nostalgia for the old innocence and trust. As a child I believed in
God; as a teenager I had come to accept that God is irrelevant. But I would

have been relieved if some powerful emotional experience had restored me to my old belief.

This struck me when I read Myra's account of how Ian, after one of the murders, had shaken his fist at the sky and shouted: 'Take that, you bastard.' The sentiment is illogical for someone who professes to believe that God is a delusion; yet it also reveals a sense of betrayal.

The same thing struck me when I listened to a tape he sent me of extracts from his favourite films, which included *A Christmas Carol* (he still read the book every year at Christmas) and *Carousel*. Both seemed to offer a key to his personality. I also used to love *A Christmas Carol*, and must have read it a dozen times. But listening to the end of the film soundtrack, with Scrooge looking out of the window and learning that it is Christmas Day, and suddenly being filled with love and generosity towards his fellow men, was unexpectedly moving. The fact that Ian loved it so much indicated a longing for lost innocence, a desire to put back the clock, as Scrooge did, and wake up to find that it had all been a dream.

I found *Carousel* just as unexpectedly moving. It is based on a play, *Liliom*, by Ferenc Molnár, and is probably Rodgers and Hammerstein's best musical. The hero, Billy Bigelow, is an easygoing ne'er do well, who falls in love with a mill-girl, Julie Jordan, and marries her. True to his nature, he is a poor provider, but when Julie becomes pregnant, decides he has to make money somehow, and takes part in a robbery — then commits suicide to avoid arrest.

After death, Billy is sentenced to fifteen years in Purgatory. Then he is given a day back on earth to try and redeem himself. He is curious about his child, and finds her unhappy and rebellious, about to go through the graduation ceremony at school. He manages to infuse her with hope and courage, and as he watches her graduate, knows that he has not only saved her, but himself too.

As I listened to 'What's the Use of Wond'rin',' I felt that it was offering me an insight into Ian Brady's state of mind:

> What's the use of wond'rin'
> If he's good or if he's bad?
> He's your fella and that's all there is to say . . .
> Common sense may tell you
> That the ending may be sad
> And now's the time to break and run away
> What's the use of wond'rin'

If the ending will be sad?
He's your fella and you love him
And that's all there is to say.

He cannot have avoided seeing the parallel with Myra, who was spending a lifetime in jail because he had dragged her into murder. *Carousel* is about redemption, and the reason it is one of Brady's favourites is obviously because, like *A Christmas Carol*, it is about putting back the clock, about the possibility of forgiveness and blotting out the past.

But then, Billy Bigelow has merely committed a robbery; by comparison, killing children is unforgivable. Yet this dream of forgiveness and reconciliation obviously haunts him. I have to admit that after listening to the tape of *Carousel* I had a lump in my throat.

The problem is compounded by the fact that the dream is not of reconciliation with society, since — as the reader of this book will soon find out — he regards our society as totally corrupt, a community in which dishonest and unprincipled authority pose as the representative of goodness and decency. So he is caught again in the double-bind situation that turned him into a criminal rebel in the first place. It would be hard to feel genuine remorse about Myra's wasted life when he strongly feels that he did the right thing in opening her eyes to the nonsensical claims of Christianity and the corruption of the Catholic Church. I have to admit that I see his point.

But I also suspect that, in this double-bind situation, he has performed a kind of mental conjuring trick which enables him to turn his back on the possibility of reconciliation with society. In concluding that society is utterly corrupt, he can lose sight of what he actually did and why he is in his present situation.

How did he come to be in this situation? In other words, what made him a killer? There is an abyss of difference between feeling that government is corrupt and our society is rotten — a sentiment which most social rebels would applaud — and committing murder.

The answer, I believe, lies in his relationship with Myra, and in that strange psychological riddle known as *'folie à deux.'* And here it is essential to speak once again of that matter of dominance. Abraham Maslow, of whom I have already spoken, spent some time studying dominance in women. (He found they were easier to work with because they were more honest than men.) He questioned a large number of women, and soon learned that they fell into three 'dominance groups' — high, medium and low. The high dominance women were, as you might expect, precisely five percent of the total. Sexually, they were inclined to promiscuity and experimentation — many had had lesbian experiences or tried sado-masochism. They liked males of even higher dominance, and regarded the male sexual organ as beautiful.

Medium dominance women, the largest group, were basically romantics. They liked the kind of man who would take them to restaurants with candle-light and give them flowers. They were looking for Mr Right. They were capable of a certain amount of promiscuity, but it was essentially a second best — what they really wanted was a husband who was a good father and provider. They also wanted him to be slightly more dominant than they were, but not too dominant. Very high dominance males scared them. This group didn't have any strong feelings about the male organ.

Low dominance women didn't much like sex. They liked the kind of man who would admire them from a distance for years without daring to say so. They were terrified of high dominance males, and thought the male organ downright ugly.

But all three groups needed a male who was more dominant than them-selves. One very high dominance woman searched for years for such a male, and when she found him, was finally happy. But he wasn't quite dominant enough, and so she used to provoke quarrels that would end with him slapping her about, hurling her on a bed, and raping her. These sexual experiences she found most satisfactory of all.

I would classify Myra as being at the upper end of the medium domi-nance type. And since we all tend to be interested in sexual partners in our own dominance group, she would have been ideally happy with a Mr Right who belonged to the same group.

Ian, of course, needed someone of higher dominance than Myra — that is why he ignored her for a year. Then, I suspect, he decided that, since she was on offer, he may as well accept what she was so anxious to give. But merely being her lover and dominating her with his personality was not enough, and he was not satisfied until he had converted her from being a Catholic to an atheist. Myra, anxious to keep this god-like male, tried her best to please, and made no objection to posing for pornographic pictures with the occasional cut of a whip.

With the new self-image produced by Myra's adoration, I think Ian decided: 'Why not?' One of the books on the Moors case quotes him as talking about murdering a baby in its cradle. I suspect that he was actually quoting Blake: 'Rather murder an infant in its cradle than nurse unsatisfied desire.' And since Myra was willing to help by picking up children, he could see nothing to stop him putting his plan into operation.

The murders, I believe, were intended as a first step towards putting into practise what de Sade had only theorised about, and becoming a master criminal, the first great exponent of moral relativism.

This, I would suggest, was the real genesis of the Moors Murders.

———•——

A few words on how this book came to be written. During the early years of our correspondence, I found myself brooding a great deal on how Ian might find a way out of his 'double bind' — that is, the problem of being trapped in a situation that could offer no hope of improvement. In the late '60s or the 70's, I would have said, like most people: 'Let him rot. That's what he deserves.' But to actually be in the situation of exchanging letters with a man with no future made me realise that, murderer or not, Ian Brady was a human being like myself, and that he deserved something more than being allowed to rot.

Part of his problem was that it would be pointless for him to look for help from the prison psychiatrist or chaplain; he would feel, quite rightly, that he could psychoanalyse himself as well as any psychiatrist, and that since he had no intention of swallowing the consolations of religion, the chaplain would have nothing to offer either. This is the problem of most strong-minded people when they find themselves under stress — that there is no one they respect enough to ask for help.

It seemed to me that there was one possible solution: to rise above the problem by shifting his mind into the creative mode. Therefore I advised him to do the thing I would have done: to think about writing a book. Since he obviously knew about serial murder 'from the inside,' this suggested itself as the obvious subject. I even approached a publisher who is also a friend — Nick Robinson, of Robinson Publishing — and asked him if he would be interested in publishing a book on serial killers by Ian Brady. He was cautiously interested, but pointed out a problem I had foreseen myself: that since the Moors Murderers are still probably the most hated killers in British jails, it would obviously be impossible to publish it as a book by Ian Brady. But the solution might be to publish it as a book 'by a Serial Killer' with an Introduction by me guaranteeing that the author was indeed a notorious serial killer. And the mystification ought to guarantee enough sales to cover its costs.

Nick agreed, and I gave Ian the go-ahead. But six months or so later, Nick wrote to me to say that he had read the typescript, and decided that he did not want to publish it. I asked Nick to send me the book, and when he did, saw immediately what was wrong. It was like a book by any competent journalist, but did not live up to the words 'by a Serial Killer' would seem to promise. It seemed to me that Ian had simply failed to stamp his own personality and insight on it. But it also seemed to me that if I worked with him as an editor, the problem might be overcome. So I wrote and suggested this.

The result was a violent explosion. He replied that he had not given Nick permission to show me the book, and would be grateful if I would keep my nose out of things that were not my business. He asked me to return the typescript immediately.

The tone — of an exasperated headmaster giving orders to a stupid sixth former — incensed me, even though I knew from experience that he was prone to blow off the handle. A few years earlier, he had forgotten that I told him I was going abroad for a month. The day I returned, I sent him a postcard saying I was just back and would be writing soon. This crossed with a furious letter from Ian, demanding forthwith the return of all his letters. I was glad I had already written, since it made explanations and excuses unnecessary. A few days later, I received a slightly sheepish letter, saying 'Well, no harm done,' and passing on to other things as if nothing had happened.

So now I wrote back a rather irritable letter, telling him that my patience was not inexhaustible, and that if he wrote to me in that tone again, it really would be the end of our correspondence.

In due course the quarrel blew over, and I assumed that was the end of the idea of a serial killer book and of further writing. (I knew he had already written an autobiography, but have never been allowed to see this.) So I was surprised to hear, sometime in year 2000, that he had written another book, and was willing to let me read it. It was sent to me by his solicitor, Benedict Birnberg, a man I have always found helpful and charming.

Within half a page, I could see that we were back to the kind of thing he and I have been arguing about for the past ten years: whether criminality is excusable on the grounds that society commits all kinds of crimes under the cloak of legality. So as I went on reading, it was with an increasing sense of *deja vu*.

But when I came to the second part, on individual serial killers, I received a pleasant surprise. The chapters on Lucas, Gacy, Sutcliffe et al struck me as excellent. The chapters on Dean Corll and the Mad Butcher of Kingsbury Run had the kind of insight that I had missed in the first volume.

I decided that Adam Parfrey of Feral House, a publisher for whom I had written Introductions to other volumes on crime, was the likeliest publisher of my acquaintance to view it sympathetically, so I sent it off to him. I was delighted when, after a few weeks, he said he would like to publish it.

I was doubly pleased because by this time, Ian's circumstances had deteriorated badly. There had been a time when he was by no means uncomfortable — when I first wrote to him, he was typing books for the blind in Braille, and was allowed books, videotapes, and his own television. Later he was even allowed a computer.

About three years ago, the computer was taken away from him without explanation. This, almost certainly, was due to the fact that he was 'making trouble,' writing to the press about the corrupt regime at Ashworth, and even appealing to the European Court of Justice. This was at the time that it was revealed that a girl of eight, daughter of an Ashworth employee, was allowed onto the ward with convicted paedophiles.

It all led to an enquiry costing £7.5 million, whose 1999 report by Judge Peter Fallon declared unequivocally that Ashworth should be closed completely. It spoke of 'years of abuse, corruption and failure,' and said that although the inmates were forbidden to have money, there was about £10,000 in banknotes circulating around, which was used to purchase drugs, alcohol and child pornography. Three earlier reports had also been highly critical of Ashworth, and in one case, only nine pages out of 385 were made public.

The Fallon Report was ignored or overruled by the government; nothing more has been heard of it.

On September 30, 1999, several warders rushed into Brady's cell, pinned his arms, and strip-searched him, breaking his wrist. The reason, he was told, was that a knife had been found taped under a sink elsewhere on the ward.

Now in fact, he would have had nothing to gain from owning a knife, and had never attacked a warder or prison officer. Nevertheless, he was placed on a psychotic ward, and when he went on hunger strike as a protest, was force-fed. Guards talked in loud voices outside his door all night, preventing him from sleeping.

There was a time when, if I had something private I wanted to say to him — for example, about his projected book — I could make sure the letter was not read by the prison authorities by putting it in a book parcel, which was handed to him unopened. After the 'knife' incident, everything was opened and read. In any case, there would have been no point in sending him books, since he was not allowed more than six. Just before Christmas 2000, I sent him a parcel full of envelopes, with first class stamps. They simply never reached him. I had to send another lot by recorded delivery.

As I write, the hunger strike goes on. Brady's own temperament guarantees that he is in a no-win situation. Because the basic characteristic of the 'king rat' is that he refuses to give way an inch, he will continue to charge brick walls until he collapses with exhaustion or dies of a heart attack.

Now this has been true of Ian at the time of his arrest. Since then, his self-esteem has been severely battered. His life in prison has been as miserable as even the parents of his victims could wish. At the time of writing it has reached the lowest point yet, where — as he says — 'I'd be satisfied to be a beggar.' And although I feel that there has always been an element of absurdity in his tirades against society, I also suspect that there is a mite of justification in his present protests. It looks to me as if his situation today is not due to taping a knife underneath a sink, but because his refusal to be silenced has made him a nuisance to the authorities.

In an article I wrote for the *Daily Mail* in October 1999, I suggested that Brady should be allowed his wish to starve himself to death. Now I am inclined to reconsider that suggestion. His death would be too convenient for too many people.

Ian Brady cannot possibly live long anyway. In a letter of a few days ago, he wrote to me bitterly: 'My life is over, so I can afford honesty of expression; those with a future cannot. If I had my time over again, I'd get a government job and live off the state . . . a pillar of society. As it is, I am eager to die. I chose the wrong path and am finished.'

As this book shows, that, at all events, is untrue.

The Gates of Janus by Ian Brady
Part One

> JANUS: the Roman god of doorways,
> passages and bridges. In art he is
> depicted with two heads facing
> opposite ways.
>
> **Collins English Dictionary**

> 'Let us to it pell-mell; if not to Heaven,
> then hand in hand to Hell!'
>
> *Richard the Third*, **Shakespeare**

If we are to have a serious discourse on murder and some of its practitioners, we should first broadly define our terms.

Murder is the premeditated killing of one human being by another, outside the law and without official sanction. It therefore follows that the premeditated killing of one person by another, inside the law and with official permission, is not considered murder. Whether or not this nice distinction has actual *moral* validity the reader must judge in the chapters to follow, where I shall, perhaps characteristically, don the mantle of Devil's Advocate, a role so frequently attributed to me by the established order and mass media.

The question as to *legal* validity is of little consequence — Auschwitz, the fire-bombing of Dresden, the atomic holocausts of Hiroshima and Nagasaki, the deluge of napalm rained upon Vietnam and all other examples of wholesale global slaughter throughout the ages were, and still are, performed under the tattered umbrella of legality.

Self-evidently, too little law and order leads to freedom only for the few, the fittest; too much law and order has largely the same result. The powerful, wealthy and influential stay on top like oil-slicks, by hereditament and oligarchy, rather than merit. Greed and lust are bi-partisan.

According to official statistics in most Western countries, the corporate activities of this elite minority, aided by the best attorneys and tax evasion/avoidance experts, annually deprive the economy of more wealth than the total aggregate of all blue-collar crime. Yet few of that elite group will ever see the inside of a prison, and politicians of either party have yet to be heard demanding harsher penalties for these white-collar criminals. One contemptuously greedy exception, whose main error was public arrogance, nicely summed up the philosophy of the whole class: 'Only little people pay taxes.'

One obvious reason why we so enjoy the fall of such public paragons and private criminals is that it happens so seldom. We may envy them their great wealth and power, but we never quite admire them as we do the relatively more honest, disadvantaged, blue-collar criminal who runs the risk of severe penalty.

However, as a brief preamble to discourse proper, let me first state what I believe to be universally acceptable, orthodox parameters.

Morality and legality are decided chiefly by the prevailing ruling class in whatever geographical variant, not least because a collective morality is too unwieldy and difficult to maintain. I prefer individual systems of principles rather than a collective set of precepts largely impossible to quantify or enforce.

Compulsory state education is, in effect, a form of mind control. Particularly enforced religious instruction.

The majority of people, rightly or wrongly, regardless of geographical location, believe that we all know instinctively what is the right thing to do in all matters simply by standing back and applying our own decisions to ourselves — 'Do unto others as you would have them do unto you.' But Bernard Shaw spotted the flaw in that idealistic argument:

'Do not do unto others as you would have them do unto you. You might not share the same tastes.'

And, unfortunately, most people are not positioned to do what they would like to see done to the high and mighty who invariably escape the rigours of the law as though by divine right.

Notwithstanding, we continue to believe we know what is cruel or kind, selfish or selfless, fair or unfair, etc. Yet we endlessly struggle to explain — to ourselves and to others — why we are in conflict with such behavioural norms.

There are differing accents within the moral boundaries of one's own unavoidably subjective system, whose familiarity makes what we do personally acceptable, particularly if our actions are consciously part of a larger, though expediently veiled, socially-dictated pragmatism.

Self-interest and self-absorption has people blindly adhere to legality and morality, and not because of some innate saintly or metaphysical quality. By and large, the most common aspect of morality is compulsion, fear of crossing boundaries and doing the generally unacceptable.

I believe it is axiomatic that the majority are too lazy, intellectually and constitutionally, to oppose the accepted order of things. Conformity is passive. Dissension demands energy and dangerous commitment.

The central reason why many prefer to have the good opinion of others is: (a) the natural wish to be liked and popular, (b) the social and material advantages which follow from that, (c) the personal pleasure derived from being needed.

By seeking the comfort and advantage that follows from being accepted as a normal member of society, the individual is merely striving, at primal level, to have his self-opinion reinforced by others.

Ironically, the attempt to attain a consensus of good opinion simultaneously generates the envy, and therefore, the resentful vindictiveness, of others competing for the same good graces. Man socially advances himself invariably at the expense of others, for the pleasure of feeling superior to others.

And those who exalt themselves through the good opinion of their superiors, do so chiefly by deferring to the judgment of same rather than relying upon their own. Good reputation — or public virtue — can reasonably be perceived as being rooted in applied flattery, personal vanity and self-interest.

Man's primal instinct is to obtain as much pleasure from life as possible, whether by self-sacrifice or the sacrifice of others. Whether termed good or bad by external moral and legal criteria, every action a person commits is determined by the amount of personal pleasure it gives.

Random acts of kindness or cruelty, which seem to surface from the individual of their own volition, often result from a clash between our personal system of beliefs and the artificiality of subconscious social conditioning.

Unfortunately, many people sleepwalk through life without conscious awareness of their own system, if they have one at all, and are therefore susceptible to external notions of right and wrong imposed by others, particularly members of the often eminently unqualified upper class and their support system, mass media.

Laws and morals based on honour are superior to those rooted in social expediency.

Thankfully there are some individuals who consciously resent and resist anything that conflicts with their own system of morals and ethics. Especially if the conflicting notions emanate from people who do not believe the pious platitudes they are trying to force or persuade others to accept.

The more dictatorial the state, the less capacity for individual discernment, and the greater the prevalence of erroneous self-sacrifice to a purely political imperative.

In my opinion, professional criminals are more prone than most to think for themselves in a morally eclectic manner. Society prefers to foster the contra-idea that, by definition, criminals are oblivious to moral and ethical values.

The fact is, many criminals know more about morality and ethics, via the process of opposition, than the conforming masses do from acceptance. I would even predicate that it is the criminal's astute understanding that the morality and ethics of the powerful is purely cosmetic, that persuades him to emulate their amoral plasticity.

In effect, the criminal seriously studies the largely unscrupulous moral standards practised by ostensible 'pillars of society,' and modifies his values accordingly. He thereby becomes a player. Albeit, by force of circumstance and lack of privileged upbringing, having to adopt less sophisticated but no less ruthless methods than his social superiors.

Conformists who observe, deduce and vaguely bemoan the immorality of their superiors are largely too afraid of penalty, or are too lazy to run the risk of acting upon their conclusions.

People are not so remorseful or ashamed of their criminal thoughts; they are more afraid of criminal thoughts being ascribed to them by others. To compensate, they rationalise their timidity or indolence as an indication of moral character, and their vociferous clamour for harsher punishment of criminals is mob retribution against a will to power they covertly envy. This envy is exacerbated by the media's colourful, exciting stories about criminals riotously enjoying every forbidden pleasure the 'decent citizens' can only dream about.

Good and evil might therefore be presented simply as a matter of what we think we can get away with without sacrificing reputation. To all intents and purposes, the majority regard themselves as law-abiding, decent, god-fearing people — right up to the moment they are caught.

Capture makes the criminal. A person may blithely break the law whenever it suits them, but still do not reject a personal sense of morality. The strictly law-abiding may still be subject to covert criminal tendencies. We all desire what we cannot have or are forbidden to have.

Naturally the polarised values of good and evil constitute a paradoxical, interdependent unity, an indivisible entity of internally-opposing tensions which constitute the vital essence of life: contrast and variety.

Every act, good or evil, is a reflection of our most natural characteristics and genuine psyche.

A relativist viewpoint — rather than surrendering to statute — enhances a more profound understanding of this schismatic variegation, in which legality and illegality are unceasingly examined, and not only morally, but *metaphysically* (preferably devoid of obfuscating religious connotations).

It is independently documented that I *instinctively* began this relativistic thought process at the age of five. The law-and-order brigade would probably regard such teachings as heresy. Bovine conformism is indirectly responsible for unjust and alien legislation, laws made to be broken, laws denying or unsuccessfully trying to suppress the intrinsic dynamic nature of the individual.

Every dictator knows to strongly emphasise the advantages, over the disadvantages, of obeying law. But the only laws that matter are those based on universal usefulness rather than immediate expediency. The only law-givers worthy of respect are those who own the necessary degree of honour to exclude their personal desires from principles and act as a collective conscience.

Good laws left to the interpretation of evil men are no longer good. Therefore it follows that good laws should be framed as clearly and as unequivocally as a written constitution, to obviate any possibility of deliberate misinterpretation and nullification. Such laws should be applicable to all, including politicians, intelligence services (foreign and domestic) and every agent of law enforcement. Exceptions lead to general contempt.

Those who aspire to have immutable rules of conduct, good or evil, are nevertheless secretly plagued by doubt like everyone else. Only the church believes in saints. Absolutists are invariably absolute fools. And not least because they absolutely expect to be absolutely believed. As stated, all but the insane are well aware whenever personal actions conflict with their true beliefs, as opposed to their socially-conditioned responses.

I believe every intelligent individual, whether predominantly good or evil, possesses a mostly idiosyncratic moral gyroscope which reminds him whether he is in conflict with his *own* moral and ethical convictions or merely those of others. Individuality is the supreme value, in my opinion, not regimentation or servile social assimilation.

In case my use of the words 'good' and 'evil' be misconstrued in a narrow theological sense, I must explain that they are meant to be interpreted, as previously implied, within the wider framework of moral and metaphysical philosophy. I examine religious teachings through the microscope of psychology, psychiatry, criminology, anthropology, literature, zoology and the principles of forensic science in general. Religion taken neat can be toxic. People drink a lot on Sunday evenings to get rid of the hangover left by attending church.

Am I alone in experiencing that the dirge-like cadence of a preacher's delivery induces drowsiness, an acute sense of absurdity, an uncomfortable suspension of disbelief, an emetic voiding of natural vitality?

In an obviously uncertain and chaotic world, those who smugly believe preachers are delivering the gospel truth represent, in my eyes, an insult to intelligence and a manifest example of criminal delusion. Even the most elementary refutatory evidence of modern medical science and eclectic philosophy appear not to affect the religious fanatic. Not so much faith versus free will, but faith versus common sense.

Had Christ been crucified in the manner commonly depicted, it is a phyiscal fact that his body weight would have immediately ripped the iron nails straight through his hands. The precepts and concepts of the gospels, written decades after Christ's death, were plagiarised from Judaism and Hellenism. Modern moral philosophy has not added significantly to the tenets of the ancient.

Prophets and preachers would do better to practise a more profound degree of humility and scientific introspection, hopefully resulting in humanistic insight and less dogmatic prohibition. However, as Luke states, even 'He that humbleth himself wisheth to be exalted.'

———————

By dwelling lightly upon morality and ethics up to this point, mainly in relation to examining, through relativistic principles, their orthodox/unorthodox interpretation and application by the minority upon the majority, you may be assuming that I regard such synthetic codes of conduct as the prime values and purpose of life. I do not. To me, as previously indicated, they are simply inescapable conditioned aspects of whatever country you had the good fortune or misfortune to be born into. Governments, with their whimsical, Populist morality and ethics, come and go, but bureaucracies eternally survive by more dependable amoral principles.

Had you been born and spent your life up till now in, let us say, the rainforests of the Amazon, you would not be devoting so much of your life and energy to conformity with the convoluted moral abstractions of others. In such primal circumstances, the individualistic urge to experience all one can, before losing the race against death, would naturally evolve as paramount. Individual quality of life is more relevant than quantity, both physically and intellectually.

Zest is the vital ingredient one should seek. Some are born with it.

———————

As previously indicated, most people observe legal, moral and ethical boundaries for immediate personal comfort or from timidity. The criminal is more attracted and stimulated by the excitement of challenging the norm, of stepping into forbidden territory like a solitary explorer, consciously thirsting to experience that which the majority have not and dare not.

Nature abhors not only a vacuum but right angles. Likewise, unconditioned human nature is inclined towards, and more fascinated by, the crooked.

Many are content to confine such forbidden journeys to the mind and, frankly, by so doing, most probably achieve more pleasure and satisfaction than they would from committing the deed itself.

Being in the position of having tasted both fantasy and deed, I can candidly testify that fantasy is invariably more hedonistically superior, its creator having the advantage of omnipotence. The safer one feels from interruption or capture, the more intense and rounded the act.

I can also state with authority that, contrary to popular belief, much crime is tedious and repetitive hard work, wearing on the nerves and an anti-climax. In the words of the song by Peggy Lee, after the completion of each successive, escalating crime, the criminal is left spiritually asking himself: 'Is That All There Is?' Pervasive emptiness accentuates a nihilistic syndrome. The hunt for the chimerical key to knowledge, life, power or the ultimate sensation becomes a never-to-be-satisfied addiction.

In performance of the deed itself, the perpetrator is either greatly preoccupied and distracted by the constant danger of discovery, the fear of leaving some clue behind, or, in some instances, the psychological impact of confronting the enormity of the crime's reality. It is not uncommon for perpetrators to overestimate their own callousness.

The determined professional's surest way to overcome physical and spiritual weakness is to programme himself in advance by auto-hypnosis techniques — which I shall expand upon as we advance.

There are of course a minority of criminals who enjoy the danger most of all, like lovers who add piquancy to sex by performing in public locations. To such aficionados, the main purpose of the crime is almost secondary.

I contend that most people, criminal or otherwise, consciously/subconsciously regard aesthetics as the dominant physical and metaphysical value of existence. They may simultaneously pay lip service to legality and morality whilst atavistically regarding them as irritating hindrances to primal biological inclinations. Only the compensatory delusions of theology attribute moral and ethical values to a patently indifferent universe.

The doctrines of Christianity synthesize a death-cult, an hallucinatory invitation to corruption and decay. Its adherents sing songs of praise to empty skies which rain visions of hell upon heretics, diverting attention from the all-precious present. This suicidal concept should be made criminal were it not already dying of its own accord.

Nowadays, belief in the possibility of a higher intelligence on other planets is more acceptable and appealing than the concept of a Creator responsible for our earthly bedlam.

The hope is now for physical rescue rather than metaphysical redemption. Children believe more devoutly in the magical benefits of Santa Claus than the verbiage of Christ and the dirge-like intoning of moralistic parables by his far-from-joyous servants.

To paraphrase Shakespeare, Christianity is increasingly regarded as a tale told by an idiot, full of inhuman ideals and absurd prejudices, signifying nothing. Its main social function of course is to delude and keep order among the justifiably malcontent. But even prison should be seen as preferable to religious lobotomy.

Show me someone who would hesitate to lie or commit a crime in order to protect or help a loved one or friend, and I will show you a truly inhuman criminal or madman. Laws and externally enforced moral and ethical norms are put into their proper secondary perspective in affairs of emotion when it makes one feel *good* to break the law if need be.

By this route, breach of law is gradually perceived as *relatively* acceptable, and statutes not at all as sacrosanct as many would have you tamely believe. Everything made by man can be unmade.

Longevity or universal acceptance is of no essential relevance in the context of endlessly fluctuating anthropological and biological values. Ubiquity should not be equated with merit, nor conformity with virtue. We are, at this stage of human knowledge, merely myths created by religion. Viewed scientifically, the death of a human being is of no more significance than that of any other animal on earth.

Superior human intelligence is no mark of divinity. Empirically, it reveals a superior savagery. No other animal on earth is so inclined to slaughter its own kind in regular global conflicts, apparently subject to the Orwellian expedient that some people are made more in the image of God than others.

The plain and perhaps regrettable fact is that it is part of the eternal human psyche and cycle for the normal individual to derive cathartic satisfaction and enjoyment from savouring the crimes of others, and from luxuriously dreaming of personally committing them. Similar cathartic satisfaction is afforded by contemplating the punishment of those who are caught. Nobody likes a loser and therefore we believe they get what they deserve.

What do you believe you deserve for the undetected crimes and secret moral outrages you have committed in thought or action? Absolution?

Chapter Two

One must have a good memory to be
able to keep the promises one makes.
One must have a strong imagination in
order to feel sympathy. So closely is
ethics connected with intellectual
capacity.

Nietzsche

The allied judges at Nuremberg, in justifying their condemnation of German war crimes, proclaimed, 'Any immoral law must be disobeyed.' But, as the history of warfare has profusely illustrated since, the countries responsible for this grandiose principle of judgment meant it to apply only to Germany and not themselves.

To the free-thinker or relativist, *personal* beliefs and principles — rather than external social dogma — dictate action. Truth be told, we owe genuine loyalty only to our loved ones and close friends. It is to whom we give our word that matters, not the giving of it.

People often blind themselves to the harsh moral dichotomy that the harms they would *not* do to a loved one or friend can be perpetrated, without any significant qualm, upon strangers.

Whatever laws you *believe* you have a right to break, accepting the possible social and legal consequences, you will do so willingly and without remorse. But it is patently superstitious to believe that all law-breaking automatically exacts some degree of personal remorse. In general, politicians, intelligence personnel and criminals only bother to heed laws when they're not attempting to bend or circumvent them. Law, to such individuals, is likened to an interesting and often irritating obstacle course.

To be bound by law distinctly advantages those who are not. It is therefore the duty of the powerful and over-privileged to frame laws that exploit and maintain this status quo. The social elite, like the criminal, allow no law to deflect their purpose and are adept at using legality against those who oppose them.

Will you not admit that sometimes it's a most stimulating experience to do something you don't want to do, don't approve of, and are legally proscribed from experiencing — just to discover new aspects of yourself and others? This is something which I will presently refer to as spiritually switching on the dark. The forbidden fascinates all, naturally attracting rather than repelling. As we all know, banning or censoring draws crowds. This reflects the low intelligence of the censorious in many instances, or political corruption and greed, as in the case of the powerful alcohol and tobacco lobbies, whose products kill millions annually, but who advocate the outlawing of less harmful drugs such as cannabis purely to maintain high profits and tax yield.

Does virtue have its own reward? You may live a blameless life, and perform charitable deeds for three-score years and ten, but if you ultimately commit one crime, you are nevertheless become a 'criminal.' Those of you who are forever baying for harsher laws and punishments should remember the blatantly obvious truth that the very wealthy and powerful are the law-makers, and that no one accumulates such a high degree of wealth and power by honest and legal means.

'Crime Does Not Pay' — except for the elite, of course. With the under-classes even deprived of the hope of honest work, crime remains the only feasible option for survival. The American private prison industry also operates on that premise. Glossy brochures to shareholders proclaim: 'While arrests and convictions are steadily on the rise, profits are to be made from crime. Get in on the ground floor of this booming industry now! . . . With the advent of a new administration, stocks for the private correctional management firms, crime-fighting sector and security industry will jump even higher than their current growth rate . . . Just consider the current inmate populations in adult facilities combined with population growth of juvenile detention centres. Invest now!'

Shareholders have a vested interest in making sure that prisons do not reform and rehabilitate. Society need not worry about unemployment or care about the underprivileged, as long as enough prison warehouses are constructed to store those forced to commit crime in order to survive. This mercenary political programme, inducing others into crime rather than providing jobs and adequate welfare, could be construed as a criminal offence in itself.

The age of reason and hope is in terminal decline. The ruling elite are abandoning even the paternal pretence of thinking in terms of general welfare. So why should anyone else?

Robbed of traditional identities and social cohesion, the underclasses of the West are now spiritless in their submission. Yawning gulfs have come between the very rich, the middle class who serve them, and what one might cynically describe as the economy class, which is now replaced by robotic technology.

As the dispossessed turn more and more naturally to crime, it becomes financially expedient to imprison them in service to corporation, an even more faceless dictator than the state. But the time is fast approaching when demand will outstrip supply, chaos shall have its day, and brute force its revenge.

Whatever section of society is out for blood, one thing should be kept in mind: 'Before seeking revenge, dig two graves.' Prisoners have relatives and friends in the outside world ready and willing to balance accounts. What better circumstance and material could a resentful, hopeless prisoner ask for to school in the study of crime and revenge? He has at his constant disposal a veritable army of budding psychopaths and psychotics serving short sentences, ardent for knowledge and instruction, eager to re-enter the community and try out their new-found ideas of social justice.

Justice? During the Vietnam War those who burned their draft-cards were jailed for refusing to kill, and sat side-by-side with convicted murderers. Different cause, same effect.

——◆——

Should the thought occur to you, this book, and every view, sentiment and expression in it, is written by my own hand from a cell in which I've spent the past three decades and will remain in till I die. Any adverse criticism you may form over the contents will not cause me to retract one measured word.

You will presently discover that this work is not an apologia. Why should it be? To whom should I apologise, and what difference would it make to anyone? You contain me till death in a concrete box that measures eight by ten and expect public confessions of remorse as well? That species of feigned repentance extorted at show trials? Rid your mind of that expectation. I will not cater to the moral pretensions of the bovine; nor will I flatter retarded authority.

Remorse is a purely personal matter, not a circus performance. Who can truly distinguish the point where self-pity ends and compunction begins? The certitude of my death in captivity paradoxically confers a certainty of belief, a freedom of thought and expression most so-called free people will fail to experience in their lifetime. Unlike the merely *physically* free individual, no hellish circles of social graces and ersatz respect bind me to censor beliefs. I am not under the least obligation to please by deceit any individual whomsoever. To all practical intents and purposes, I am no longer of your world — if, as you might suggest, I ever was. I am now simply a curious observer, resistant to 'thirty years of blur and blot.'

Is it so perversely singular to postulate that compassion for mankind in general is empirically inconceivable? That such ostensible human empathy, when so widely distributed, loses all meaning and substance? Is such an over-ambitious, compensatory claim of universal benevolence in reality a clear admission that one has, in fact, no deep feelings worth speaking of?

Even Jesus smote the moneychangers. But that metaphysician habitually preached the impossible anyway. Know thyself? We find it far simpler, and more emotionally satisfying, to believe we know others; it deflects self-analysis.

If a psychiatrist is leading a worthless private life, a failure even to his family, he could be of far more assistance to his patients by explaining his own faults, his own mistakes in life, from which the patient might benefit through avoidance.

I am applying variations of that principle in these opening chapters, by the end of which perhaps some of you will know my faults and strengths. The majority will think they know them better than I do.

The reader rightly expects to share the psychic, ethical and moral perspective of the serial killer for a change, anticipating that beliefs and rationale are expressed with articulate candour, devoid of any attempt to gain sympathy or acolytes.

I have never seriously set out to corrupt anyone. I believe the seed of corruption is already within all, requiring only the right primal incentive, circumstance or utilitarian stimulus in which to blossom. The degree, nature and cultivation of corruption depends almost entirely upon the innate criminal propensities of the individual recipient. The extent of his/her natural predatory instinct and capacity for independent thought and social/relativistic analysis. In this particular, I am unavoidably in unholy accord with the theological doctrine of original sin, but from a secular premise.

My present state of psychic evolution should by now be distinct to some; one purpose of these opening chapters is to assist a few in appreciating the routes of my reasoning.

When most people approach middle or old age, as I am, they opt for increasingly greyer decisions, in contrast to the vibrant black and white of younger years. Some obtusely regard the tendency to compromise a sign of wisdom or tolerance. I regard it as selling out, and retirement to the comfortable grazing of the flock.

Thanks largely to authoritarian stupidity and the spectrum of human savagery and absurdity witnessed and experienced by me in decades of imprisonment, and an absence of personal ambition, my relativistic beliefs and philosophy are therianthropically preserved in convictions of glacial ice. At this moment I continue to value personal loyalty and friendship even more. The coining of golden rules is not always the prerogative of those with the gold.

We can now resume in a deeper condition of mutual understanding, I hope.

To further early ambitions pragmatically and at maximum speed, I must confess that I selected associates who visibly possessed advanced 'criminal' potential.

A test question was, 'How much money would you kill for, considering you would do it for a pittance in the army?' The amount chosen was irrelevant. The act of positive choice paramount. Any moral or ethical equivocation I encountered led me to bantering disengagement, when I falsely implied that discussing murder was hypothetical, a philosophical indulgence.

'I wonder what it's like to kill?' many would ask. And, naïvely, 'Am I capable of killing and getting away with it?' The stuff of amateur detective novels. Beyond good and evil there is no self-doubt, the opposing values being complementary sides of the same coin. *Self-conscious* good or evil is equally counterfeit. *Spontaneity* in the enactment of both is the essential mark of purity and distinction. Only self-flattering poseurs claim predominant owner-ship of good or evil. Without exception we fluctuate between the two, both qualities being regulated mainly by social conditioning. The vibrancy of evil requires the threat of external force for its containment, and the drive to be good requires narcissistic self-interest or delusions of grandeur.

The majority of people naturally enjoy the *idea* of running with the fox. But their heads, their pack instinct and keen sense of self-survival, urge them to ride more safely with the hounds.

The vast popularity of crime in the media and entertainment industries suggests most people spend their lives envying the certitude of belief and ability for action possessed by the professional criminal. They are, as it were, impatient for the villain to appear on stage to liven things up. And if he appeared in real life, what then? Shock and trepidation.

For instance, if someone you trusted were to offer to rid you of a life-long enemy, a nagging wife, an obstacle to your promotion or some other important ambition, giving a complete guarantee that no suspicion would fall upon you, would you feel tempted to accept? I believe most people would initially at least be tempted.

The notion would emotionally attract. Then delayed caution would prompt secondary considerations: (a) is the guarantee genuine? (b) accepting that it is, what if something goes wrong? (c) is someone who makes such a proposal sane or to be trusted and, if not, would I eventually be regarded as a danger and disposed of in similar manner or be blackmailed? (d) can I even afford to show for one moment that I am the sort of person who would seriously contemplate such a proposition?

These and many other imponderables predominantly reflect concern for *self*, not the criminal act or the fate of the intended, annoying victim. However, I believe the majority of people would eventually, albeit grudgingly, begin to feel deep unease. A sense of stark, disturbing, stomach-churning reality they had never before been forced to experience. A daunting consciousness of alien power and personal responsibility. The absolute prerogative of a Caesar or divinity. To decide someone's fate with casual ease and indifference. A cold-blooded, primal capability they amorally and even proudly *assumed* they and everyone else possessed as a birthright.

Most people do possess the capability to kill, when given government *permission* which obviates or diminishes personal responsibility and penalty. Or in the collective irresponsibility of a mob.

Significantly, in my unorthodox experience, almost everyone, after considerations of self-interest, consciously or subconsciously approaches the academic question of murder on mainly *aesthetic* grounds. Not moral. They will enthusiastically discuss or ingest every conceivable horrific method of successfully destroying their enemies. Experiencing no moral pang, only keen enjoyment at exploring and contemplating the fatal possibilities and painful variations.

Philosophical parlour games and semantical acrobatics soaring free of moral gravity also proliferate. For instance, if a killer of six proved that he had consciously refrained from killing a dozen other victims he previously had at his mercy, why should the dozen acts of clemency be of lesser moral significance than the six fatalities? Are good and evil primarily matters of arithmetic; is their significance, like success, measured by a stopwatch?

The following moral question is a well-known moral parlour game. Say, before the start of World War Two, you were standing beside Hitler with a concealed gun, knowing or believing that fifty million people would die in a future war, would you have killed him? Would you have considered the assassination a criminal act or felt remorse? Would you have realised that, by killing him at that crucial period in history, Hitler would be respected today as one of the world's greatest statesmen and strategists?

Do you have an inner statute of limitations for your own crimes? As years have passed and you are no longer the person who committed or would repeat such crimes, do you believe you should not be punished? Would you honestly sacrifice yourself simply to satisfy the abstract principle of public deterrent or divine/secular justice? In which case, do you still believe that a captured criminal who has similarly altered with passing years should continue to be punished regardless?

As already indicated, law-abiding souls must have their victims, too, experiencing no guilt at how pleasurable it feels to punish others for crimes they themselves have contemplated or succeeded in getting away with. Further, in punishing others for these crimes, they actually feel they are making retribution of some sort for their own. That's why punishing others subconsciously feels so good.

Beneath the civilised veneer, man remains the supreme predator. Cursed with what he believes is understanding, his true soul blossoms god-like in the heart of the nuclear inferno. Again, only does punishment and retaliation frighten him, not the crime.

———◆———

Practically everyone believes they could write a book or compose a song if only they put their mind to it. They believe this simply because they can easily comprehend the finished products of others. It is not until they attempt the task of creation themselves that they become conscious of their own limitations, lack of imagination, abysmal powers of self-expression and how unaccustomed they are to thinking deeply about anything at all.

Becoming aware of the vast gap that exists between understanding and personal creativity — and the intellectual effort required to capture and express a complex idea in simple terms — is humiliating.

The art of psychological profiling is also subject to a misapprehension as to its complexity. As soon as something is interpreted for them, readers or listeners tell themselves it was obvious anyway. They blithely credit themselves with the author's insight or common sense, in a psychic precinct most people self-protectively avoid approaching anyway, in case they bump into themselves in the dark alleyways of the mind.

Had they been asked to interpret the psychological aspects of a murder, the result would probably have been a long confused silence. The subconscious defensive inertia to self-analysis combines with a social reticence to admit, even remotely, of sharing and understanding the psychological drives and thought patterns of a serial killer.

In liberal guises, the law-abiding masses will assure you that they do wish to understand, but that such atrocities are far beyond their pristine comprehension and delicate sensibilities, even if they work quite happily in armaments or biological warfare industries. Distance ameliorates any responsibility for monumental carnage, but the act of an individual killer shoves the spilled guts right under their noses.

Bad manners is the crime.

Chapter Three

This truth within thy mind rehearse,
That in a boundless universe,
Is boundless better, boundless worse.

Tennyson (1809–1892)

Deep thought is anathema to most people. They are too self-absorbed, too deeply immersed in their own immediate appetites and mundane problems to exercise a spark of originality or a capacity for extended abstract cogitation, and are content to regurgitate second-hand or generally popular opinion. Such people seek safety in the stale clichés and platitudes programmed into them since childhood.

Television interviews with the so-called 'average man in the street' suggest that he is facile in almost every respect, prone to say what he believes 'nice' people would expect him to say, displaying a social awareness that would flatter Attila the Hun. In effect, an aspiring clone.

If you disagree with this general assessment, perhaps you should think again. We *all* believe we are unique. Relatively speaking, that is of course correct. Likewise we may regard someone as a 'character,' but that does not necessarily mean that they possess character.

Many serial killers think in terms of such adverse value distinction *all the time*. Their superiority complex is, it could be argued, paradoxically a symbol of inferiority. A closed mind. Almost completely self-consumed, insular in a psychopathic or psychotic stasis; they, much like patronising politicians, can pass public muster, but privately devalue others around them by habit or reflex. They regard people generally as obstacles to be surmounted by all available means, their victims appreciated intrinsically as existential commodities.

———

'Good morning, sir. Why have you put out your lamp?'
'Those are the orders,' replied the lamplighter.
'Good morning.'
'What are the orders?'

'The orders are that I put out my lamp. Good evening.'
And he lighted his lamp again.
'And why have you just lighted it again?'
'Those are the orders,' replied the lamplighter.
'I do not understand,' said the little prince.
'There is nothing to understand,' said the lamplighter. 'Orders
are orders. Good morning.' And he put out his lamp.

— *The Little Prince*, Antoine de Saint-Exupery

Policemen, penal psychiatrists, prison guards, pulp authors, TV crime
pundits, newspaper reporters and other failed academics and social misfits
who make a profitable, parasitic living from the crimes of others, may conde-
scendingly claim special insight into the criminal mind — and why not? —
since they have no doubt vicariously enjoyed committing every crime under
the sun in thought and spirit themselves, and perhaps many in actuality.

Those who make a make a 'respectable' living from crime are in many
respects more corrupt, culpable and self-deluded than the criminals themselves.

Therefore, by virtue of extensive study of the human animal, I might counter-
claim insight into the mind of the serial academic and commercial crime scavenger.
The self-appointed scholastic expert but practical amateur. Or the penal dustbin
men, too inadequate to make a living in the real world, bolstering their insecurity
by locking people up. Policemen who lack the intellect and nerve to commit their
own crimes but feel free to steal and extort stolen money from criminals. And, last
but beastlier, the local and national politicians who graft a career from loudly condemning criminals and crime — as a general rule the more corrupt a politician is,
the more vociferously they condemn and exploit criminals to divert attention from
their own iniquity. In short, corrupt police, judges, lawyers, judges, customs men,
etc., who are on the take are not particular whether their bribes originate from
drugs, prostitution, murder, gambling, robbery, extortion, or whatever other criminal pursuit, so long as the dirt doesn't show under their nails.

Second-rate authors and journalists hacking towards media prominence
via the serial killer risk nothing by the encouragement of crime through commercial exploitation and sensationalism. Like tail-notes to a comet, they seek
by association to share the historical longevity certain serial killers achieve in
the collective subconscious. Academics in this category, resenting dependency
upon the savage, transmute their salacious guilt and lack of self-esteem into
sanctimonious vilification of the specific killer chosen as their personal vehicle
to fame and fortune.

Police chiefs are subject to the same self-aggrandizement syndrome, habitually fighting amongst themselves not only to claim major personal credit for capturing the serial killer, but also to cash in by having a book ghost-written about their own imaginary powers of detection — though in reality, most criminals are caught through police informers.

Even eminent judges jostle unashamedly for the distinction of trying particularly notorious murderers, hoping to be remembered in something other than infrequently read, dusty tomes of jurisprudence.

Such is the competitive alchemy of fame and infamy . . . the stroke of a bloody axe often outliving that of the pen.

As previously intimated, the serial killer is unavoidably a failure in many normal walks of life. Particularly if stoical acceptance of tedious subsistence is the prime criterion commonly sought and admired. He lacks the patience to compromise and bear the stultifying lassitude of ordinary modern life. He — or she, though women's lib prefers to claim less than equality in the field of murder — wants more NOW, without wasting time on social decorum or strategy, in what is clearly perceived an extremely uncertain and short life.

This acute awareness in the serial killer of precious time passing creates an existential urgency which counter-productively sublimates the knowledge that one mistake may deprive him of life, or terminate the freedom he hungers to exercise. In actuality, subconsciously or consciously, the serial killer has emotionally chosen to live one day as a lion, rather than decades as a sheep.

Once he believes that if he does not determine his own destiny some fool will determine it for him, the dice cannot be recalled. Legality and morality are transmuted almost magically beyond strictly irrelevant human barriers. No one had better try to hinder his riding roughshod over such impediments to existential fulfilment. He has declared war.

Psychologically, there may be some social conditioning which still hinders his obsessive and, therefore, contradictory quest for spontaneity. A debilitating metaphysical impulse may still stubbornly inhabit his subconscious. An impulse which paradoxically compels him to openly challenge a Supreme Being he consciously does not believe exists and, in some instances, may wish did, so that he might either smite the antithetic entity directly, or beg for a forgiveness he would never stoop to ask from man. At this initial stage, some serial killers may still retain the common human tendency to luxuriate in fear-induced guilt.

But once the killer has committed the first or second act of homicide, unchallenged by any divine or increasingly contemptible secular power, he will gradually accept his own acts as normal, or supranormal, and that of the rest of humanity as subnormal and weak. He will in effect begin to regard society in much the same way as professional soldiers do an enemy state. He has created a microcosmic state of his own in which he alone governs, becoming as careless with other people's lives as are most rulers.

The serial killer perhaps attains a degree of amoral, ruthless detachment on par with, say, a state-security doctor employed to ensure a prisoner under torture does not die before divulging the information sought. By a process of logical extension, the killer sees himself as following the example of society's legalised killers, only freelance. But he considers himself superior to legal killers in that he accepts responsibility and the risk of penalty from which the officially-sanctioned are exempt. He might also validly come to the conclusion that crime is a logical variant of capitalist free enterprise, simply a lucrative and often exciting form of illegal self-employment.

I personally can testify to having had boundless energy for criminal pursuits, just like any avid businessman could work from dawn till dusk on projects offering high financial or existential rewards. Crime is a natural extension of *laissez-faire* culture.

Having a passion for travel, my long journeys from city to city to recruit and organise the required labour and logistics of a crime were acutely stimulating, an aesthetic bonus. I particularly enjoyed the old-world romanticism of travelling by steam locomotive, and the mysterious, sooty atmosphere of railway stations vibrant with bustle and purpose. I also experienced a unique sense of licence when taking anonymous possession of a fresh city from which I would be departing the same night. The kinetic panache of total possibility. Several authors independently likened my passion for travel and certain other traits and characteristics to that of Stavrogin, the pivotal figure in Dostoevsky's novel, *The Possessed* (aka *The Devils*), a satire on the revolutionary mind.

Whether the comparison holds any validity or truth does not trouble me one way or the other, and in fact affords the opportunity to underline some salient psychological points, being an ardent admirer of all Dostoevsky's works and their unique psychological depths.

Most intelligent people have the tendency to believe they are masters of their own destiny to a greater or lesser degree. As to whether this concomitantly signifies a greater or lesser degree of insanity or sanity is an imponderable to other than the wilfully blind. Further, whether any individual's beliefs are considered sane or insane by others is of no basic relevance to the individual concerned.

Peripherally, we all change with time, but the deeply-held central beliefs forming the gravitational core of each unique personality rarely undergo significant modification. Whole nations and individuals regularly defend their beliefs to the death. Sometimes the victors are admired and venerated, and sometimes the defeated. Transient historical perspective is as fickle and modish as morality and legality, sanity and insanity. Acceptance of society's idiosyncratic norms can be accounted a virtue one moment, a crime the next, and only the individual has the supreme right to decide which, and accept the consequences of his/her considered acts.

The visionary or dissident is more admirable than the conformist or social hypocrite. The same can be said of Stavrogin, regardless whether or not his actions are generally pronounced selfish, irrational, immoral or criminal. He at least holds the interest as being uncommon. The compliant have always been more stimulated by criminals than by saints, preferring the intoxication of wine to the bland sustenance of milk. Without temptation what value virtue?

Ye who suffer, suffer from yourself. No one else compels.

— Buddha

Stavrogin cannot tolerate ordinary existence. He turns life into a cartoon where anything is possible, experiencing only scorn for the followers he is turning into caricatures, revelling in the absurdity that they take his revolutionary games seriously, even to the extent of risking their lives.

Thirsting to believe in something, Stavrogin is incapable of believing in anything and finds life meaningless, in effect preferring to accept no hope to false hope; this colours his every action, yet paradoxically fails to deprive him of the ability to inspire hope in his followers. Negative dynamism creating positive effect.

The author Colin Wilson, in his brilliant but derivative literary critique *The Outsider*, misconceives important aspects of meaning and motivation in *The Possessed*. His interpretations seem more concerned with reflecting his personal, somewhat eccentric philosophical ideas which lack the eclectic elasticity of moral relativism. In addition, he has deficient grasp of the necessary multi-dimensional psychic factors of empirical thought required to conduct a comprehensive diagnostic into such matters.

Wilson's obsession with writing about murder, outsiders and criminals is perhaps subconsciously explained by the fact that his own beliefs and opinions are surprisingly mundane and lacking in controversy, and he has never used his writings or influence to champion a social cause.

Making a lucrative living from criminals and their crimes should engender a guilt complex, yet he appears to possess no moral scruples about demeaning the victims of the crime by lovingly describing every horrific and intimate forensic detail of their final moments. Some authors invariably rationalise their prurient intrusion in the name of science and the furtherance of human illumination. I believe most serious students can discern when that line has been crossed and morbid sensationalism begins.

Having proclaimed himself a genius suggests psychotic overtones, and, perhaps because of this, Colin Wilson apparently fails to appreciate and extrapolate the importance of psychotic influence in *The Possessed* — the very title echoing it — and states that most great criminals and guerrillas turn out to be mindless Freudian neurotics. A rather disturbing hypothesis when one considers that the majority of present world leaders, particularly in the third world, were former 'terrorists.' Conversely, the political doctrines and actions of many of the more exalted world luminaries in the West are frequently, and often justifiably, termed 'criminal' by the politically/socially informed and eminent intellectuals.

From three decades of practical study, I have found that it is generally applicable, especially amongst the vast majority of lesser criminals who can be described as inadequate, that life imitates art. The film actors do not act like gangsters, the gangsters act like their film counterparts. By externalising dreams and modelling themselves upon celluloid images and stage projections, they effectively alter and lose touch with reality, increasing their chances of apprehension. Essentially such aspiring criminals fail to develop sufficiently the third eye and ear, consequently creating a personal microcosm with insufficient pragmatic defences.

Further, it is facile to use the word 'Freudian neurotic' in a blanket derogatory context. Neurosis is an innate survival mechanism. Only when developed to a morbid degree is it regarded as detrimental and the seed of psychosis. Psycho-neurosis also nurtures a predisposition to dissociative reaction, surrender to irresistible impulse, a state of temporary insanity. I am certain that even seasoned psychopathic and particularly psychotic serial killers can fall prey to dissociative reaction, faced with a victim so physically attractive or psychologically appealing that they literally cannot resist the impulse to attack.

Stavrogin's erratic social behaviour, his impulsive physical attacks of varying categories on others, can certainly be classified as psychotic episodes. Wilson seems unable to appreciate, or make allowances for, altered states of affective mental aberration and invariably applies narrow philosophical or moral criteria, thus demonising rather than apprehending.

Outsider tendencies can be attributed to many fluctuating psychological imponderables devoid of philosophical rationale. Without wishing to pathologise, Stavrogin is more the victim of his impulses than Wilson will allow him to be. He examines Stavrogin from the outside rather than attempting to enter and look out from within. Stavrogin is an open book to those who have shared his psychic experiences.

Impulsiveness is not a conscious act, therefore Stavrogin's spontaneous frolics into criminal mode are essentially reflexes lacking in thought, self-interest or strategic intent. More a satisfying of primal appetite. Stavrogin's real crime is his inability to curb anti-social impulses.

Criminals can be as impulsively good or evil as the 'normal' person but are, for expedient social and political motives, always defined exclusively by their evil acts. The Byrons and Rimbauds escape criminal categorisation by merit of accepted artistic genius; politicians and amoral officialdom escape by merit of power. Most common criminals possess neither of these social absolvers, and the type of serial killer whose determined crimes lead to notoriety regard their acts as justifiable within the framework of their hidden agenda, and do not seek or require the absolution of others who live by a different credo.

Whether their acts might be interpreted by an opposing culture as 'insane' or 'depraved' is, as already indicated, of no consequence to them. It is not that they lack a morality but that they believe in a strikingly different and individual form. Even amorality is a mode of morality. Wittgenstein's struggle with language exemplifies its eternal paradox.

The word 'psychopath' is a case in point. Ask most people to define the word and the majority will — thanks to the mass media, pulp fiction and decades of film and other theatrical depictions — immediately opt for 'killer.' This is erroneous.

Further on I shall deal with the essential personality traits and characteristics of the criminal psychopath and psychotic, but I now take the opportunity to define briefly the identical psychopathic traits and characteristics shared by both the criminal psychopath and the socially-acceptable psychopath.

It should be noted that this book deals with serial killers, therefore future use of the term 'psychopath' throughout I shall be referring exclusively to the psychopathic killer. If I were writing about habitual criminals other than killers, application of the term would be in the context of whatever type of habitual criminal behaviour was being dealt with. For the word 'psychopath' can be applicable to *all forms* of habitual criminal and anti-social behaviour.

As the term 'psychopath' defines an affective form of deep-seated personality disorder, its valid application is not confined solely to the so-called 'criminal classes.' There are many ways to commit all crimes, murder included, without the least danger of being caught or even having one's actions branded 'criminal.'

In the field of devious criminality the socially-acceptable psychopath reigns supreme.

Such socially-acceptable, highly successful psychopaths are in fact common in the upper echelons of every society, for it is that very state of mind that helps them to succeed in the first instance. It is the psychotic who is out of tune with reality, not the psychopath. It is the psychotic who is legally termed 'insane,' not the psychopath.

Each one of you, whether high or low, regularly rubs shoulders with socially-acceptable clinical psychopaths every day without the least awareness, not only accepting them as 'normal,' but also as people to be admired and highly respected by virtue of their success and positions of authority. But should you look beyond their prestigious trappings and study their personality traits and characteristics, you would find it quite easy to identify the socially-acceptable psychopaths amongst you.

Beneath the exterior of self-serving charm and urbanity — which most psychopaths can usually switch on and off at will — the crocodile smile, which doesn't quite vitalise the eyes, there exist only negative emotions, all of which are primarily concerned with personal ambition and the will to power.

The most salient traits and characteristics of the psychopath are coldness, calculation, manipulation, lack of sensitivity, natural deviousness, facile mendacity, amorality presented as moral flexibility, pathological anger and envy rationalised as altruism or logic, all-encompassing greed, assumption of personal superiority over all others, a dictatorial and bullying attitude relying on power and authority rather than intelligence, suspicion and lack of trust to a paranoid degree, inexorable ruthlessness, an egocentric conviction that they are always right, sexual promiscuousness, complete lack of remorse.

These traits and characteristics are most likely to surface unwittingly when the psychopath is contradicted, frustrated or blocked.

Does any combination of these salient features of the psychopathic personality remind you of someone in your household, a relative or friend, a person at your place of work, a politician, a bureaucrat, some minor official, a judge, a teacher, an author or journalist, a member of the armed forces or the police, some person with practically everything they could possibly need but who always wants more?

Or even yourself?

———

Research into psychopathology conducted by psychiatrists and psychologists is almost exclusively based on selected captives — imprisoned, failed psychopaths, who have not had the high measure of power, authority and privileged opportunity requisite to inflict upon society the same degree of widespread damage of which the socially-acceptable psychopath is capable on a daily basis.

Naturally, the psychopathic elite are in an almost unassailable position to refute any charge or suggestion of mental abnormality. Even in the unlikely event of such powerful people agreeing to psychiatric examination, they would certainly ensure their eminent lawyers, and personal doctors would, by application of every threat in existence, silence and quash any adverse diagnoses.

As indicated, the whole of society, backed by the power of the mass media, is geared to concentrate public attention and hostility upon the captured, relatively small-time psychopaths, and particularly serial killers, using them as popular entertainments to distract public scrutiny from the infinitely more dangerous, socially-acceptable psychopaths who hold high office throughout society.

Governments have always employed socially-acceptable psychopaths to good effect, particularly in the special armed forces and intelligence services and, of course, expediently present the actions of such special servants as being 'for the good of the country and the people.'

America, forever glorying in its international reputation as a democracy, employs the largest army of security/secret police in the Western hemisphere — the FBI, the CIA, the NSA, undercover civilian police, SWAT riot squads, Special Service units, the National Guard, State Troopers, etc., etc.

To safeguard its international commercial empire the government frequently uses naked aggression, employing the CIA to 'destabilise' foreign countries not subservient to American foreign policy/influence, and replacing democratically-elected governments with American-financed military dictatorships.

Axiomatically, a crucial sector of the American economy is based upon a thriving arms industry. When Henry Kissinger publicly announced, 'It is not *economically feasible* for America to end the war in Vietnam at this present moment,' there was no public outcry at the clear implication that, faced with the choice of scaling down the American arms industry, or continuing to allow thousands of its own and foreign nationals to be slaughtered weekly, the latter course was preferable. And when President Nixon was carpet-bombing Cambodia for many months while solemnly assuring the American people he was not, there was insufficient moral concern within the political establishment to demand impeachment.

Shareholders, executives, technicians and labourers in the arms industry exemplify the zoological fact that any form of mass destruction is perfectly acceptable to respectable people so long as they earn a good, 'honest' living by it. Not 'guns or butter,' but guns for butter.

Any government which, at any given time in office, necessitates law enforcement agencies to protect it from the majority of the people, is not a government for and by the people. Any law enforcement agency which protects a government, at any given time in office, against the majority of the people, cannot be for the people.

Study your leaders more, your prisoners less. Be more concerned about the beliefs of the Inquisitor rather than those of the heretic. The barbarity and power of the state thrives upon lack of public understanding and organised repudiation.

Chapter Four

God so commanded, and left
that command
Sole daughter of his voice;
the rest we live
Law to ourselves, our reason
is our law.

Paradise Lost, **Milton**

Who can deny having experienced moments when, had you owned the power, you would have gladly destroyed the world and every living creature on it in your anger and despondency, like a thwarted, disgruntled child?

In retrospect, when the blood has cooled or circumstances brightened, you may self-flatteringly asseverate, 'Oh, but I didn't really mean it.' Nonsense! Had the world-extinguishing button been under your thumb at that particular moment of inspired rage or evil brilliance, you would have pushed it with grateful exhilaration, even joy. The Götterdämmerung syndrome.

I offer this to illustrate further that there is no great gap between the law-abiding and the criminal. It is man's expedient or delusional nature to parade lack of omnipotent power as evidence of innate virtue, well knowing the latter formed no motivational part of his thoughts or emotions at the moment of resentful revenge.

Given the right conditions and circumstances, particularly when frustrated and depressed, do we not all harbour the homicidal, megalomaniacal urges of Nero hidden deep within?

'If the mob had one throat, I'd cut it!'

Or the ferocious inclinations of the Marquis de Sade:

'How many times have I longed to be able to assail the sun, snatch it out of the universe, make a general darkness, or use that star to burn the world. Oh, that would be a crime!'

Such extreme examples of criminal candour scorn the parameters of stereotypical bromides and threadbare truisms with which theologians, moralists and sanctimonious tyrants seek to exculpate or cloud material motives.

One should try to be honest with oneself almost as a daily devotion.

Forget the moral pedants. Many shrivelled academics attempt to measure the human psyche with crude calibrators, much like those television grotesques with swingometers you see on election night.

If history teaches anything, it is: In every war or ideological conflict both sides genuinely believe themselves to be right. They deny purely selfish stimulus, paying lip-service to lofty moral concepts, but unwittingly reveal, by their *actions*, the true and universally empirical belief that the end *does* justify the means, that might *is* right, that the victor *does* dictate morality and legality; that often two wrongs *do* make a right and two rights a wrong. And, of course, that the spoils always go to the victor. Equivocations to the contrary are patently cosmetic, and falsely egalitarian.

Bored by the futility and inertia of prolonged, reasoned argument, and having unsuccessfully explored and deployed every devious and deceitful stratagem to defeat the enemy, your eminent 'statesmen' invariably regard war as the natural extension of diplomacy. They seek vain consolation in cathartic extravaganzas of bloodletting, whose sole moral exoneration lies in the superior brutality of martial victory. This reveals them to be cyclically vulnerable to the same primal instincts as serial killers. But murdering on a so much grander scale, of course, and being honoured for it to boot.

If I were wont to play Pontius Pilate, and asked you to choose between Richard Nixon and Charles Manson, who best would deserve crucifixion?

In the context of nuclear global conflict, where both sides know neither side can win, mankind self-evidently owes his continuing survival not to *virtue* but to *evil*: the balance of *terror*.

Can there be any objective doubt, in those of you wisely conversant with the wiles and ways of human nature and man's infinite capacity to rationalise every atrocity there is, that the main psychological reason why most people do not pray to the Prince of Darkness, had they robust spirit to do so, is that it would be tantamount to worshipping themselves, thus confirming a nature they would piously deny?

Is not evil man's true element of delight, the dominating psyche he naturally luxuriates in and is drawn inexorably to embrace? A source of spontaneous vitality and verve, evil banishes the mundane barriers of 'normal' existence, galvanising the senses and lending a fresh vibrancy to the world. It is a facet of character man thoroughly enjoys in the darkness of mind and bed most of his life. Intoxication without artificial stimulants.

Man secretly thrills to, or derives profound psychic comfort from, the satisfaction of successfully convincing others he possesses little or no evil in his intrinsic character, but is expert in detecting and condemning it in almost everyone else. So cohesively corrupt is this moral schizophrenia that even his indignant, sporadic criticism of evil is momentarily experienced as genuine; aesthetically rooted as it is in the smug satisfaction of having caught out someone less adept in duplicity and hypocrisy than himself.

But, at a deeper level, evil, like its opposite, must be sustained by illusion, for it brings with it an understanding of the futility of life when all actions are permissible and equally meaningless. Emptied of forbidden desires, we still desire contrast, the illusion of meaning.

If we fail in our attempt to create and stimulate the illusion of contrast and meaning, the psychic dynamo rusts and grinds to a halt. Why bother to exist or act if all is indeed vanity? But if we intend to persist in existing in a meaningless world, the logical extension to disillusionment is delusion, where only insanity divines meaning.

I believe most serial killers have, consciously or subconsciously, trodden this labyrinthian course, resentfully deciding to impose personal meaning upon the world's façade by acts of destruction which invite, or approximate, self-destruction. A reversal of Buddhist principles, attempting to purge each desire by gratification, but sharing the common goal of Nirvana. Oblivion.

The serial killer regards both the wilful destruction of others and of himself as human/cosmic triumphs which establish mathematical equilibrium and psychic meaning.

What gives *your* life meaning?

———•◆•———

Losers are considered fair game to mankind in general. People must have someone, anyone, to throw to the lions as a reward for their own grudging adherence to public 'virtues' — tiresome virtues, the observance of which infuriatingly devours most of one's brief existence on this insignificant speck of spinning dust. Such people, unlike the serial killer, have chosen to allow other people to guide their destiny, and must pay the price of expedient subordination.

It is perhaps comforting to realise that even those citizens who achieve the zenith of wealth and power by moral languor are still too afraid to freely enjoy its rewards, because of the public image of probity they weightily forged for themselves and are forced to maintain.

Man is an unswerving moral hypocrite in many other fields of dishonest endeavour.

He perversely despises imitation whilst in the very act of duplicating;

claims originality in the midst of his own mediocrity; searches out opposites against his will, seeking an otherness he truly does not wish to find. He then compounds this chimerical assortment by inventing in his own image false gods to placate, fanatical dogmas to prosecute and absurd prophecies to fulfil. All this convolutional jousting is performed primarily to avoid confronting his true nature. It makes little difference, for he fretfully remains the scourge of the earth.

On the other hand, it is mostly in the quiescent company of the atheist, the sceptic, the cynic, the nihilist, the existentialist, those self-absorbed who are content to propose and preach nothing, that we may sometimes escape the obsessive demands of synthetic morality and the jarring irritations of theological presumption. They cast aside the ridiculous banality of metaphysical minutiae striving beyond man's feeble comprehension, and instead opt for that comfortable, sensual silence known chiefly to old friends, lovers and opium addicts, which is so often much more stimulating and inspiring.

It is in the spiritual vagaries, the paradoxical heights of poetry and music, that we sometimes glimpse, and fleetingly believe we have reached, our true potential, almost touching the power of gods. But the descent back to sullen earth and the babble of the rabble soon depresses and enrages our sensibilities, and all seems meaningless once more.

This profound conviction of human absurdity, in harness with an ineffable sense of eternal boredom, visits us all at times, of course, usually departing in due course as preoccupation with more demanding appetites returns.

But to the criminal, and particularly the serial killer, the 'ordinary' is an emetic less to be stomached than potassium cyanide. Leaden uniformity is slowly crushing and suffocating him. Action becomes imperative. He has to prove he exists beyond the control of all. Even of himself. That self which is a programmed contamination, a synthetic conscience, arguably his own greatest enemy. He must systematically neutralise this alien intruder before it betrays or destroys him, as it surely will, on the dangerous path of extreme individualism he has chosen to pursue.

Like Dostoevsky's anti-hero Raskolnikov, the criminal not only wishes to taste the extraordinary, but also longs to know whether he possesses the will to dare reach for it. Hamlet-like, tortured by doubt and indecision, the longer the serial killer procrastinates, the greater becomes the urge to resolve matters by cathartic, homicidal action. He can 'resist anything except temptation.'

It would be quite natural for most people to believe that the serial killer regards murder as the ultimate crime and the greatest challenge of all. But such a generalization is too simplistic.

Serial killers, like it or not, can possess just as many admirable facets of character as anyone else, and sometimes more than average. The majority of criminals have hidden agendas, as has practically every intelligent being. They also have their own personal code of ethics and morals, albeit eccentric to the ordinary individual.

For instance, I regard personal disloyalty as the worst crime of all, and have killed some guilty of it without a qualm.

Yet members of the public, in guilty self-awareness of their own criminal fantasies, and secretly envying the criminal's ability to act them out, eagerly accept the mass media's self-flattering, demonizing projection of criminals as an inferior species.

Humiliating though it may be to accept, the serial killer's leap of faith pivots primarily upon identity as an independent entity — with everyone else perceived entirely as extras. The fate of some nameless victim is secondary to his purpose, simply a means to an existential end. In the pursuit of his hidden agenda, he is as indifferent to the fate of others as others are to his in the pursuit of theirs.

'It's business. Nothing personal,' as the Mafia would say, in concert with other honest businessmen. Whether a man dies by a bullet or the merciless decision of a bank, the result is the same. There are many men in the upper echelons of finance, industry, politics and the military who are more psychopathically ruthless than any Godfather, leaving a higher body count in their wake.

More or less, all but the constitutionally inadequate possess the wish for power, but many lack the will. The *desire* to be insubordinate and autonomous, reach mercurial heights, psychically transfuse the blood of gods into the veins, is more common than the ability to do so. Conscience confounds the majority. The remainder, in my opinion, seizing whatever they wish by means legal or foul, careless of the consequences to others, are as culpable as the criminal. In brief, sanctioned by law or no, elitism is the soul of criminality.

The spiritual best in life is perhaps conceived in silence, but the same can be true of the worst. Whatever gains are conceived in the silence will eventually be interrupted, for good or ill, by the approach of some frenzied believer in something or other, anything at all, who will not desist until he has pressed his delirious delusions upon you, no matter how fatuous.

This species of Inquisitorial prophet would almost rather kill you than let you elude conversion to his moral/political/philosophical deformations of character, the corrosive obsessions which feverishly torment him to proselytise every person in sight.

Your tolerant indifference, peace of mind, or independent spirit would be interpreted as a personal affront in the arrogant eyes of such religionists, who supposedly believe in original sin yet appear to consider themselves exempt. The born-again Christian (or, worse still, convert) is so zealously pleased with himself that he apparently has little time left to please anyone else.

Such people represent in microcosm the psychological mechanisms, dogmas and fanaticisms which have helped ferment ideological wars throughout the ages and to this very day. They recognise no middle ground.

What do I believe in? I reiterate, moral relativism in all matters other than personal loyalty to chosen individuals.

Studying humanity with the objective detachment of a spectre — my active, free participation in the human comedy now being constrained by manganese-steel bars and electronic eyes — I have observed nothing in the social evolution of mankind to shake my lack of faith in human nature in general.

The age of positive progress in human affairs has long gone, I conclude, and shall never return. Crime will forever increase in ratio to the escalating corruption and unbridled greed in the upper echelons of Western social order. This will inevitably lead to ever-increasing brutal repression and suppression of the masses, who will react in kind.

If you indifferently choose to isolate criminals, prepare yourself to be isolated by them. Permanently.

The dispossessed and disadvantaged shall become progressively more nomadic, alienated and resentful. Mobile serial killers will flourish like the flowers in the field. It is happening in America and other Western countries at present. Overpopulation, once periodically diminished by wars, will mainly be regulated by famine and perhaps more ambitious man-made plagues of the AIDS variety, to which only the ruling elite shall be immune.

> If you can always remember danger when you are secure, and
> remember chaos in times of order, watch out for danger and
> chaos while they are still formless and prevent them before
> they happen, this is the best of all.
>
> — *The Art of War*, Sun Tzu

The obscenely rich are already in full retreat, heavily fortifying their private domains. Even the affluent middle class of America has begun constructing whole towns for themselves, encircled by high fences and guarded by private police forces who allow no inhabitants to enter without an identity pass, and no strangers in without a written invitation from an inhabitant.

Extreme polarisation has resulted in sporadic urban warfare in America since the sixties, of course, but it is becoming more commonplace.

Technological advances, particularly in the field of smart computer software, are now a weekly occurrence. Cameras and electronic bugs have evolved to insect-size and are almost as ubiquitous. Equipped with heat-seeking video cameras and probing searchlights, police helicopter gunships prowl the city skies after dark like Martian invaders, whilst in all the streets and buildings below yet more video cameras pry constantly.

The disenfranchised city populations bitterly resent their ever-increasing lack of personal privacy, but no longer seem interested in fighting for civil rights through the enemy's 'normal channels,' perceiving anarchic destruction as perhaps the only form of effective self-expression remaining, and, from their hopeless perspective, almost certainly the most spiritually satisfying — even to the extent of nihilistically burning down their own ghetto prisons. Cohesive social concern and consensus are rapidly being rendered extinct.

> United thoughts and counsels, equal hope,
> And hazard in the glorious enterprise.
> Yet not for those
> Nor what the potent victor in his rage
> Can else inflict do I repent or change,
> Though changed in outward lustre; that fixed mind
> And high disdain, from sense of injured merit.
>
> — *Paradise Lost*, Milton

Though I have become used to being watched by prison security cameras, etc., both inside and outside the blocks, I can still identify with how supposedly free people *should* feel at constant electronic encroachment. So much so that I am certain I would not meekly tolerate it if in their position, and would oppose it by all effective means. Soon the only people left with privacy will be those behind the cameras and listening devices.

I deem myself fortunate in the belief that the supreme individualist should not only choose his own life but also the manner and timing of his own death. This Bushido code, the kamikaze spirit, Samurai stoicism, shall, I am

sure, proliferate and exact a heavy death toll amongst the wealthy and privileged classes. When one accepts, in pursuit of a chosen goal, the possibility or
certainty of one's own death as of no consequence, one has total freedom to
manoeuvre and exact maximum retribution. Only by coming to terms with
death do you grasp the essence of life.

One determined, motivated individual can inflict significant psychic
destruction upon a city or country. Others will note and emulate. The domino
effect gathers momentum.

Observing the human condition with a strong sense of absurdity, I appreciate the solution to man's ills when offered by that wonderful comedian W.C.
Fields, who splendidly suggested:

'Instead of having wars, the world leaders should be put into a stadium to
fight it out amongst themselves with socks full of horse manure.'

In Hellenistic and medieval times many territorial disputes between
warring nations were settled by king's champion fighting king's champion —
peoples' champions in the story of David and Goliath. We naturally find W.C.
Fields' solution highly amusing mainly because of his choice of weapons and
the image of pompous, decrepit politicians wielding them. Conversely, the
present advanced stage of 'civilisation' invariably demands nothing less than
the total destruction of the enemy state and the flower of generations.

Wars of vast destruction are now fought as though they were children's
computer games, by impersonal pushbutton heroes whose names we hide
from public scrutiny and inscribe on no roles of honour. For instance, can any
reader spontaneously call to mind the name of the pilots or crew who bombed
Hiroshima or Nagasaki?

The machines are now the real heroes. Their victories over enemy
machines are lauded, not only for defeating the enemy but also for boosting
the economy by increased weapon sales to other 'civilised' countries. The
unavoidable war dead are brought furtively home crammed in giant freight
containers, political embarrassments to be hastily buried and forgotten. The
merely maimed and crippled are then cosmetically removed from the PR-
managed glory of the victory parade. Nondescript politicians, mere stock
clerks for the arms manufacturing industries, smile and wave airily from bal-
conies in their lucrative brave new world. They beam and dream of high poll-
ratings whilst working out the schedule for the next war, staged to test fresh
weapons and use up old, envisioning future election victories soundly based on

'patriotism,' economic prosperity and the blood of the dead, the latter performing a final sterling service in reducing the 'surplus population' and future unemployment statistics. Festivities concluded, the upstaged wounded anonymously wind their way home to oblivion through drooping bunting and drunken rednecks. The politicians then begin work on their second stalwart platform, 'law and order,' urging the death penalty and longer sentences for less enterprising criminals than themselves.

Those social engineers and optimists, who propose that a more widely-available system of higher education in every country will lead to an equally elevated standard of global human/humane conduct and culture, are impractical dreamers who conveniently ignore the numerous lessons of modern history which illustrate the contrary: the more sophisticated the society, the more impersonal and grandiose the savagery.

Those who rely upon ideological education and an ever-increasing degree of authoritarian order to eradicate the criminal and predatory instincts of mankind, are wilfully blind. The death camps of Nazi Germany were conceived, organised and very efficiently run by highly-educated men who venerated a form of conservative law and order they planned and expected to last for over a thousand years. These men, such as Rheinhart Heydrich, SS founder-head of the Reichsicherheitsdienst (RSHD and SD — SS Reich Security Department and Gestapo), and prime organiser of the extermination of Jews in German-occupied territories; Dr Josef Mengele, chief selector of victims for the gas chambers, and performer of thousands of fatal eugenic and sterilisation experiments on male and female concentration camp inmates; Dr Ernst Kaltenbrunner, SS successor to the assassinated Heydrich — all had the highest university education. They were pillars of society, men of high culture, possessing aesthetic sensitivity and genuine appreciation of the classical arts. The six or seven million Jews, gypsies, homosexuals, communists, criminals, lunatics and other undesirables they enthusiastically exterminated by poison gas, shooting, hanging, medical experiment and lethal injection, which was performed perfectly legally under German law.

In modern-day America, criminals, per capita mostly Negroes and other ethnic minorities, are being just as legally sentenced to death by cyanide gas, lethal injection, hanging, shooting, electrocution, by similarly well-educated 'civilised' men and women, with clergy and doctors in attendance to sanctify the ritual.

Further, the respectable giant pharmaceutical companies in the United States are allowed to use American prisoners as human guinea pigs in medical experiments to test the possible adverse side-effects of untried drugs. And it was recently exposed that eminent American medical researchers are using the captured medical records of Dr Josef Mengele, tabulating the results of his fatal medical experiments, to assist them in similar American programmes of research at present being carried out.

Many German 'war criminals' were tried and sentenced to death by American judges at the Nuremberg Trials in the late 1940s for 'crimes against humanity,' under laws specifically invented by the victorious allies to condemn the vanquished retroactively. Amongst the listed 'crimes against humanity' were euthanasia, and the legal sterilisation and execution of patients in German mental hospitals.

Those same American judges could not have been unaware of what a judicial colleague of theirs had pronounced on the subject of dealing with the mentally subnormal, many years prior to the Nazi regime in Germany. He was the eminent American Supreme Court Justice, Mr Oliver Wendell Holmes, from Cambridge, Massachusetts, former professor of anatomy and physiology at Harvard University, distinguished essayist, biographer, poet and novelist, whose literary works were described by American critics as 'kindly, humorous and sagacious.' Perhaps 'ironic' should have been added. His final solution to the problem of mentally retarded American citizens reads as follows:

'We have seen more than once that the public welfare may call upon the best citizens for their lives. It would be strange indeed if we could not call upon those, who already sapped the strength of the state, for these lesser sacrifices in order to prevent our being swamped by incompetents. It is better for all the world if, instead of waiting to execute the general offspring for crimes, or to let them starve from imbecility, society can prevent their propagation by medical means in the first place. Three generations of imbeciles are enough.'

The justification or rationalisation of wrongs performed by the leading lights of so-called civilised society — be it in wars, persecution, discrimination and general law enforcement concentrated upon the ferocious punishment of predominantly blue-collar criminals — does more than suggest that, on the whole, it is the highly-educated conformists, not the dissenters or 'criminals,' who represent the greatest danger to humanistic culture and the very existence of mankind.

A truly enlightened society, allowing for the varying degrees of intelligence and diverse psychological inclinations of its population, should actively foster and increase ranges of freedom and tolerance. Instead, the politicians contrive to pass increasingly punitive laws, apparently in a futile attempt to deform human nature entirely.

An eclectic society which allows its schools and universities to teach the appositive or contesting works of, let us say, Taoism, Nietzsche, Zen, Wittgenstein, Kierkegaard, Sade, Jung, La Rochefoucauld, Blake, Dostoevsky, Adler, Plato, Machiavelli, Rimbaud, Teilhard de Chardin, Sun Tzu, Stendhal, Marx and many other philosophical, metaphysical and psychological sorcerers who galvanise and illuminate with bolts of aphoristic paradox, should, I reiterate, be prepared to tolerate a more hazardous degree of natural conflict and turmoil.

It is the absolutists and censors who are the bane of progressive thought. Men of genius transcend the tempting knowledge that all is vanity, resist its concomitant urge to suicide, and retain the will to contribute original concepts which may slowly further the evolution of the species.

On the other hand:

> In Italy under the rule of the Borgias for thirty years there was bloodshed, war, terror and murder, which produced Michelangelo, Leonardo da Vinci and the Renaissance. In Switzerland they had five hundred years of brotherly love, peace and democracy. And what did that produce? The cuckoo-clock!
>
> — Orson Welles, *The Third Man*

This, perhaps perversely, illustrates that those whose nature thrives on creative destruction also serve to strike inspirational sparks in the surrounding darkness. Contrast and paradox radiate dynamism.

Chapter Five

The reasonable man adapts himself to
the world; the unreasonable one per-
sists in trying to adapt the world to
himself. Therefore all progress
depends on the unreasonable man.

George Bernard Shaw

Many variations of the amoral interpretation of dualism are found in the sphere of criminology. For instance, is it not self-evident that the detective, in order to outwit the criminal he hunts, must not only be able to duplicate the — for want of a better word — *abnormal* thought processes of his quarry, but also strive to excel in corrupt faculties?

The serial killer and the detective, to a significant extent, necessarily share many characteristics, including a common unorthodox philosophy in tandem with solitary dedication and commitment. Both protagonists must be ruthless in purpose, astute in deceit, clear in strategy; temper self-confidence with caution; cultivate doubt where there is certainty and certainty where there is doubt; feign incompetence to provoke overconfidence; nourish arrogance by fake humility; deny, affirm and divert with dexterity as tactics dictate; incite anger to obtain the unguarded response and sow confusion; exude synthetic sympathy for trust whilst doubting everyone; regard all individuals as essentially corrupt and guided by self-interest; live and breathe moral and legal relativism whilst projecting moral and legal rectitude; and, above all, as already postulated, believe and act in the certainty that the end always justifies the means.

Not that any homicide detective would publicly admit to owning most of the above amoral qualities or killer instincts. In this they are much like their brethren in the vice squad who, in reading and viewing pornographic material every day, year in year out, to assess whether they are liable to render the public depraved and corrupt, nevertheless claim self-immunity. To successfully deceive others they must to a significant degree deceive themselves.

Reason's a thing we dimly see in sleep.
— *The Birds Fall Down*, Rebecca West

The captured serial killer, with no hope of freedom, invariably sloughs off the debilitating scales of hypocrisy and sanctimony, hazards self-analysis, and indulges the luxury of cynical honesty which can no longer further or hinder lost ambition. Disinterest keens an omnipotent view of the human chessboard.

> By thy cold breast and serpent smile,
> By thy unfathom'd gulfs of guile,
> By that most seeming virtuous eye,
> By thy shut soul's hypocrisy,
> By the perfection of thy art
> Which pass'd for human thine own heart;
> By thy delight in others' pain,
> And by the brotherhood of Cain,
> I call upon thee! and compel
> Thyself to be thy proper Hell!

— Lord Byron

The term 'serial killer' is used to describe a person who kills spasmodically over a comparatively lengthy period of time, as opposed to the 'mass murderer,' who usually kills all his victims in one bloody scenario.

It is generally accepted that the FBI's National Center for the Analysis of Violent Crime headquarters in Quantico, Virginia, originated the formal concept of psychological profiling, a method of projecting the probable traits and characteristics of an unidentified, usually violent criminal.

This art has given rise to quite a lucrative industry, popularised by such box-office successes as *Manhunter* and *Silence of the Lambs*, both of which films featured the fictitious, insane serial-killer-psychiatrist Dr Hannibal Lecter (played by Brian Cox and Anthony Hopkins, respectively).

Psychiatry, being an art, is only as good as the individual practitioner. Mediocre forensic psychiatrists, particularly those in penal and academic circles in America and Britain, smitten by the popular Lecter Syndrome, have jockeyed for fame and fortune by loudly proclaiming they have some special psychological insight into the 'criminal mind'; ironically, one could therefore interpret such a claim as inadvertent admission that they themselves possess more criminal traits and characteristics than average.

If lucky enough to have had even one success out of several hundred stabs in the dark, these exponents magnify it by self-publicity and try to found a profitable media career on it. In my opinion, this commercial factor taints and colors all of their works. In reality, the less they perceive, the more others believe — especially police upper echelons, their brains atrophied by abuse of power and expense-account alcohol. Based on a study of such self-serving amateurs, I do not hesitate to state that one could achieve a higher percentage of success with a Tarot pack.

While it is to some extent praiseworthy that urban police outfits recognise the positive potential of expert psychological profilers (namely the FBI unit at Quantico), it is also somewhat perplexing. The scientific methodology refined by expert profilers should be used automatically by anyone claiming to be a professional detective, instead of further straining the thinly spread resources of the Quantico facility.

Last but not least, the methodology of second- or third-rung prophets of serial killing profiling is usually plagiarised from research published by the formidable FBI Psychological Profiling Center at Quantico. The media's vested interest is to deliberately inflate, out of greed to sell newspapers and boost TV ratings, an immense and often dangerous public hysteria and panic regarding the serial killer.

Can one reasonably doubt that a great volume of sensational publicity generates an unhealthy ethos, in which serial killers are so glamorised, their methodology so widely disseminated, as to tempt others to copy them, if not revere them as the prophets of risk and individual action, in a society overwhelmed and bogged down by the dull courtiers and ass-kissers of celebrity culture?

To my certain knowledge, a minimum of six impressionable individuals have sought to emulate my crimes; two killed, were caught and committed suicide; another two are serving life sentences for multiple murder; the remaining two are still free and the body count continues to mount.

The mere accumulation of forensic information in itself does not predicate expertise. A good profiler must possess instinctive dexterity to juggle multiple concepts and associations with some originality. Genius. The FBI, recently accused of shabby incompetence and misconduct, is not infallible.

One very important factor has been completely overlooked by both the shallow and the professional profilers.

All intelligent individuals, criminal or otherwise, have a hidden agenda. Something so precious to the psyche that it can be confided to no one. Forensic science has not yet triumphed over 'the stuff as dreams are made on.'

Therefore most captured serial killers will confess to any motive in order to conceal the hidden agenda. This not only leaves a significant gap in psychological data but also introduces wild cards.

What is more, it is axiomatic that many criminals themselves have an instinctive or acquired grasp of the forensic sciences. Some are ardent students of published forensic research. Understandably so — their continued freedom or very life literally depends upon keeping up to date. Theoretically, the criminal and his empirical practices should always have a competitive edge over academic assumptions. The innovative or inspired pupil invariably drains the master of knowledge and adds it to his own practical expertise.

In the course of time, leaps in understanding forensic science are double-edged. A pair of gloves can take care of fingerprints, but how does the killer achieve the more complex task of hiding a crime signature or personality print from the expert profiler?

Most of the traits and characteristics that create the crime signature are rooted at a subconscious level, influencing the *modus operandi* increasingly, especially when murder ceases to be a novelty and becomes merely an unsatisfying contest with the law of diminishing returns.

Most power, once attained, becomes a curiously empty experience. Routine is the greatest danger to the security of the serial killer, decreasing his alertness, innovation and caution. He becomes sloppy.

This syndrome also helps to explain, in many instances, why the killer's crimes become more frequent or outrageous; he is chasing a chimera, a homicidal ideal, becoming more frustrated with each successive failure.

The murders of Jack the Ripper exemplify both aspects of this syndrome. He, in common with other uncaught serial killers whose crimes mysteriously ceased, perhaps was insightful enough to realise the futility of his search for the ultimate experience, or, conversely, perhaps it was discovered in the final murder.

Accepting this premise in general, one might tentatively suggest that the successful criminal student remains undetected mainly by virtue of knowing when to stop.

But what of others who do not possess this faculty? How have they avoided capture? Once this type of killer has mastered the psychological principles involved, knowing precisely what the profilers are searching for and tabulating, his next logical step would be to discover the most effective way not only to neutralise the danger but also shape it to his advantage, like any competent chess-player.

For instance, as already opined, he may adopt auto-hypnosis techniques to selectively modify the psyche at a subconscious level, and systematically create the thought processes of a second personality. Or, in Jungian terms, assume the identities of multiple personae to a clinically affective extent, masking and transiently modifying his true thought patterns and emotions, whilst retaining the essential criminal consciousness to exert comprehensive control over his multiple creations.

The achievement of conscious control of the subconscious may seem paradoxical or theoretical, but I assure you, from personal study and experience, that it can be accomplished. Raskolnikov, had he applied such auto-hypnosis techniques, would not have been troubled by 'conscience,' the unregulated influence of subconscious social-conditioning.

Variations of this practical methodology, of converting a potential disadvantage to personal advantage, could well be applied even more simply in the sophisticated field of genetics, now that law enforcement agencies have publicly (and, in tactical/strategic terms, foolishly) affirmed their belief that each individual's DNA is practically as unique as their fingerprints. In which case, to fabricate innocence, the criminal need only (a) ensure he leaves no samples of his own DNA at the scene of the crime; (b) prior to the crime, obtain by recondite means the DNA substances/traces of some innocent individual to plant on the victim or at the crime scene.

Thus, in judo fashion, the strength of almost every advance in forensic science can be turned against itself by the educated criminal.

After all, in a general philosophical/theological sense, education is the first step on the road to corruption: the loss of innocence. And, as already touched upon, objective observation of the powerful and influential inculcates that higher education/intelligence should never be automatically equated with higher humanism, or lack of criminal tendencies.

Further advances in the sphere of genetic research have prompted those with vested interest (political and financial) in the lucrative law enforcement industry to set up expensive research programmes to isolate the 'killer genes' that allegedly develop 'cold-blooded killers.'

One must assume the researchers arrogantly mean cold-blooded criminal killers, as opposed to cold-blooded legalised killers, and that they can differentiate between the two. In which case, the research becomes patently absurd — a sort of genetic fortune telling, in which the psychic scientists will claim to see invisible black hats on illegal killer genes. A concept crazier, you might think, than the imaginary 'Star Wars' defence system dreamt up by President Reagan to ward off the 'evil empire' of Russia.

It is therefore significant that the scientists hunting 'killer genes' have begun their research in asylums for the criminally insane, where presumably they feel more at home, less open to criticism, and less constrained by moral and ethical considerations. These genetic boffins, arguably suffering from delusional disorders themselves, hope, rather than more justifiably dread, that one day they will be able to identify 'killer genes' in babies and apply preventative drugs — or, more Reagan-like, shoot laser beams at the 'evil' genes.

I should point out that I for one would not assist in any such research. If they require 'abnormal' personalities to experiment upon, let them use their own, or those of politicians and other power-brokers.

I believe it was Woody Allen who advanced the theoretical connection between excessive masturbation and those who enter politics. The human propensity to see evil in all others needs no form of further encouragement.

———◆◆———

Self-delusion is an almost inevitable consequence of life in the modern world, or perhaps even a necessity, to stave off encroaching madness or a collective lemming-like rush to the brink.

In my assessment, any person nowadays who does not suffer from some form and degree of personality disorder should, by definition, be regarded as highly suspect, dangerous and possibly certifiable.

At this juncture, let me again partly define my relativistic perception/conception of what is meant by 'criminal.'

Essentially, to one believing in legal and moral relativism, legalities, moralities and ethics are simply questions of geography, passing modes of fashion and taste, shaped and dictated by the prevailing ruling class of whatever country one happens to be in at a certain time.

In some instances, more from political expediency than altruistic generosity, a few of the laws and morals may, unavoidably as it were, reflect the wishes and interests of the population as a whole. It therefore follows that criminality is not necessarily indicative of innate evil in any person, nor is an *ostensible* lack of criminality illustrative of innate good; both of these polarised conditions are merely personal responses to artificial, externally applied criteria or stimuli, imposed by a political minority or capriciously extant majority of conformists upon a more discerning minority of non-conformists.

This further postulates that criminality is not always the inherent attribute of a specific act, but often the consequence of a variable power or majority successfully defining the said act as 'criminal.'

Laws and morals are not guided or decided by divine tablets handed down from the Mount but by secular power or tyranny of numbers.

Audience reaction, rather than the discriminating wisdom and inherent superiority of individual judgment, is the critical factor in defining a 'criminal,' an 'outsider,' someone not running with the herd or going with the prevailing popular flow.

> Treason doth never prosper, what's the reason? For if it
> prosper, none dare call it treason.
> — Sir John Harington (1561–1612)

If this is accepted as true and valid, one can better understand why the serial killer just as selfishly reasons: why let one's actions be constrained by basic mathematics, vote-hungry politicians, superstitious fear of a Supreme Being, or indeed anyone at all?

Moreover, he may logically conclude it was obviously fortunate that the majority should let their thoughts and horizons be thus restricted. Their critical disability would enhance his personal advantage, existential vitality and initiative, as well as adding an aesthetic, rounded satisfaction to life in general, and zest to the hunt in particular.

He experiences the exhilarating superiority of the *freelance* predator; each act not only affirming his unfettered existence to the world but also the failure to succeed by extant codes and rules of society. Knowing his strengths and limitations, he has determined to prove himself a villain, that being the only natural sphere in which he can shine.

It is rather significant to note that those members of the lower classes who assiduously adhere to law and prevailing morality usually display a smug self-righteousness, which appears to be based on the patent delusion that their virtuous qualities are inborn, rather than evidence of a servile constitution predisposed to the influence of social engineering.

Mostly politicians need to be concerned about programmed 'public opinion,' a fickle state of collective consciousness chiefly created and exploited by themselves and the media for financial/political reward. In reality the only individuals who have freedom of the press are those who own one.

Paradoxically, this pious delusion of innate rectitude, in the as yet not caught out population, manages to persist in conjunction with a voracious addiction for every prurient detail about criminals and their crimes, from which the public obtains vicarious enjoyment and sexual stimulation.

In this respect, it could be cynically advanced that criminals provide a necessary cathartic service to society and, when captured, also serve as sacrificial exhibits on which to heap collective guilt and sexual frustration, not to mention primal bloodlust.

The unpleasant truth, I venture to reiterate, is that many envy the esoteric pleasures and excesses enjoyed by the criminal, who translates their darkest fantasies and desires into action.

The common individual craves prohibited sensation minus responsibility and risk. And, perhaps the most psychologically intolerable aspect of all, such people resent inner knowledge that they will spend all their life as timid spectators, never players.

They can't quite pull off the trick of fooling themselves or others all of the time, no matter how hard they try to rationalise the unedifying reflection of themselves as insatiable voyeurs, luxuriously participating (or *panticipating*) in forbidden pleasures, and deriving compensatory comfort from the misfortune of others. Reading of the murder of strangers makes them feel good to be alive, particularly if sex is also part of the crime. The resulting guilt spurs them to fresh zeniths of clamorous righteousness and revenge.

In effect, by entering into a form of collective personality of retribution and purpose, they subliminally absolve themselves of evil recompense and intent, assuaging guilt by self-deceit.

Those subject to mob mentality are usually of low intelligence. They fail to recognise that they themselves are victims, of the politicians and their minions in the law and order industry, who have personal careers to advance and fresh powers to seek. Having deliberately provoked public panic, the same politicians egocentrically and geocentrically milk it for votes in the role of saviours, creating harsher penalties and promising the mob more to come. A circus.

The soft-porn tabloids and other sensational media require no remit other than financial gain to daily devote whole front pages to sex crimes — doing so in loving, salacious detail, exploiting man's lowest instincts and sexual imperatives. Sex crime is reduced to the status of a spectator sport, publicly stimulating for profit the very same feral instincts supposedly possessed by the perpetrator.

Such coverage subliminally incites the spectator to gloat over the physical charms of the victim in every respect, imaginatively projecting into the victim's eyes whatever changing reflections of horror or pleasure most excites their recondite inclinations.

At breakfast tables all over the country the sexual appetites of millions of 'decent citizens' are sharpened by such press reports, their readers luxuriating in vivid visions of debauchery, rape, murder and sado-masochistic perversion, sometimes as perpetrator, sometimes as victim. Death being perhaps the greatest aphrodisiac, feel-good factor and appetizer there is, readers wolf down the bacon and eggs with additional relish; a secular parody of the communion wafer, celebrating life in the midst of random murder.

Whenever prurient reporting acts as a catalyst to some latent killers and rapists, as surely it must, the mass media, with or without the least connecting evidence, conveniently places all the blame on mythical 'video nasties' or hardcore pornography, simultaneously utilising the opportunity to print or televise many titillating samples of that which they sanctimoniously condemn.

It is big business. Morality does not enter into the equation except in the shoddy guise of derisively pious editorials, reminiscent, in shallow sympathy and ersatz horror, of the lucrative ramblings of the late Edgar Lustgarten. This self-styled media 'criminologist,' a jaundice-jowled, lugubrious little specimen with the eyes of a carp, the ethics of a minnow and the ambience of a ripe red herring, physically personified what every media sensationalist should be *obliged* to look like as a warning to others.

The sensationalists shrewdly appreciate that when it comes to serial killers or killings, the general public has the infinite attention span of lower primates assiduously searching for fleas. As a rule of thumb, conservative politicians, tabloid reporters, pimps and other strangers to ethics, who regularly and loudly pontificate on law and order or matters of public morality, bear closer investigation. They invariably fulminate in the not so ingenuous hope that hot air will waft attention from their own unprepossessing activities, and that their bluster will be mistaken for personal virtue and probity. They protest too much. The more they profit from crime, or the darker their hue of chosen vice, the louder they rave for ever-harsher penalties for the working-class criminal.

The illusion of having a 'good reputation' to maintain can be a most *corrupting* preoccupation, whereas confessing to a bad reputation is often highly virtuous.

Honest criminals are much preferable, more refreshingly wholesome and cheaper to sustain than conservative politicians. You should never doubt your own experience in favour of other people's opinions, no matter how loftily they berate you with them. Hypocrisy adores exalted heights to condescend from.

Experience and instinct caution that one should invariably beware of those who *talk* much of friendship, loyalty, honesty and other admirable qualities; they devalue the coin by usage and abusage. Virtue requires no messenger, particularly not a Mercury of the press.

The man who reads nothing at all is better educated than the
man who reads nothing but newspapers.

— Thomas Jefferson

An editor is a person employed on a newspaper, whose business it is to separate the wheat from the chaff, and to see that
the chaff is printed.

— Elbert Hubbard

Did you ever notice that when a politician does get an idea he
usually gets it all wrong?

— Don Marquis

A Sympathizer would seem to imply a certain degree of benevolent feeling. Nothing of the kind. It signifies a readymade
accomplice in any species of political villainy.

— Thomas Love Peacock

In close daily association with psychopaths, psychotics and schizoids, I
personally find it easy to differentiate between them, to read them accurately.
Your life depends upon it.

I have previously listed the salient traits and characteristics of both the
criminal and socially-acceptable psychopath/sociopath — broadly synthesized
as lack of concern and emotional depth in all but self-interest. Devoid of
humour, they can nevertheless simulate laughter, bonhomie and all other
social niceties as part of their practised public persona. But the experienced
observer will usually detect the hollow tone, the unsmiling eye. In general they
are not susceptible to psychiatric treatment.

It is sometimes the case that they slowly mellow with age. But, with equal
validity, this process could be attributed to declining physical strength in a prison
culture where brute force is perhaps the highest value. The deadly monotony
and social stagnation of a prison regime naturally debilitates, with its mindless
repetition and stale conversations. In addition, there is nothing worth striving for
if, as many psychopaths are, imprisoned without the possibility of parole. The
withering of ambition, desire and life-force in general might generously be
regarded by the authorities as 'mellowing.' Dying is a more honest word in a
caged place where sleep is the best part left of life, dreams defeating the walls.

In such artificial, insular conditions, the psychopaths are generally the least dangerous, as should one always remain alert in their company, never turning one's back, especially on those with paranoid delusions of grandeur or persecution complexes. They may kill you simply to break the boredom, to have something momentarily exciting to do.

Contrary to popular belief, not all psychopaths are prone to violence. As previously explained, the general public erroneously connects the term psychopath with murder, when in fact it can be applied to all recurring patterns of criminal behaviour coupled with an inability to learn from past mistakes.

Those classified in the remaining psychopathic categories are dangerous in other ways, obsessed with secular power in all its forms. The socially-acceptable psychopath, immune from serious prosecution by virtue of influential power and wealth, differs from the more vulnerable criminal breed to whom money is something to spend freely and enjoy life with, rather than hoard as a power base.

In this particular respect, the orthodox criminals are at least more human, more easily satisfied. Child-like, less sophisticated, if you will. They exhibit identifiable desires far easier to comprehend, no matter how abhorrent and selfish their chosen means to an end. They are also, of course, more likely to be caught and heavily punished.

The socially-acceptable psychopath is quite another kettle of fish. This category shares the same basic pathological traits and characteristics possessed by their less exalted brethren, with some added.

Secular power being their aphrodisiac, they can never be satisfied. Obsession drives them relentlessly.

> Power tends to corrupt and absolute power corrupts absolutely.
> — Lord Actin (1834–1902)

In prison I met those few politicians and financiers careless enough to be caught. Their whole manner denoted the conviction that they were not only above the law but also the architects and swayers of it. They regarded prison as a brief, unjust, temporary setback, which their power and wealth would eventually overcome — a slight slip-up their influential friends would not hold against them when released to re-enter the high social strata.

As previously indicated, statistics show that this elite category of socially-acceptable psychopath collectively deprives society of more wealth than their blue-collar opposites. And with less excuse, the former having had superior education and a privileged upbringing. Their easy air of effete affectation was reminiscent of the French aristocracy before the tumbrels and heads began to roll. However, unlike their decapitated approximates, the confidence of these modern-day tyrants is rather more justified, so securely are they protected by the forces of law and order they themselves create and treat with such contempt.

Mass communication rubs salt in the wounds of the servile almost daily by reporting how the high and mighty invariably escape imprisonment or suffer no stigma when released.

Ousted dictators can flee to the West with billions of dollars stolen from their country's treasury, confident they will be received like visiting royalty, whereas some little gangster trying to escape justice abroad would be imprisoned immediately.

Steal an apple, you are a thief; steal a country, you are a statesman. Moral relativism therefore indicates the bigger the crime, you do no time.

Those very same pillars of the community who bay for harsher prison sentences and capital punishment for petty criminals, obsequiously wine, dine and lionise exiled financiers and plundering dictators.

Such moral, legal and social distinctions have always clearly illustrated that judgment and penalty are tempered according to wealth and privilege, an irrefutable fact that should reinforce relativism in all discerning individuals.

The Manson family effectively taught the wealthy that they are not beyond the reach and reproach of the activist subculture. As evidenced, 'Anyone can be killed, even the President.'

Society, if you believe such a thing exists, trains and constrains the individual to counterfeit surface respect for powerful personages and outmoded conventions which, in truth, the large majority abhor and despise.

Therefore, there exists in every free-thinking person a tenacious tension between that which they know to be their genuine beliefs and desires, and the grotesque proprieties and social protocols they reluctantly pay homage to under duress. The resulting psychic conflict creates a neurotic self-contempt, a mordant doubt that they possess the will or spiritual strength needed to throw off such tight bridles and assert unconditional individuality, even at the risk of their disconsolate lives.

Contrary to Ian Fleming, you only live once. Therefore, a person should consciously choose whether to exist as a grey daub on a grey canvas, or as an existential riot of every colour in the spectrum. You know which of these alternatives the serial killer selects, action-painting with his knife on a human canvas, each slash-splash creating a unique masterpiece. Not for sale but nevertheless widely viewed with fascination by most.

One should be fully aware of the respective relative merits of those complementary qualities deemed good or evil before daring to pontificate upon them. Society demands, for reasons of social control, that the criminal, having experienced, enjoyed and practised both good and evil with more or less equal enthusiasm, should recant his unorthodox beliefs and actions simply because an error of judgment led to his capture. Had he not been captured, would the criminal then have been expected to renounce all his good qualities in similar manner?

This essentially artificial, impossible demand for a moral dichotomy, which excludes one of two contrasting qualities that in reality constitute a unity, is the height of human folly.

By all means punish or execute transgressors, but do not bore them to death with concepts based entirely on social engineering flatteringly disguised as divine wisdom.

———•◆•———

Returning to forensic matters, paranoid schizoids are, by definition, less predictable than psychopaths, and are therefore, in some instances, more dangerous.

Many are lost in a whirlwind cycle of hallucination and grand delusion, tranquil and normal one moment, raging and violent the next. Beyond accurate prognosis, they can nevertheless be stabilised to an effective degree by drug therapy, but on the whole must be regarded as an almost permanent potential menace to themselves and others.

Sometimes many appear normal for such lengthy periods that one becomes careless and relaxes — then the explosion of violence catches you off-balance. Yet certain other schizoids are comparatively harmless, reacting mainly to their imaginary inner experiences rather than their surroundings.

Many under strictly supervised medication can be kept as normal as the next person. But one still has to remain alert for those who decide they no longer need medication and surreptitiously spit it out.

I personally consider psychotics the most interesting. When not in a state of cyclical manic-depression, or lost in a schizophrenic fugue, they are energetic in mind and body, swinging from tears to laughter, constantly bubbling with ideas and startling momentary insights, treating morals and legalities as malleable playthings. They often exhibit a high sense of absurdity combined with acute observation of man's foibles. This invariably results in a cavalier, bold and arrogant attitude to all matters — including murder.

They 'view the world as from the edge of a far star.' Should they respect or learn from the conduct of their sane mentors, who exemplify and justify tribal mayhem? Over fifty million people died in World War Two — it reads more like a league table than an Everest of bodies.

How many centuries would you suppose it would take for freelance 'criminals' and 'madmen' to equal the numerical carnage the 'law-abiding' and 'sane' can achieve in such a comparatively short space of time? One should cultivate discrimination in accepting or respecting one's moral 'superiors.' So often they are certainly *not*.

————— · · —————

Do you not find it at all intriguing and incongruous, as I do, that political and military killers show none of the guilt or remorse society so eagerly demands from lesser criminals?

Why is this?

Because society has given the former *permission* to openly indulge, glory and exult in unlimited slaughter and panoramic devastation.

For an intelligent discussion of this question, we should ignore such absurd rationalisations as 'But that's war.' Convenient psychological sophistry manifests itself in other bewitching ways.

Why are the mass media and the general public so fascinated by serial killers, yet show not the least interest in, and, quite frankly, absolute boredom with, far more prolific legalised killers? Say, an American pilot in Vietnam, whose daily routine task was to fry alive in napalm thousands of men, women and children; or the American Special Forces, who habitually cut off the ears of the enemy as trophies and made necklaces of them.

The American public displayed no shock over such atrocities, but expressed horror and revulsion over a *simulated* mutilation in the film *Reservoir Dogs*, where a character cuts off a policeman's ear.

It becomes transparent that the reason why the media and public are so fascinated by serial killers is that these people kill at will, requiring no legislation, without asking for or needing permission, the very concept never entering their mind.

The same morbid syndrome exists in all other countries, of course. The five murders committed by Jack the Ripper in England over a century ago are found to be far more internationally intriguing than the six million murdered in the German concentration camps of Heinrich Himmler. Everyone knows about the Boston Strangler murders, but how many people can as easily recall who was President or Attorney General at the time?

Fickle fame and infamy.

You may have already deduced that the teams of prominent psychiatric consultants who have attempted to interview and categorize me over the years classify me as psychotic. A rose by any other name . . .

> Though they go mad they shall be sane,
> Though they sink through the sea they shall rise again.
>
> — Dylan Thomas

Even the wildest spirit is, in action, unavoidably crippled by what moralists term 'conscience.' And also by one of the most debilitating, insidious cankers of all — timidity.

The Napoleons are exceptions, as Dostoevsky's Raskolnikov belatedly discovered to his cost. At the point of death, I suggest that most of you will not regret what you have done in life but what you have left *undone* through defective anxiety and trepidation.

You, too, shall 'rage against the dying of the light,' cursing a lifetime of missed opportunities and the dourness of sanity. Many cultures believe, rightly or wrongly, that the 'mad' have a touch of divinity about them — that they perhaps reach upwards, and downwards, just that little bit farther than most of their 'sane' brethren. That they enjoy a richer experience of life. The 'Fool on the Hill' syndrome.

Putting to one side the caution of legal definition, intuition suggests that a great many members of the public equate serial killing with insanity, but atavistically desire to execute the perpetrators anyway. I have no quarrel with this. Official murder is the triumphant exoneration of relativism.

However, let us examine a few misconceptions.

I believe the term 'serial killer' is highly misleading, in that it implicitly suggests to the general public that murder is the paramount object or motivating urge in the mind of the killer.

The vast majority of the public never having experienced what it means to kill another human being in cold blood — or hot, for that matter — nevertheless readily assumes or accepts that the serial killer's main object must be murder. They naturally attribute this motivation partly because they value human life above all else, and partly because, as their endless fascination with the subject suggests, they have a vague conception of murder as being a somehow mystical, highly dramatic or even nebulously romantic experience, with sophisticated or unimaginable connotations of eroticism. And guilt must be paid for in full.

People mostly dream of killing a hated enemy, not realising that it would be far more satisfying to inflict significant injury, leaving the enemy alive to endure it, or commit suicide. This concisely illustrates the predatory compulsion to view the taking of life as the be-all and end-all. But it also exemplifies there are crimes far worse than dealing out blessed oblivion.

Of course there are many serial killers to whom murder is the prime motivation. Perhaps they lack the capacity to ponder the matter in abstract philosophical terms, probably because the metaphysical aspect — the sense of making their mark in the universe, metaphorically challenging God — is the most powerful. This significant metaphysical factor is, to a greater or lesser degree, innate not only to all serial killers but also the majority of thinking individuals. Which accounts for the popular captivation or enchantment of murder.

But personally, I have met only a few such death-fixated serial killers, despite having rubbed shoulders with a considerable variety over the years. And contrary to current notions in popular fiction, I believe most serial killers seldom 'develop a taste' for killing *per se.*

Ironically, however, it is within the ranks of the domestic murderers, non-serial killers, that you will find many whose main purpose was murder, perhaps to rid themselves of a nagging or unfaithful partner, or collect life insurance, or marry a lover, etc. Obviously the motivating factor in such cases is *personal gain* of some sort, but by deliberate homicide.

What the average (if one can use the term in this context) serial killer seeks above all is power and the will to power. In this psychic ambience, power and sex are often synonymous or complementary.

Commitment to a personal system which relegates external legality, morality and ethics to mere serendipity — random leaves blowing from a moribund tree — can be arrived at via disparate emotional routes or roots.

Some may find a philosophy of cosmic uncertainty joyful and stimulating, and dance happily and harmlessly through life, their innocence a positive inspiration and boon to their fellow voyagers. Yet a lack of moral and ethical certitude is automatically assumed by most to be on the whole undesirable, something either akin or equivalent to evil. The colour of a guide dog may be black or white, but what matters is that it takes us in the direction we wish to go.

I think it can be stated with certainty that the serial killer's consciously or subconsciously chosen path is towards perdition and desirable oblivion. However, he may travel that road just as exuberantly and light of heart as the innocent travels his.

Having determined and resigned himself to the fact that life is meaningless, and that synthetic systems of probity only tend to make the journey more tedious, what could be more natural than that he consciously decides to sample every variety of spiritual and physical excitement that attracts his interest, perfectly aware of and willing to accept the secular consequences of his actions? The rewards of good or evil are just as satisfying to the adherent of either.

Essentially, I posit, there is no such thing as an unselfish act, though theologians and moralists might argue otherwise. We do whatever we enjoy doing. Whether it happens to be judged good or evil is a matter for others to decide.

———•◆•———

Returning to the psychological and physical logistics: once the serial killer's power/sex urge is satisfied, he is left with the unfortunate living witness to it, the victim. He is therefore logically or emotionally compelled to kill the victim simply as a secondary expedient, to escape the legal and psychological consequences of what he perceives to be his major crime.

The first killing experience will not only hold the strongest element of existential novelty and curiosity, but also the greatest element of danger and trepidation conjured by the unknown. Usually the incipient serial killer is too immersed in the psychological and legal challenges of the initial homicide, not to mention immediate logistics — the physical labour that the killing and disposal involve. He is therefore not in a condition to form a detached appreciation of the traumatic complexities bombarding his senses.

You could, in many instances, describe the experience as an affective state of shock. He is, after all, storming pell-mell the defensive social conditioning of a lifetime, as well as declaring war upon all the organised, regulatory forces of society. In extinguishing someone's life he is also committing his own, and has no time to stop and stare in the hazardous, psychological battlefield.

In another very significant sense, he is killing his long-accepted self as well as the victim, and simultaneously giving birth to a new persona, decisively cutting the umbilical connection between himself and ordinary mankind.

Having fought his former self and won, the fledgling serial killer flexes newfound powers with more confidence. The second killing will hold all the same disadvantageous, distracting elements of the first, but to a lesser degree. This allows a more objective assimilation of the experience. It also fosters an expanding sense of omnipotence, a wide-angle view of the metaphysical chess-board.

In many cases, the element of elevated aestheticism in the second murder will exert a more formative impression than the first, and probably of any in the future. It not only represents the rite of confirmation, a revelational leap of lack of faith in humanity, but also the onset of addiction to hedonistic nihilism.

The psychic abolition of redemption.

Chapter Six

For here the lover and killer are
mingled. Who had one body and
one heart.

Keith Douglas (1920–1944)

From a specific point in spiritual and intellectual commitment, the serial killer is subconsciously evolving towards becoming his own god and executioner.

With each subsequent killing, the homicidal drug, blunted by habitual use, creates a diminishing and disappointing impression. The extraordinary becomes increasingly ordinary.

This confirms my view that most killers do not find the act of murder itself pleasurable. Increasingly, it is viewed more as a *necessary* conclusion to an exercise of power and will. Ironically, having striven for absolute freedom, he has found its antithesis. A categorical imperative. A wearisome cleaning up after the feast. Or, more fatal to his welfare and continued freedom, he may view the necessary task as an irritable imposition exacted by those he increasingly regards as the inferior enemy ranged against him.

An additional minority of serial killers may kill not only as a measure of self-survival but also to provoke greater public storm, having also become addicted to their own publicity and undergone a complete personality change in the process.

Just as society believes itself justified in punishing the criminal for the hurt he has inflicted, so also does the serial killer in relation to society.

He is out to exact post-traumatic vengeance, compensation for the real or imaginary injuries he has experienced at the hands of society, and is essentially exulting in the cathartic joy of finally declaring open war. He rationalises and excuses his barbaric behaviour in the same terminology as the state: 'This is war.' Except that, by virtue of acting alone against great odds, pitting his wits and his life against all the organised power of the state, he feels morally superior to the state.

It is this quality of extreme individualism that fascinates the public and excites their secret envy, fear and hatred. But who is the hero, who is the antihero?

We cannot avoid the quandary:

> Whether 'tis nobler in the mind to suffer
> The slings and arrows of outrageous fortune,
> Or to take arms against a sea of troubles,
> And by opposing end them?

———•◦•———

Incongruously, as mentioned, the sadistic type of serial killer, if he allowed his instincts for self-survival to be overwhelmed by pathological desire, would much rather inflict *life* than death upon the victim, so that he might savour the knowledge that the victim has been forced to suffer the memory of the ordeal for the rest of his/her days.

The living victim would serve as a psychic, sentient trophy of the crime, thus prolonging the intimate relationship, or psycho/sexual link, between victim and perpetrator.

The sadistic perpetrator would be perfectly aware that it would further torture the victims to know that the person who inflicted such traumatic indignities upon them is still alive to remember or, perhaps more important, publicly divulge. This mutual fear of public testimony and sensational dissemination of the intimate facts of the crime also intensifies the relationship between victim and perpetrator. Thus the latter's clemency would be ostensibly humane, but for inhumane motives. Mercy has its cruel side.

Similarly, the captured sadistic killer may ask, is life imprisonment without the possibility of parole really more compassionate than a quick, honest execution?

Sadistic purists among members of the public would prefer a lengthy revenge. In fact, they would probably like to enjoy both if it were possible: execution *and* life imprisonment, or to take pleasure from the vision of him rotting in Hell. Therefore, the logical extension of their desires would be execution by lengthy torture, their savagery possibly surpassing that of the killer to whom they believe themselves morally superior. Again, philosophically and psychologically, this would play into the hands of the killer.

The concept of hell and endless torment is popular with those who believe they aren't headed there.

Unlike Dostoevsky's character, I would rather be dead — *Thelma and Louise* style — than stand for eternity on a ledge staring into the abyss.

Which would you choose?

Many serial killers believe in hell on earth, consequently administering it to those who appear never to have tasted its gall — those who seem to have cornered all the luck. The killer might believe democratically in the equal, abstract, random distribution of misery, as it were. The reverse side of feeling yourself unfortunate for having no shoes until you met a man with no feet.

———

I intend to weave the factor of mental illness throughout the broadcloth of this factual and philosophical discourse, without unduly distracting or taxing the reader by use of overmuch psychological/psychiatric terminology; I wish to communicate, not obfuscate.

This I partly hope to achieve by foraging through the criminal psyche in individual instances, particularly in the realm of psychological/psychiatric profiling, both as a past criminal *participant* and a present objective observer.

> Thus I live in the world rather as a spectator of mankind than as one of the species.
>   — Joseph Addison (1672–1719)

Whether or not some forensic facts, conclusions and interpretations disturb the mental equilibrium of the reader in the process, is an abstract factor which cannot be allowed to intrude if we are to have a clinical examination of reality, or a perception of reality. A dissection of what murder is really all about, from the point of view of a serial killer, for a change.

Many of you, sitting out there in cosy easy-chairs, with a drink at your elbow and the prospect of vicarious excitement ahead as you settle down to read, have probably assured yourself in advance that there is no danger of you identifying with, or even empathising with, anyone you are about to encounter in these pages.

Indeed, you already feel intellectually and morally superior because this is a book written by a criminal about other criminals, creatures of the underworld, a distant subculture, whereas you have nothing to hide or be ashamed of, have you?

That inner glow of sanctity feels almost as good as a large glass of double-malt whisky, but not quite as genuine or fully matured. The plain fact is, heavens above, the criminals feel exactly the same way about you. In spades.

I reiterate: common sense should caution that if you indifferently isolate criminals and pretend you cannot identify with them even in human terms — when freed they will isolate you, with extreme prejudice.

Even as you read this, one may be travelling through the night toward you, maybe trying your doors and windows at this very moment. If so, too late to repent or recant. You have created the enemy within, and within he will come. Ready to stare you out of countenance. Mark his eyes. The indifference reflecting your own of some minutes ago. You belatedly understand. That sinking feeling. He has no more mercy for you than you had for him. You are staring at your alter-ego for the first, and perhaps final, time. You are thinking of all the things you will probably never see again, just as he did in prison. You begin to feel sorry. Mainly for yourself, but also perhaps just a bit for him. He may recognise it. See you as a human being rather than an object of abstract revenge in solitary prison dreams.

———•◆•———

Did you ever share the same innocent obsession that I have? Forever being drawn back compulsively to places of childhood. Localities of spiritual renewal. Touchstones to recharge the flagging batteries. Places where the feet itched to make contact with the soil of your roots, hands ached to caress the texture of old buildings and trees you once knew well but had almost forgotten? They look much older and smaller than you remembered them, of course, more vulnerable, in need of tactile comfort. It is mutual. A touch of sympathetic energy spans the lapsed years. For that moment you forget your quarrels with the world.

You are innocent again.

And so is mankind.

———•◆•———

In childhood years I was not the stereotypical 'loner' so beloved by the popular media. Friends formed round me eagerly in the school playground, listening to me talk, and I took it as natural. Apparently I had a descriptive talent and contagious enthusiasm. All harmless, adventurous stuff, no devious intent. No sense of superiority.

Later, in my early teens at senior school, matters changed imperceptibly. Gangs formed round me. Similarly I had no conscious sense as to why, only that again I took it as a natural process. I was not consciously aware of being out to gain followers but follow they did, obviously predisposed to go where I led.

That our activities became criminal was also accepted as natural. The more money we stole the more fun we had. Only when we were caught by the police did a minority drift away, mainly at the behest of their restrictive parents. I hardly noticed, nor did the remaining others; replacements joined us, and we continued to enjoy the fruits of our activities.

Gradually I began to adopt a more studious, professional attitude towards crime. My instinctive form of relativism developed into a pragmatic philosophy. I began to choose my followers. This book is not an autobiography, but these passages form a brief personal introduction before tackling the main subject.

The purpose was to explain why, on those occasions when I returned to childhood haunts as an adult, I couldn't get enough of people, roaming the old bars and cafés, soaking up the atmosphere and delighting in overheard conversations.

Each face I then observed seemed to radiate unique character. I felt truly *alive*, all criminal inclinations and ambitions forgotten, erased by temporarily regaining the vitality of seeing the world through the eyes of a child. That microscopic form of vision where nothing is unimportant and almost everything is fascinating.

Does this seem rather foolish to you? Somehow, I don't think so. Too much of life is wasted in pretending we are something we are not — that we know everything instead of relatively nothing. Are invulnerable and in total control of all we survey, and capital at caring for nothing. Are beyond good and evil and proud of it.

We are what we believe we are at given times.

But we are always reluctant to admit that the child is still there deep in each of us, occasionally peeping out to laugh at what we have become. And we take no offence at it, but joy from being reminded. It helps us recognise that, without knowing it at the time, we created a barren role as we travelled the years, have inexorably *become* that role, and are stuck with it. The past our future. Vainly play-acting our lives away for the benefit of other people, even total strangers.

As one cannot afford to show weakness in the prehistoric ambience of prison, at least I now have *pragmatic reasons* for persevering in my beliefs. Kindness of any description is invariably interpreted as weakness. This tendency is also prevalent in the outside world, as is fear of the truth.

Prince Myshkin, in Dostoevsky's *The Idiot*, is regarded in what is laughingly termed 'polite society' as being a simpleton because of his habit of saying what he thinks and believes without due deference to a culture in which social suppression is regarded as a virtue.

His honesty not only disarms his peers but also scares them, exposing their avaricious shallowness and threatening their defensive lifestyle. To them, Myshkin is too in touch with his feelings for comfort; they are too close to the surface, and that enables him to express his thoughts and emotions without cosmetic social adulteration.

That is also a characteristic of the criminal, who cannot silently or passively accept the transparent hypocrisy and greed of those who rise to control society and preserve the status quo in their favour. Hence, the expedient term *sociopath* is applied to him.

> The only absolute knowledge attainable by man is that life is meaningless.
>
> — Tolstoy

What do you, the reader, really believe in? And would you dare express it publicly?

———•———

Now it's time for you to accompany me into the esoteric territory you have chosen to enter. An Hieronymous Bosch landscape. The abyss you already know much more of than you care to acknowledge. Seduced by repulsion. The vision gives form to the act.

> Thou shalt have one God only; who
> Would be at the expense of two?
> No graven images may be
> Worshipped, except the currency.
> Swear not at all; for, for thy curse,
> Thine enemy is none the worse.
> At church on Sunday to attend
> Will serve to keep the world thy friend.
> Honour thy parents; that is, all
> From whom advancement may befall.
> Thou shalt not kill; but need'st not strive
> Officiously to keep alive.
> Do not adultery commit;
> Advantage rarely comes of it.
> Thou shalt not steal; an empty feat,

When it's so lucrative to cheat.
Bear not false witness; let the lie
Have time on its own wings to fly.
Thou shalt not covet; but tradition
Approves all forms of competition.

— 'The Latest Decalogue,'
Arthur Hugh Clough (1819–1861)

Chapter Seven

The desire of the moth for the star,
Of the night for the morrow,
The devotion to something afar
From the sphere of our sorrow.

Shelley (1792–1822)

As I shall be examining the cases of serial killers who have been caught and ones who have not, I will now explain as briefly as possible both the subjective and objective methodology of psychological/psychiatric profiling and the relevance of its forensic subdivisions.

I conduct this preliminary in order to demonstrate that psychological/psychiatric profiling is both a behavioral science and an art, not a haphazard system of mere guess-work or hindsight concocted after the killer has been captured.

In addition, I shall introduce personal, empirical innovations to the existing methodology of psychological/psychiatric profiling, integrating them into the central profiling system, and then logically extending and dividing functional/organic conclusions into two main categories, namely, the psychopathic and the psychotic.

The personal modifications and interpretations, combined with a psychological/psychiatric emphasis on pathological patterns of thought and behaviour, will perhaps marginally enhance the future possible quotient of prediction and detection in the pursuit of serial killers.

I personally appreciate the study more when the opponent is unorthodox and versatile:

The chessboard is the world; the pieces are the phenomena of the universe; the rules of the game are what we call the laws of Nature. The player on the other side is hidden from us. We know that his play is always fair, just, and patient. But also we know, to our cost, that he never overlooks a mistake, or makes the smallest allowance for ignorance.

— T. H. Huxley (1825–1895)

The player is hidden but his acts are not, and the primal motivation behind the acts is essentially unoriginal.

The crime scene should be studied with a degree of atavism. What has taken place has taken place before. What has taken place shall take place again. The answers are within that conviction. That cycle of eternal recurrence.

Opportunistic homicide, in the context of the emotive terms 'good' and 'evil,' should be removed from the realms of mysticism.

There are basically three types of people. The optimist who has the naïve expectation of universal altruism. The pessimist who has a morbid conviction of universal malevolence. And finally, the remainder who exercise a pragmatic, humanistic approach.

In which category do you believe you belong?

Your answer will of course largely be dictated first by personal vanity and, second, by which category you believe the criminal or serial killer belongs. Now conjure up the secret urges, images and fantasies which exist in your own mind, and think again.

———•◦•———

Pierce Brooks, ex-captain in the Los Angeles Police Department and Chief of Police in Springfield, Oregon, and Lakewood, Colorado, respectively, had spent over two decades formulating and practising a personal, and therefore necessarily limited form of psychological profiling to help track down and capture serial killers and other violent criminals. In later years he was to have many conferences with FBI chiefs, particularly members of the Behavioral Science Unit (BSU) at the FBI Training Academy in Quantico, Virginia.

As early as 1974, Brooks had also attended conferences at the Justice Department to propose the setting up of a computerised system and Task Force which, years later, was to become known as VICAP (Violent Criminal Apprehension Program). Experts in all fields of national and local law enforcement also attended the conferences and expressed enthusiastic support for the concept.

William H. Webster, then Director of the FBI, was instructed by the Subcommittee on Juvenile Justice of the Senate Judiciary Committee to examine the VICAP concept, with a view to incorporating it into the administration of the FBI Behavioral Science Unit at the FBI Academy. The subcommittee heard the testimony of innumerable expert witnesses from police agencies nationwide, all enthusiastically in support of setting up the VICAP Task Force under the control of the FBI BSU, and funded by them.

It was disclosed to the subcommittee that the FBI BSU in Quantico had already researched and instigated a restricted, computerised national crime analysis unit, in tandem with a special FBI team researching the concept of psychological profiling. The FBI psychological profilers were already interviewing in depth many serial killers in prisons throughout the country, attempting to ascertain common characteristics and traits they shared. This project remained obscure to the American public until the films *Manhunter* and *Silence of the Lambs* appeared.

Meanwhile, back in 1984, the Reagan administration finally agreed that the VICAP project would be set up under the auspices of the FBI BSU at Quantico, in conjunction with the psychological profiling unit already in existence there, and that the resulting computerised data would be made available to all national and local law enforcement agencies.

The vision first conceived by Brooks Pierce in prior decades had at last come into being. Psychology and technology had joined forces and become a formidable weapon to combat all violent criminals, particularly the high-profile threat of the mobile, trawling serial killer.

When a definite pattern of killings is detected by state or local police, a team from the FBI Behavioral Science Unit is called in to assist. Their prime task is to study the crime scenes closely and assess whatever forensic evidence has already been collated, then to look for anything that might have been overlooked or not properly interpreted at a local level.

It is by tabulating and evaluating the where, when, how and why of the murders that the serial killer's personality print and crime scene signature begin to emerge, and a possible rhythm to the killings detected, perhaps leading to a working hypothesis or subsequent prediction of where and when the killer is likely to strike next.

For instance, from the series of in-depth interviews the FBI Behavioral Science Unit conducted with captured serial killers who were sexually motivated, some of the following statistics were tabulated:

1. Almost 90% had received psychiatric treatment at some stage in their life.
2. Over 50% had family members with a psychiatric illness.
3. 35% had at some time attempted to commit suicide.
4. More than 40% had been sexually abused as children, and this figure almost doubled in the instances of psychological abuse as children.

5. 45% had a criminal record at an early age.
6. 75% did not have a steady job.
7. 30% were Caucasian.
8. 44% came from a one-parent family.
9. 70% had a strict mother.
10. 75% had a strict father.
11. 70% had an interest in pornography.

These figures, and many other additional criminal statistics, assisted the Behavioral Science Unit in formulating a table of traits and characteristics which would help to identify a serial killer.

But that is not to say, as some authoritarian schools of thought might expediently argue, that a violent criminal or a serial killer can be identified as such by reference to his/her childhood behaviour before an age when a sense of conscience, aesthetics or idealism has been given a chance to evolve. If that were the case, you might easily confuse the serial killer with a far more aggressive and dangerous future general or politician!

However, as can be clearly predicated from the above statistics, if a child is physically/psychologically abused or rejected in early childhood either by parents or (as the statistics carefully neglect to mention because of the political implications) social deprivation, the chances of him/her reacting violently against 'authority' in later life is dramatically enhanced.

As previously stated, I have constructed a table divided into two main categories, the 'Psychopathic' and the 'Psychotic.' However, this does not mean that the two categories are mutually exclusive.

A psychopathic killer may have secondary affective symptoms of psychosis; the psychotic killer may have secondary affective psychopathic symptoms. Further, very occasionally, a schizoid serial killer may emerge who possesses, almost in equal quantity, affective psychopathic and psychotic traits and characteristics.

In another more general instance from my experience, the initial murder(s) by either a psychopath or a psychotic invariably takes place in or near the area in which the killer lives or works, as familiarity breeds both desire and self-confidence. Therefore, expert assessment of what can be ascertained to be the killer's first ventures into homicide will produce the most *comprehensive* personality print or crime scene signature of the serial killer. From study of the crime scene data, one should at least be able to make a tentative estimation as to which main category the killer belongs.

Obviously, computerised national records would be exhaustively cross-referenced to establish whether previous crimes bearing the same — or similar — *modus operandi* had been tabulated in some other part of the country. Tracking back on a national scale, to establish and intensively study the forensic evidence of the initial murder by the killer is made no less important by distance. The 'first-strike' principle of proximity still applies.

<hr>

The high I.Q. serial killer is a complex, eclectic individual who is not ruled by mere consistency or routine. He is likely to resort to pragmatic innovations where necessity or intellect dictates. Therefore, this category of killer is so much more difficult to predict or trap by mere pedantic or academic adherence to the textbook. One must be extremely careful never to equate insanity with stupidity.

There is often a grandeur in insanity, and an insanity in grandeur. The seed of genius (which, I hasten to add, I do not claim to possess) can thrive just as robustly in the dark as in the light.

The pathological killer affectively influenced by cyclical factors axiomatically gives advantage and proactive initiative to the detective. But the killer to whom the universe teaches chaos or absurdity is unlikely to fall victim to an easily recognized pattern or less than sophisticated proactive strategy by the police.

By definition, the very fact that the killer thinks in universal, existential or *cautiously* omnipotent terms widens the mindscape in which his acts are likely to be committed.

Essentially, belief in either chaos or absurdity creates the same vision of man: an ant trying to fathom the mysteries of the cosmos and dismally failing. Therefore, the acts of such a killer will probably be as much a product of intellect as of passion. Far harder to comprehend or predict.

If he conceives murder as an art, he will naturally perceive his acts as spontaneous creative destruction, and therefore he himself possibly has no idea where or when his next brushstroke shall fall, or whether the result will be aesthetically pleasing. If not pleasing, he will not repeat the hue.

How then can the detective anticipate in such a case?

If the killer is so consciously mindful of effect, his subconscious will nevertheless leave identifiable psychological traces, personal traits and characteristics. The more complex the creation, the more information his subconscious shall reveal. His 'paintings' will become identifiable primarily by their brushstrokes rather than the subject matter.

There will doubtless be killers aware of this trace element who will attempt to create diversions, in much the same manner as some people can appear to converse a great deal about themselves as a method of concealing their true nature.

However, all in all, despite such precautionary tactics, the subconscious will nevertheless reveal more than the serial killer consciously wishes. Even silence reveals evidence by omission.

The worst possible scenario for the detective would be a killer educated in the employment of auto-hypnotic techniques, which would enable him to modify and programme his subconscious to a controlled, effective degree, like a chameleon capable of consciously altering the colour of his personality at root level. This concept is not simply theoretical. I myself used it successfully.

———•◆•———

The practical mechanics of examining and analysing the crime scene presented by any serial killer naturally requires insight as well as deductive skills. The most important answers are already within the psyche of the investigator. Within us all, in my opinion. The serial killer is in effect your alter-ego, that facet of character you strive so hard to conceal and repress.

You study serial killers not only to understand him/her but also yourselves.

Like every other individual, the serial killer doesn't wish anyone to know something until he is ready to reveal it himself.

The collating of crime scene information with whatever other factual, physical and circumstantial evidence routine police work has managed to come up with also requires expertise, the prime object being to build a psychological portrait of the type of killer who would commit a particular type of murder — his probable pathology and motivation. And, by tried and tested principles, to attempt to chart and predict the possible course, cyclical parameters, choice of environment, type of victim and general methodology his next crime is likely to include. In short, his crime signature.

In reality, the investigator is asking why *he himself* would commit that particular kind of murder.

Ideally, the detective should always assess the killer in both psychological and philosophical/metaphysical terms, in order to determine what the killer believes in, or what he believes he is accomplishing, or aspiring to accomplish, by his crimes.

We can safely predicate that the serial killer *has* confronted the chaos or absurdity of existence, as previously mentioned, the spiritual abyss — whether it be religious or secular in nature — and is trying to impose upon it some meaning and order of his own. Although there have been serial killers whose crimes were motivated by orthodox religious fanaticism or visions, in my experience they are a small minority.

But there are killers who, not believing in any orthodox god, create one of their own. Or, more accurately, who believe in a form of personal philosophy (predominantly nihilistic in character) so devoutly that it has the psychological power of a religion. This category, in my opinion, constitutes the majority of serial killers.

Seeing no divine order of things, no hidden significance to life, other than the hedonistic or existential, they create their own spiritual or aesthetic microcosm. Metaphorically gods in their own kingdom, whimsically sampling everything that was once forbidden, eventually taking the lives of those who have entered their private domain, witnessed their darkest desires and, therefore, must never be allowed to leave or testify. The killing also affirmatively defines their new powers. That is why, in this primarily metaphysical context, some can often regard destruction as an act of creation — an 'act of God.'

Man created God in his own image, then claimed that God created him in His. The serial killer juggles dreams and fantasies in similar fashion. He is impatiently withering under the confinements of what is generally accepted as ordinary reality. Most people are.

He daily observes people throwing their entire lives away on repetitive jobs, territorial obsessions, promotion to a particular desk, key to the executive toilet, etc. To his eyes this is *insanity*. He craves excitement. Vibrant meaning. Purpose. But it never seems to come.

He cannot wait indefinitely. Life has become a funeral cortège. Indifference and ubiquitous mediocrity provoke him. He appoints himself possessor, enlightened inhabitant, of a vacant universe. A cynical Don Quixote tilting at any laws and customs questioning his newfound sense of nihilistic integrity.

Time has been squandered. Time to catch up. A hidden agenda to foster, personal accounts to settle, dormant fantasies to fulfil. He thirsts for the realm of total possibility.

Where should he draw the line? Unconditionally and spontaneously far beyond any border which others have had the arrogance to draw for him.

Ideally, he must perform the dualistic feat of proving to himself that he is literally capable of anything, whilst knowing he is not. Dream as reality. Life a work of art. The attempt, all.

He has a vivid sense of seeing farther and deeper than most. Other people seem to be somnambulistic. He resolves not to be dragged down by numbers. Endurance of others must cease. Slough off the last vestiges of servility. Vigorous with resentful intent, as though an inner generator, hidden deep within since birth, has been switched on, his spirit expands to encompass the vaster gestalt.

Most people have vague intimations of this recondite power. Standing on a vacant shore, staring over oceanic plains, the soothing surge of the void fills them with renewed life. Unknown presences whisper. Arcane meanings beyond language are experienced. Silent music.

Some may interpret the metaphysical revitalisation as a religious experience. Others as a pagan power source, causing them to laugh and dance with savage delight at the cosmic insignificance of humanity. The nature of unconditional freedom is instinctively seized and wielded.

And there you have an amorphous soul/psyche portrait of the unknown serial killer — designer chaos and idiosyncratic subversion. To him, morality reduces life more than it enhances. It could be impartially argued that he inhabits an almost poetic fourth dimension, where dreams and reality naturally meld, a world of esoteric certitude and applied will. A psychic state in which common reality is seen merely as a lace curtain, visually recognized and noted but too insignificant to interfere with the more fascinating visions he sees beyond. He intuits that those around him can only see the lace curtain, and he keenly appreciates his advantage. While they blankly daydream behind the lace, he acts . . . the natural prize due psychic penetration and a superior altered state. .

It amuses him that conformists, whom he regards as sanctimonious timid bores, preach morality, remaining unaware of his own.

Once the victim has been chosen and action commences, the serial killer enters into an abnormal dimension: one in which he is viewing the world as a dynamic scenario, a theatrical event or happening, in which he is the prime mover. Both artistic creator and sole spectator of a production yet to be viewed by the general public.

At another level the play is an independent production, taking on a life of its own. A hazardous, cathartic drama in which the script is impromptu —

neither the killer nor the victim knows for certain how it will end, nor whether a member of the unseen audience (the public) will decide to participate or not. The passing world has become much like television with the sound turned off, only half intrusive. As already stated, he believes no act in itself has inherent qualities of good or evil that is not made so by an audience. Does a falling tree make a sound if there is no one there to listen?

The audience is the value and quality of the act. During the process of artistic creation, in the killer's psychic dimension beyond good and evil, the audience is merely a possible offstage threat. If his 'play' is a success, he will read the critical reviews with interest, not least as a technician in search of dangerous, structural flaws.

Some people may interpret these expressed, multi-dimensional qualities of the serial killer as denoting the supernatural, others the inhuman.

Public fear of the species is ambivalent. On one hand, the atavistic dread of the abnormal is deliberately magnified in the public mind by the mass media. On the other, the astounding popularity of news, books and films on the subject indicates that the public must thoroughly enjoy being 'shocked,' 'terrified' and 'sickened.' In fact, the popular current demand for extravaganzas of innocent blood is obviously outstripping supply.

It is human nature to derive comfort in the misery of others, and the nature of those in the media to derive maximum profit from it. Some serial killers are obviously intent upon a more equal distribution of misery. Therefore, if the concept of even-handed justice were paramount in the killer's mind, it is surprising that so few victims have been selected from the media milieu who exploit and profit from gore. This curious neglect appears to indicate that the serial killer regards the media as his confederate in crime — his Boswell, as it were.

Logic confirms there is not such a gulf between the instincts of the serial killer and those of the media and public. A common bond of interest and satisfaction exists, the critical variant being, as in the theatre, between those who watch and those who act. Yet thoughts of murder are obviously psychologically and atavistically satisfying to the individual. If only they had the inclination and time to spare, they too would be capable of murder, and certainly would have no shortage of suitable candidates in mind. Indeed, they would feel silently insulted if anyone suggested the contrary.

Unlike the serial killer, few feel compelled to prove the point. But murder nevertheless remains probably the most popular, primal form of public entertainment there is or ever shall be.

Which perhaps helps one to understand why official statistics in practically every civilised country show that you are 99% more likely to be murdered by the person sitting next to you at home this very moment than by a serial killer — a revealing fact I will expand upon shortly.

> One may indeed lie with the mouth; but with the accompanying grimace one nevertheless tells the truth.
>
> — Nietzsche

On this further advanced plateau of mutual understanding, let us now examine some of the basic psychological guidelines for trying to outwit and track down the serial killer in his chosen field of recreation or retribution.

I have no compunctions, no sense of betrayed fellowship or breach of loyalty, in assisting the opposition, so to speak. After all, the killer knows the risks and is prepared to take them. He has the initiative and should keep abreast or ahead of current forensic developments and other scientific advances. If he makes a miscalculation he must accept the penalty, but not necessarily the judgment of others — a Christian ethic, of course, put to pagan use.

First, there now follows an initial reference table of characteristics and traits which help to identify the psychopathic serial killer. When we get down to individual case histories, this and subsequent tabulations will facilitate speedier understanding of significant factors. A surer grasp of these multiple associations will also assist in understanding the means by which a psychological/psychiatric profile of the killer being hunted is constructed. (Bear in mind that the more you tell someone, the more dangerous they become to you and, therefore, the far more dangerous you become to them.)

Psychopath Personality Print

1. Organised, emotionally controlled and methodical.
2. Of average or above-average intelligence.
3. On the surface, socially competent, persuasive and manipulative.
4. Usually a skilled worker or self-employed.
5. Sexually adequate heterosexual/homosexual/bisexual.
6. Often an only child.
7. The father or mother usually erratic/irrational/unstable at work and at home.
8. Subject to inconstant/capricious discipline as a child and used to getting his/her own way. The same selfish and amoral attitude extends into adult life.

9. Emotionless, controlled mood when committing a crime.
10. Moderate use of alcohol before/after a crime if stress builds up.
11. Usually married, divorced or living with a partner.
12. Owns/uses a reliable, functional vehicle.
13. Liable to change jobs quite often and move from one area/town/city to another. No sense of social awareness or community.
14. Takes an interest in media reports about his crime, especially news of police tactics being adopted.
15. By creating a fantasy, sexual or otherwise, and putting it into action, he believes he creates his own highly controlled, existential reality, his personal microcosm.
16. He is likely to return to the scene of the crime either to recreate the crime in imagination, or to check whether the crime scene has been discovered/disturbed or holds some originally overlooked clue/danger.
17. He will usually personalise the victim, talk to them, to give added significance, emotional and intellectual depth to the crime. Unlike the psychotic, he has little to fear from his conscience by personalisation of the victim.

Psychopathic Factors at Scene of Crime

(a) Indications that the crime was carefully planned and organised.

(b) Initial victim probably chosen in a district in or near where the killer lives/lived, works/worked, or is/was otherwise highly familiar with. He will probably correct this mistake when he sees the police in his home ground, and strike next in a more distant area. The initial victim may ostensibly be a stranger, but is more likely to be someone he knows, even if only by sight. He may initially kill the victim — not as part of his fantasy but simply to avoid leaving a witness who could give a description of him to the police. When he has killed once, it will be easier the second time, and killing will probably gradually become either (i) an habitual self-protective measure, a compulsive part of his *modus operandi*, or (ii) a metaphysical or psychological experience he has grown to appreciate.

(c) He deliberately personalises and terrorises the victim either to gain easier control, experience a further dimension of power, add emotional depth, or obtain sadistic satisfaction from their fear. The more insecure he is, the more likely a weapon will be brandished. Talks to them in an abstract, controlled manner, issuing threats or describing their probable fate if they don't comply with everything he says. Conversely, he may falsely reassure them by promising they will come to no harm so long as they keep quiet and do as he tells them. This may be done for expediency or as a sophisticated form of sadism in the knowledge he is going to kill the victim anyway. Sado-masochistically he is deriving pleasure from what he knows the victim is experiencing — fear, shame, hope, despair, wishing an end to the experience, hoping to live, a surrendering to deliberate sexual stimulation against their will and experiencing pleasure without guilt.

(d) Above all, he wants total submission from the victim.

(e) If insecure he is likely to use restraints — handcuffs, rope, gag, etc.

(f) Obtains his satisfaction by rape or other violence prior to death of victim. Despite appearances, the central motivation is power, not sex. Sex and violence are both expressions of his will to power. He may wish to dominate and control his victim totally as part of his fantasy. This compulsion also indicates deep feelings of insecurity.

(g) Takes methodical pains to leave no forensic clues at the crime scene. Will hide or bury the body to minimise risk. No body, no crime.

(h) Rarely leaves a weapon behind. Will normally destroy or dispose of it in a river, etc., usually some distance from the crime scene. If he keeps the weapon, it is likely to be for some obsessive, ritualistic reason.

(i) He will probably take a trophy from the victim — a ring, garment, lock of hair, etc — for use as a catalyst, to re-enact and savour the memory of the crime. This re-enactment also serves to satisfy him psychologically, extending his cooling-off period between murders.

(j) A vehicle will be used to convey the live victim or the body to the disposal area.

(k) Contrary to popular detective fiction, if the killer is of average or above average intelligence, it is highly improbable that he will risk keeping any press cuttings about his crimes. Trophies are likely to be hidden in an obscure, secure place, such as a safe-deposit box, second address, a lock-up garage, etc.

———— ·•·•———

There are psychological/psychiatric subdivisions and secondary symptoms in every broad category profile. These shall be considered further on. Let us first tabulate the traits and characteristics of the second broad category.

Psychotic Personality Print

1. Volatile, spontaneous and disorganised. Usually seriously maladjusted, emotionally and intellectually. May experience hallucinations, reacting

chiefly to inner experiences rather than external, perceiving a delusionary concept of reality. Often suffers from cycles of manic-depression or profound melancholia.

2. Can be below or above average intelligence, depending upon the affective degree and subdivisions of psychosis involved, but in certain cases can soar to well above average.

3. Normally prefers unskilled work.

4. Sometimes sexually inadequate by normal standards but, stimulated by abnormal fantasy, can be sexually rapacious and violent.

5. Father socially erratic or incompetent. Son tends to emulate the father.

6. Probably experienced harsh parental discipline or psychological/sexual abuse.

7. Suffers from stress or emotional anxiety during crime.

8. Rarely uses alcohol during crime.

9. Usually lives alone.

10. Dramatic fluctuations in behaviour.

11. Normally lives or works in the area in which his initial crimes were committed.

12. Takes no real interest in media reports of his crimes or police tactics.

13. Usually neither owns nor uses a vehicle. Commits his crimes opportunistically/spontaneously in whatever spot or area he happens to be.

14. Being unable to square his personal perceptions and conceptions with surrounding reality, he consciously and subconsciously erects protective mental blocks and creates his own distorted version of reality, one which fits the ideal image he has of himself and the personal microcosm he inhabits.

15. Usually depersonalises the victim, by deliberately perceiving her/him as an object, attempting to eradicate any twinge of conscience, which he almost certainly regards as a sign of weakness.

16. Extreme character polarisations. May hold religious beliefs but reconciles them with criminal acts he commits.

Psychotic Factors at the Scene of a Crime

(a) As the disorganised psychotic usually kills erratically within a window of opportunity, hastily innovating as events dictate, the scene of the crime reflects general disorder and should furnish important clues to the profiler.

(b) He will usually not even bother to conceal the victim or, at best, do so in a cursory, sloppy manner, either (i) because he simply does not care about the victim, or (ii) does not fully appreciate the consequences of his act and the increased risks involved, or (iii) wishes to further degrade the victim by discarding them naked to public view, or to shock those who discover the body.

(c) Despite the fact that he normally knows one or more of his initial victims and lives/works in the same vicinity, he is usually not aware of the obvious dangers inherent in killing a victim in his home territory; this will depend upon the degree of mental maladjustment involved and the strength of affective influence exerted by the subdivisions of his psychosis. Therefore, unlike the psychopath, he will be tardier in strategically selecting other districts in which to strike. This is an important point to note, as it leads to faster psychological classification of the killer, denoting whether he is predominantly psychopathic or psychotic, and often strongly suggests the probable direction in which to concentrate to search for his base of operations, and the detection of a probable pattern revealing where and when he is likely to kill next.

(d) Rarely uses restraints on victim.

(e) There will usually be pathological, ritualistic or some esoteric factors at the crime scene which will reflect aspects of the killer's fantasy fulfilment, his psychosis and perhaps some of its subdivisions and secondary symptoms.

(f) Where the organised psychopath nearly always chooses isolated or secure areas in which to kill or take his victim to, the psychotic will often kill in places fraught with obvious dangers — streets, busy parks, subways and other public venues. The nature of his psychosis often generates a total or partly affective delusion that he is being protected or aided by supernatural forces of some description.

That completes the initial basic tabulations which help to identify into which of the two broad categories — psychopathic or psychotic — the hunted serial killer fits, and some of the further significant indications which have to be looked for at the crime scene.

The next required step in building a comprehensive psychological/psychiatric profile of the particular killer being sought is a precise evaluation of his *modus operandi* from start to finish.

This is naturally achieved by an exhaustive survey of each crime scene, compiling a highly individualistic personality print/crime signature from the conscious/subconscious methodology he employs throughout.

Evidence of symbolism, ritualistic or sadistic fantasy is of special relevance. We are, as previously evidenced, searching for and creating, from explicit and implicit evidence, a physical and psychological after-image of the killer.

Modifications may be required as investigations progress or further murders are committed, providing additional data to test against the original hypothesis.

In the process of constructing a psychological/psychiatric profile under one or other of the two main categories, Psychopathic and Psychotic, evidence of secondary symptoms and additional sub-classifications of abnormality assist in determining the nature of the fantasy the killer is acting out.

In the case of psychotics, some category of schizophrenia is usually present — simple, acute, hebephrenic, paranoid, etc.

Every variety of psychoses should be considered — organic; functional; hallucinatory; delusional; melancholic; general paresis; alcoholic reactions; pathological intoxication; acute alcoholic hallucinosis; Korsakoff's Syndrome; senile dementia; psychotic depression; involutional melancholia; the male climacteric; manic depressive psychosis; psychotic mania; hypomania; etc. Some of these symptoms may also be found in the psychopath to a non-affective degree.

Thus we axiomatically enter the field of compulsions, obsessions, phobias, dissociated personalities, fugues, traumatic neuroses, multiple personality, psychosexual behaviour, sexual symbolism, sexual aberrations, and resort to all the main schools of psychology — structuralist (psychophysical); functionalist; psychoanalytic; gestalt; behaviourist/behavioural (in the context of psychological profiling, the most important).

Some individuals erroneously believe that if they master logic they will master life.

Logic is merely a tool. The science of argument. In that context it can be used to deduce what argument the serial killer is trying to put across by his actions, what he is trying to prove or disprove.

A syllogism presents two parts of an argument in which the premises may be stated before the conclusion. Therefore the serial killer's successive murders can logically be developed as the premises from which one must synthesize conclusions that may lead to his capture.

Even though most serial killers are not guided by logic, his pursuers are constrained to be. Logic plus inspired insight is a much greater threat to the quarry, no matter how ultra-modern technological research is likely to become.

As stated, much valuable information can be amassed from extended interviews with serial killers, though obviously a great deal depends on how proficient the psychiatrist or interviewer is, or how forthcoming the killer.

One must understand that there is little intellectual or spiritual inducement for the captured serial killer to cooperate in any way. To all intents and purposes his real life is over and done with, as he knows he shall never be free again, so why should he volunteer information or reveal aspects of his personality to the authorities?

Most killers will be intelligent enough to realise that the penal authorities will mainly use such information as control points against him. Therefore he is most likely to reveal only that information which may persuade the authorities to understand his better side and treat him more humanely.

Naturally, prior to interviewing, all aspects of the serial killer's case must be exhaustively studied — family and educational background, pathology reports on victims, police interviews, trial transcript, how he spends his time in prison, what he reads, other hobbies, brand of cigarette if a smoker, favourite chocolate bar, relationship with guards and prisoners, observed general attitude to his crimes, etc.

Essentially you will read him by his actions. Avoid use of questionnaires and an overtly structural approach. Much more will be revealed obliquely in relaxed, free-flowing conversation, touching upon politics, general philosophy, topical social questions, authors, films, controversial personalities, universal moral dilemmas.

The aim is to generate, as far as possible in the artificial circumstances of captivity, the sort of spontaneous atmosphere and genial conversation of a bar, avoiding the self-consciousness of formality.

Do not make instant notes. Create interest and it will snowball. That's the time to be a good, observant listener. One careless display of fish-eye or impatient disinterest by the interviewer can destroy the whole relaxed ambience. Therefore eyes must be constantly candid and receptive, ready for the unexpected dart of eye contact. All these and additional techniques should be second nature to a seasoned interviewer.

Many of these very same techniques are also used by serial killers to lull and snare victims. The interviewer will in effect be faced with the difficult task of deceiving a skilful deceiver.

The serial killer shares to a significant degree a common characteristic of the schizoid, namely, a marked lack of tension in reconciling polarised opinions or beliefs. This relativistic dexterity is an advantageous aid both to deception and self-deception, the latter enhancing the persuasion of the former. The higher the vocabulary and ability to articulate with apparent validity, the more convincing the argument, independent of truth, as every lawyer and expert logician knows.

In short, expressed even more cynically, it is the impression that counts, both in the eliciting and delivery of information. Personal interaction and observation will indicate the best psychological method to mine information from an adversary, and the information will instinctively form the basis of the most effective structure of persuasion to be adopted. Negative or positive responses, semantical nuances, body language, etc., all reflect or infer significant covert data for hypothesis, reapplication and ever discrete testing, never underestimating the opponent's own powers of observation and interpretation.

As previously betokened, one careless word or gesture, a solitary false note, can damage or neutralise a painstakingly nurtured ambience beyond recall. It is therefore largely safer to maintain a cautiously interested, confidential tone of underemphasis, unless otherwise is specifically or tactically indicated. The inner gyroscope of counter-transference is usually accurate and reliable.

You will note that I have kept this in general terms, as opposed to that of interrogating a serial killer exclusively. By and large the serial killer, like the socially sanctioned killer, regards himself as normal, except to the extent that he has transformed thought/fantasy into action.

Naturally an attitude indicating you regard him as an alien species will achieve naught except his regarding you similarly. In fact, even without given cause, the serial killer will at inception regard the interviewer as hostile anyway, by force of adversarial circumstance, and this dualistic defence mechanism is something the interviewer has to overcome.

Personally I could/can evaluate the integrity and calibre of a psychiatrist usually within the first ten minutes of a discussion, and decide whether to persevere or dismiss him/her as mechanistic.

Ironically, in some instances the psychiatrist himself evinces a serious personality disorder. So it should not be surprising that, according to official statistics, psychiatrists as a group have the highest suicide rate. Obviously a schizoid hazard of the profession, perhaps mainly due to patients injecting persuasive, relativistic philosophy into the field of inevitably limited psychodiagnostics and upsetting professional mental equilibrium.

A structurally impaired professional ego can quite easily be forced from its complacent tracks by psychodynamic intuition expressed in forcefully emotive and impulsive terms. The spoken word can possess a psychic penetration far beyond the reason of the written — as exemplified by the hypnotic oratory of Adolf Hitler and other great manipulators of primal emotion whose vocal delivery takes on the mystical power and sway of music. A psychosemantic symphony.

> Then the thing of courage as roused with rage with rage doth sympathise, and with an accent tuned in selfsame key retorts to chiding fortune.
>
> — *Troilus and Cressida*, Shakespeare

In the following pages I shall not tax the reader's patience with abstruse medical terminology without defining clearly, in plain language, what is meant.

As the prime purpose of this book is a study of the forensic evidence relevant to compiling a psychological profile of the killer, I shall not unduly clutter these pages with the name and biography of every victim of each killer (unless the killer is targeting a certain category of victim). Other authors most often do use such victim biographical material, but in many instances simply as humanistic or artistic padding. In this particular case it would only serve to distract from the prime object.

This volume is not intended to be a psychological/psychiatric textbook. If further constrained to classify the book's contents and intent, I am forced to resort to sporting terms. It is a modest manual for helping to track and capture the greatest and most dangerous animal in existence: the human predator.

I am understandably aware that tabulated techniques of the hunt may unavoidably assist the hunted as well as the hunter. Therefore both would do well to remember:

> He who fights with monsters might take care lest he thereby become a monster. And if you gaze for long into an abyss, the abyss gazes also into you.
>
> — Nietzsche

Part Two

Chapter Eight
Henry Lee Lucas

Kill me tomorrow; let me live tonight.

Othello, **Shakespeare**

Only of brief personal interest, Henry Lee Lucas' significance comes from a sociological vantage point: the capability of mass media to create the desire in so many people to be famous at any cost, even their lives or that of others. The yearning to flicker for a few moments on television, or appear on the front page of a newspaper that wraps tomorrow's fish. 'The medium is the message.'

Psychologically, Henry Lee Lucas primarily fits the classification of the disorganised psychotic killer: of average or below-average intelligence; an unskilled worker; outcast, rootless transient with no social awareness; sometimes disoriented and confused during the crime; murders committed spontaneously regardless of risk. A resentful Charlie Chaplin. Lucas' alcoholic father abused him sadistically for years, unwittingly fashioning him into his mother's nemesis.

An abused child usually does not focus hatred upon the parent who abuses but upon the parent who stood by and did nothing to stop the abuser. The hatred towards the abuser is effectively regarded as nothing compared to the betrayal of love and trust by the second parent. We guard against an enemy, not a loved one or friend, therefore betrayal by the latter has more psychic impact.

Lucas was twenty-three, his mother seventy, when he stabbed, strangled and raped her. Obviously the viciousness of this act projected that the hatred for his mother would burgeon into a deep-seated distrust/hatred of the female species as a whole. It would also make Lucas sexually inadequate with women throughout his life.

For the murder of his mother, he was sent to a top-security mental hospital, which eventually discharged him to spend eight years in prison. When released, he became a vagrant and petty thief, forging a lasting companionship with another illiterate, homosexual hobo, Ottis Elwood Toole, with whom he aimlessly wandered and panhandled across America.

When Lucas was again eventually arrested in 1982 for the squalid murder of his fifteen-year-old common-law wife, Frieda Powell, the niece of Toole, he was asked why he had dismembered the body. Lucas revealingly replied, 'It was the only thing I could think of.' In other words, it was a murder committed in panic and without *forethought*. Hardly the pattern of the psychopathic, calculating, seasoned killer Lucas later claimed himself to be, with several hundred prior victims to his credit. Such a killer would surely by then have been an expert innovator in such basic matters as disposal.

Nevertheless, when police routinely questioned him about other possible murders, Lucas began confessing to every homicide put to him. Contagiously, eager detectives from police forces from almost every American state began converging upon this prodigious confessor and were not disappointed.

As the body count Lucas claimed he had killed mounted, it must have seemed to the gleeful detectives that Lucas would next be revealing that he was the second shooter on the grassy knoll in Dallas.

The final, grotesque total of homicides Lucas confessed to reached over three hundred. Nominally, this made him the most prolific serial killer in American history. Which is why I am dealing with his case first.

In addition, other unusual events led me to take a personal interest in the case.

An eminent author passed a message to me from a friend of his at the FBI Psychological Profiling Centre at Quantico, requesting my considered opinion of Lucas. I replied that it would help considerably and enhance accuracy if I could see or hear Lucas confessing. A video tape of Lucas being interrogated was promptly forwarded to me.

I studied the video in conjunction with forensic evidence and other documents on the case.

One of the most important factors I immediately took note of was that Lucas, when explaining away the fact that, in almost each of the three-hundred-odd homicides a different *modus operandi* had been adopted by the killer, made the astonishing assertion, no doubt prompted by his helpful inquisitors, that he had consciously contrived this system in order to mislead the police. From tramp to criminal genius and strategist in one unlikely stride. One had only to consider the prolific degree of applied intelligence and sustained concentration that would have been required to accomplish such feats of memory and diversionary complexity to see that it did not fit in with Lucas's chaotic history of psychosis.

In psychological terms, it would almost amount to Lucas possessing the ability to create literally hundreds of fake criminal personae or methods, each convincing enough to fool an army of investigating detectives actually searching for a telltale MO in each case.

In Jungian psychology, *persona* is construed as the psychic mechanism which masks a person's true thoughts and feelings in relation to the world as they perceive it. Therefore Lucas' absurd claims went far beyond the bounds of credibility, or of Jung's multi-personae theory that each persona is unaware of the existence of its fellows. In light of this, Lucas' real scenario should have become transparent to expert detectives.

Namely, that Lucas, with his record of matricide and being charged with another murder, was at least intelligent and experienced enough to realise that in such a chronic situation he faced two alternatives: death by execution, or imprisonment till death. Catch-22.

Having been previously certified insane regarding the murder of his mother, what if he could again convince the authorities that he was crazy? Second. His whole life being a dismal catalogue of failure from the day he was born, there was now a final opportunity for him to be remembered as a success in some field of human endeavour. It would not have taken him long to see that claims of prolific murder filled the bill nicely in both respects.

It is reasonable to conjecture from the known facts that Lucas did not possess any significant degree of self-understanding.

Logical extension therefore suggests that Lucas, in common with the vast majority of ordinary people, was unable to differentiate between the genuine parts of himself and those that had been imposed by reaction to circumstance.

When one adds to this his psychiatric history, his chronology of lifelong failure and that fact that his free life was at an end, it becomes obvious that the transmutation from being a nobody to a world-famous serial killer would also have been a logical and psychically satisfying escape route from reality, presenting a role to which he could easily adapt.

The mass media had made serial killers as fashionable and popular as movie stars. He too would become famous and, with luck, be certified insane into the bargain.

When his bandwagon of confessions began to roll, he probably noted how willingly the police from various states not only accepted his every word, but also generously put them into his mouth to conveniently clear unsolved murders from their files. A normal police practice and tendency.

A further incentive in this particular set of sensational circumstances, is the patent fact that mutual cooperation between Lucas and the detectives would not only make both Lucas and the detectives famous, but also the latter rich from books, newspaper exclusives, television appearances, films and other media spin-offs, including lucrative fees from the university lecturing circuit.

It is common knowledge that, after involvement in particularly notorious cases, police chiefs invariably retire early in order to benefit from commercial exploitation in this manner.

Again, crime is seen to pay very well indeed for some. Many otherwise respectable people exhibit not the least compunction in greatly profiting from the crimes and miseries of others. Even the relatives of victims eagerly cash in on criminal notoriety, employing agents to handle their media deals.

After I gave this (abbreviated) analysis and summation in response to the initial request by the aforementioned author, independent investigators and journalists belatedly began to test Lucas' claims, and the whole farcical charade began to fall apart immediately.

They discovered with hilarious ease that Lucas was actually in prison when many of the murders he confessed to were committed, and, in the case of many other murders, found irrefutable documentary proof that he was thousands of miles from the scenes of the crimes when they occurred.

The special Task Force, comprised of the legendary Texas Rangers, which had been set up specially to deal with Lucas' myriad murders, when confronted with this and other equally embarrassing evidence of monumental duplicity and inefficiency, either flatly refused to answer questions from journalists, or shifted the blame onto visiting police forces.

A lawyer who was helping to uncover these stupendous errors was suddenly arrested by the Texas Rangers and charged with a long list of unlikely criminal offences — an obvious attempt to discredit him. He eventually sued and was awarded a record $58 million in damages and, ironically, then became Lucas' lawyer!

Lucas at last made one true confession: he had invented the whole fiasco.

With unusual candour, he admitted that, once he saw how much world attention his prodigious homicidal claims were commanding, he became a publicity junkie and just kept confessing to murder after murder.

In his own words, he 'felt more famous than Elvis Presley.'

Though his false claims qualified him for inclusion here, the same exaggeration diminishes his homicidal stature, my interest and his significance in the annals of crime. When on Death Row awaiting execution, Lucas belatedly realised the price of his murderous ambitions.

The forces of law and order, from the low ranks to the political heights, having been made to appear ludicrously self-serving, are resolved to save face by making it a point of honour that Lucas does not cheat the death penalty. In the event, Lucas will in effect have been his own executioner.

> Fame is a food that dead men eat,
> I have no stomach for such meat.
>
> — Austin Dobson (1840–1921)

Chapter Nine
John Wayne Gacy

> They have swallowed us up quick:
> when they were so wrathfully dis-
> pleased with us.
>
> **The Prayer Book**

I had personal contact with John Wayne Gacy and we shared mutual friends. With an easy manner and a ready smile he could don at will, and harnessed to a recondite ferocity mostly only his victims saw in their final hours, Gacy evolved into the perfect psychopath.

He was in the psychological category known as the organised killer: of above-average intelligence; social skills highly cultivated; thought processes and emotions strictly controlled even under stress; functional in all aspects; victims usually strangers; use of restraints; bodies buried; high professional interest in media accounts of his crimes.

Like practically every serial killer, as his number of victims grew, so did his overconfidence, and he began leaving obvious clues and making serious errors of judgment. Not least of which was his burying of so many victims under his house that he ran out of burial sites and eventually created an odious sanitary problem in the immediate neighbourhood.

At the time of his crimes, the 1970s, Gacy was a successful building contractor in Chicago.

A large, powerfully-built man with an affable extrovert air, he took an active part in local Democratic politics, raised funds for charity, and dressed himself as Pogo the Clown to entertain children in hospitals.

There is no reason to suppose that his charitable activities were not genuinely altruistic. Crime is no more a full-time profession than any other, and serial killers are no exception to the rule. I will raise this point again in future pages re: another prolific serial killer, Dean Corll, to further illustrate that criminals do have a spectrum of other natural talents and genuine interests outside of their law-breaking activities. The sensationalist media and law enforcement agencies, for political and social manipulation, would have the public believe otherwise, usually inferring that the innocent enthusiasms of the criminal were in fact spurious in some way.

Gacy was a model citizen in every visible respect. But, as the tens of bodies of young men and boys buried under the crawlspace of his house oozed the sickly sweet smell of putrefaction into the sleepy suburban air, his respectable neighbours politely began to complain. In response, Gacy graciously shared their concern and distaste, blaming the drains and promising to have the matter rectified by his construction team.

It is hard to understand why an intelligent man of such resource did not foresee this logistical problem long before it became critical, and modify his homicidal methodology accordingly.

Obviously his sexual appetites had gradually overridden the instinct for self-survival. This is a common phenomenon in both the human and animal species, particularly when in the throes of immediate sexual ecstasy, or, in Gacy's case, in the coils of sexual obsession or fantasy.

The pathological depth of Gacy's addiction is evidenced by his practise of often keeping victims alive for several days in his house, needlessly increasing the risk of deduced or accidental discovery, whilst repeatedly beating and sodomising them.

One young man was fortunate enough to escape after twenty-four hours and reported Gacy to the police. Amazingly, the police simply asked Gacy a few cursory questions, as the escaped victim was a known prostitute; being a respected member of the community, Gacy's denials were readily accepted. Such is the illusionary power of good and bad reputation. The case against him was automatically dismissed. Gacy continued to torture and kill regularly and methodically.

―――――・▸・◂・―――――

Victims, picked up amiably by Gacy in bars or other public places, were cajoled by financial and other inducements into accompanying him home. As soon as he had them safely behind locked doors, the mask dropped and Gacy became threatening and violent. The victim was then forcibly led up to the attic where, using a plank of wood, four feet long with steel handcuffs at each end, Gacy would manacle the ankles of his victims apart. Sometimes he manacled their wrists to this plank and hung them from the roof rafters. The attic was also equipped with a bloodstained mattress.

When eventually tiring of them as sex objects, Gacy would strangle his victims by tying a rope round their neck and inserting an iron rod to tighten the noose like a tourniquet. Often he made their death more lingering by repeatedly loosening the noose and reviving the victim to further sexual abuse and torture. Perhaps this prolongation practice was stimulated by the fact that strangulation usually produces an involuntary erection in the male victim.

———————

The trees were festooned with Christmas lights and snow was in the air the evening that police were finally led to Gacy.

They were searching for a high school youth who had mysteriously disappeared the previous evening, and it was reported that Gacy had been heard offering him a job earlier the same night.

It is almost certain, from the hasty change of method Gacy eventually used to dispose of the body, that the youth, dead or alive, was still in Gacy's attic when the detectives called to question him.

Gacy put on a bold front and even invited the detectives in for a drink, cleverly reinforcing his highly respectable image by drawing their attention to plaques awarded to him for charity work, and to photographs of himself in the company of police chiefs, and another of him shaking hands with Rosalynn Carter, the wife of President Jimmy Carter. The ploy worked. The police eventually left without searching the house.

Gacy obviously had to work fast and disposed of the youth's body in an icy river some miles away. It would remain there undiscovered until the next spring thaw.

But one Des Plaines detective was suspicious of Gacy and ran a routine check through Chicago police headquarters. It showed Gacy had been charged twice with aggravated assault, and there was mention concerning the male prostitute he had allegedly held prisoner. The detectives immediately obtained a warrant to search Gacy's house.

Gacy greeted the detectives with an air of amused surprise, but his mood changed to one of arrogant truculence once their suspicions and intentions became apparent.

The detectives discovered and examined the 'torture board' still lying in the attic. In a downstairs bedroom they also found a drawer full of men's watches and rings — one of which bore the initials of another missing youth.

Whatever the local vagaries of the law in Chicago, it appears astonishing that these finds were not deemed sufficient evidence on which to arrest and hold Gacy on suspicion.

Charitably, one could interpret the apparent generosity of the police as a tactical expedient, to pressure Gacy into making a false move that would produce more evidence. For they put him under overt constant surveillance.

Gacy at first treated this ostentatious tailing with open scorn. However, as the days passed, and considering the amount of bodies he was living on top of and now had no opportunity to move or destroy, inner tension began to mount.

His behaviour became increasingly ferocious and reckless, like a tiger trying to escape the encircling beaters. He resentfully attempted to provoke the tailing detectives into arresting him — by driving his car at breakneck speeds, then openly smoking dope and blowing it in their faces.

Had the tactical provocation been successful, it would have enabled Gacy's excellent lawyers to file charges of police harassment, forcing them to ease the pressure a little. Shrewdly, the police refused the bait.

Questioning one of Gacy's employees, the detectives discovered that Gacy had sold him a car, which belonged to another missing youth. This was the extra evidence they had been waiting for to close in. Gacy got wind of what was happening and attempted to escape the net.

After a high-speed car chase in which Gacy was making straight for the airport, his vehicle was forcibly brought to a halt by the police and he was arrested on the technical holding charge of possessing amphetamines and other controlled drugs.

Detectives now had the opportunity to conduct a more thorough search of his house.

In a cupboard they discovered a trapdoor leading to the crawlspace below the house, where the perfume of putrefaction was so intense and overpowering that the detectives temporarily retreated.

Floorboards were eventually ripped up and windows opened to allow more air to the toiling diggers. The stench of death wafted out to the growing number of curious sightseers congregating beyond the barrier of police cars around the floodlit house.

As excavations by the police team progressed, the body count mounted, and so did the army of newspaper reporters and TV crews, stamping their feet against the hard frost.

A final total of twenty-eight bodies of young men and boys was uncovered. Later police investigations ascertained that a further five bodies had been concealed elsewhere, including the youth in the frozen river.

After being sentenced to death at his trial, Gacy, against all apparent reason, but in reality to keep the executioner at bay, continued to plead innocence and successfully fought legal battles from his prison cell for well over a decade.

In captivity his civilised veneer vanished and revealed the aura of a large trapped predator waiting to pounce. Most other prisoners gave him a wide berth. But some young prisoner thrillseekers were attracted to him like moths to a flame.

That was not surprising, as Gacy was very interesting to talk to when beyond the hearing range of prison guards. He was particularly fond of discussing politics and analysing the ulterior motives of various prominent politicians. He also enjoyed outside visits from many youths and good-looking young men who were obviously enamoured by his notoriety, and liked sexually teasing Gacy from behind the safety of a steel grill.

Gacy was intelligent enough to handle this without rancour, deriving a degree of visual stimulation from participating in the flirting, deliberately fuelling their seductive fantasies to complement his sadistically homicidal ones.

Despite being safely beyond his grasp, some youthful visitors could not quite conceal occasional flickers of masochistic dread in their wide eyes, which Gacy liked to stare into as he talked, feeding on the fear and nostalgically remembering times past.

———•◦•———

Gacy was born in Iowa in 1932. Apparently his father was not cruel but was a strict disciplinarian — which probably planted the first seed of sado-masochism in Gacy's subconscious, where it would lie dormant for almost three decades, waiting for the necessary catalyst to come along.

I believe the psychological trigger eventually arrived when Gacy, in the early 1970s, read and watched the media saturation coverage given to a homosexual killer in Houston, Dean Corll, who raped, tortured and murdered at least thirty boys and young men and then buried the bodies.

Corll, whose case is dealt with in a future chapter, invented a 'torture board,' a seven-feet square plywood board with handcuffs and ropes attached to each of its four corners. It is surely more than mere coincidence that when Gacy began his murderous career, he too constructed a torture board for his young male victims.

This serves as a perfect example of the amoral attitude/influence of the media in publishing every sordid detail of a case, including the methodology of the killer, simply to boost circulation and ratings, whilst ignoring the dangerous possibility that another killer might emulate the methods described.

Then, having been the first to publish such facts, the same newspapers do not hesitate to piously attack (yet again to boost circulation) any book which simply repeats those published details.

Gacy's mother had an entirely different personality to that of his father. She was loving and protective, and her son reciprocated in kind.

He was an apt student at school, and there was nothing remarkable in his childhood to presage what he was to become. Some pedants portentously pronounced that he lied and pilfered when young.

Has there ever been a child born who has not done both?

The media find it obligatory to please their public by always finding, or inventing, something discreditable, no matter what, in a criminal's childhood.

If the journalists I have met and studied are anything to go by, they themselves mastered little other than the art of moral prostitution and mendacity for financial gain. Most lack the intellect, insight and integrity to stray far from the mainstream and mediocre, purveying middle-class platitudes.

> An editor should have a pimp for a brother, so he'd have someone to look up to.
>
> — Gene Fowler

It was also reported that Gacy had suffered a severe blow to the head as a child. His trial lawyers naturally tried to make forensic use of this. But a brain scan conducted by prison psychiatrists showed no sign of organic damage, and further tests discovered no affective maladjustment that could be related to the head injury from that period.

That is not to say that such findings are infallible, of course, but merely that primary tests specifically designed to detect organic/causal relationship produced no positive evidence of same. One must also take into account that most of the tests conducted by prison psychiatrists expediently lean towards the requirements of the prosecution.

The human brain will always be more than we know, staying far beyond man's technological comprehension. The neurophysiological correlates of criminal behaviour obtained through the electroencephalogram (EEG), which measures or replicates electrical activity of the cortex, are not as reliable as correctional facility doctors would have the public accept.

If the EEG does discern 'abnormal' patterns of electrical activity or some apparent neurological dysfunction, there are schools of thought which argue that such findings do not necessarily correlate affective criminal behaviour, past or future.

Interpretation of abnormal patterns of electrical activity are based on comparing the brain patterns of known criminals with those of supposedly normal people, purely theoretical noncriminals. I maintain that any person without latent criminal tendencies is by definition abnormal or subnormal.

In short, some doctors argue that, as a certain person is a criminal, his brain patterns must therefore be abnormal; this is another way of saying that the crime dictates interpretation of the criminal pattern. It also implies, to the uninformed, that brain patterns are as distinctive as fingerprints in detecting the criminal. That is not the case.

It is a theory which, to me, is reminiscent of George Orwell's 'thought police.' I would like to see judges, psychiatrists, generals, financiers, psychologists, corporate lawyers, bishops, police, reporters, politicians and doctors subjected to EEG tests if, as is suggested, it is such a reliable method of detecting the criminals of society.

To my knowledge no such comprehensive testing of the shapers of society has ever been conducted, and I believe it would be safe to assume there would be very few who would volunteer to be tested against such criteria.

———— •◆•◆• ————

Gacy had been married and divorced twice. Both ex-wives had nothing sensational to say about him. However, the two confirmed that Gacy's drift from the norm was gradual.

His first wife revealed that he started bringing youths home with him occasionally. There was, in the early stages, no sexually overt change in Gacy, other than that implied by his odd choice of companions.

But finally he was arrested for beating up a youth and given a short term in prison. This led to his first divorce.

He married again and moved to Des Plaines, on the outskirts of Chicago, and set up his very successful business. However, he also slowly regained the habit of bringing homosexuals home with him.

Incongruously, the final break with his second wife took place after sexual intercourse with her one night, in 1975, when he informed her it would be for the last time.

———— •◆•◆• ————

The pathological traits in Gacy became more pronounced; he was now regularly picking up male prostitutes, first sodomising and then beating them up.

This transference of aggression onto the object of desire is common in latent or secretly active homosexuals; personal shame/guilt transmutes into violence. But in Gacy, I believe the main element was that of deriving sado-masochistic satisfaction. He had begun by beating and torturing his willing sex partners and ended by torturing unwilling ones. But why did he start killing them?

Again you have the example of gradual evolution from the relatively mild to the fatal. No dramatic overnight transformation.

Perhaps, it could be argued, not even a conscious or willed escalation. More an instinctive drive, an irresistible urge towards ever stronger sensual satisfaction, ever-increasing sadism, only to be frustrated by the concomitant disillusionment decreed by human limitations. A syndrome that could be expected to drive him, and probably most normal people, to the edge of insanity.

That is arguably a reasonable and valid interpretation of the facts but, in my opinion, a facile one. Gacy was far more intelligent, complex and danger-ous than basic analysis postulated.

As already stated, on occasion he actually allowed some of the youths he raped and violently tortured to go free, as though he were subconsciously seeking disaster and an end to the addictive treadmill he had created for himself. Again, 'Those whom the gods wish to destroy . . .'

The burgeoning sado-masochistic psychopathology was predictably demanding fantasy fulfilment of the most extreme nature. An act totally free of all moral restraints, performed in conditions of safety and secrecy.

Twice Gacy had let his victims live, and twice they had informed on him to the police. If he was to continue in his sado-masochistic practices as intended, he could not risk being given away a third time, especially as he had by then built up a successful company and a very respectable image to go with it. Naturally, he found respectability useful financially, but dull as ditch-water — and what was the point in being respectable and rich if he couldn't continue to do what he desired and enjoyed most, the satisfying of his obsessive sado-masochistic fantasies?

There was only one logical solution: he would never again leave any victim alive to testify against him.

Murder, like anything else repeated often enough times, inevitably loses any mystical, moral or deterrent dimension and simply becomes a practical habit, or an interesting and sometimes dangerous mode of recreation, like hunting.

In normal human psychology it is generally assumed there are few powers greater than that of inflicting death on another. In the psyche it can attain cosmic significance. We are all a world unto ourselves, therefore, by destroying another human being we are destroying a profound microcosmic world. Hence my referring to Gacy, at the beginning, as 'the perfect psychopath': intelligent, successful, pragmatic and, eventually, ruthlessly murderous. A practised killer of lesser microcosms.

I base the following psychological and psychiatric analyses of his character not only on the forensic facts of his crimes but also upon confidential information about his covert behaviour in prison for over a decade whilst awaiting the death sentence.

Gacy epitomized the new breed of intelligent, highly mobile stalkers for whom criminologists and psychiatrists even had to adopt a fresh term to describe: 'serial killer.'

A term for a modern satyr, a werewolf who, having contempt for humanity as a whole, is nevertheless astute and resourceful enough to camouflage his predatory nature and move freely among the herd without being detected, methodically killing at will. As surgical and alert to public niceties and social impact as a freelance politician. An updated Duke of Clarence as Jack the Ripper. Machiavelli practising the science of murder. De Quincey cultivating it to a fine art.

Surprising though it may seem at first glance, I believe it would be erroneous to assume that Gacy was a homosexual, or even a bisexual, simply because he committed homosexual acts upon his victims. A person may enjoy exotic meals without being classified an epicure; he might simply crave variety. Many prisoners practise homosexual sex but revert to heterosexual when released. We should search beyond the immediately obvious, for a cause or reason which best fits the character and circumstances as a whole.

Every man has his feminine side. In most instances it remains subliminal and does not unduly influence his essentially masculine personality. But Gacy, either at a conscious or subconscious level, began to fear this feminine part of himself.

Fear breeds hate, and hatred breeds violence. Therefore, in an attempt to neutralise this fear and reinforce his masculinity, Gacy began by choosing homosexuals to beat up, torture and degrade, his acts simultaneously distancing and definitively proving to himself that he was superior to the breed.

But the subconscious is a tenacious enemy, and the more guilt Gacy experienced the more resentfully sadistic he became.

Gradually, Gacy discovered that this form of sadistic sex was far more satisfying, making normal heterosexual sex tame and boring by comparison. So, when he abruptly informed his second wife that he would no longer be sleeping with her, Gacy was not abandoning her because he had become a homosexual, but rather that he had evolved into the enthusiastic, sadistic scourge of homosexuals. The neurotic craving deepened its roots and evolved into an addictive psychopathic cycle.

In periodically being driven to crush and annihilate a victim, Gacy was not only psychically reinforcing his sense of superiority but also attempting to eradicate his own guilty lust, caused by committing homosexually satisfying acts mainly to torture and destroy the victim. So naturally the cycle of guilt and self-contempt continued to accelerate.

In this pathological context, it is quite logical that Gacy concluded that to prove his masculinity to himself even more emphatically, and in tandem deepen his sadistic satisfaction, he had to go one step farther.

He began to ensnare young men and boys who were not homosexual. In raping and degrading heterosexuals, he was further persuading his subconscious to accept the argument that: by violently subduing and treating a heterosexual male as a woman, I demonstrate more masculinity and virility than the victim or the ordinary male.

The only problem was that he had to keep up the cycle of torturing and killing to reinforce the premise, systematically and ritualistically conditioning his pathological conscience. Further, in my opinion, it is more than likely that Gacy, notwithstanding the fact that he was quintessentially a psychopath, may also have become a victim to secondary psychosis.

As the cumulative effect of his crimes mounted, his personal behaviour became overtly erratic, irrational and self-destructive. He had in addition gradually begun to evince all the incipient symptoms of organic or non-affective psychosis.

In order to eradicate or relieve his feelings of anxiety and guilt, Gacy developed a high dependency on alcohol and medically unsupervised drug abuse. A toxic mixture used to ameliorate tension by depressing it at the source, the cerebral cortex, which is also generally agreed to be the storehouse of conscience. Alcohol, even taken without other distorting substances, immediately begins to dissolve conscience, therefore the effect of alcoholic abuse on someone who already had comparatively little conscience remaining, could reasonably be expected to be dramatically psychotic. Even the ordinary intoxicated drunk is in the grip of a temporary psychosis, the regressive behavioral effects resulting in atavistic, child-like reactions. Loss of emotional control is the next casualty, leading to escalating primal aggression. Long-term alcoholic abuse to relieve psychic attacks, as in Gacy's case, could feasibly be anticipated to create variations of a condition known as pathological intoxication, several symptoms of which are prolonged amnesia, dissociation and mounting anxiety attacks.

As alcoholic abusers eat very little, the next stage in the destructive chain would be vitamin deficiency, which can cultivate or exacerbate yet further psychotic factors and trigger the Korsakoff Syndrome, some symptoms of which are additional forms of selective amnesia, disorientation and emotional volatility. This goes some way to explaining why Gacy, in the final stages of freedom, exhibited all the signs of florid functional psychosis, being in a permanent state of overanxiety as his real and imaginary fears of disaster overwhelmed all normal thought processes.

This culminated in the drunken/drugged high-speed drive towards the airport and visions of escape, despite knowing that the police were chasing only yards behind him, and irrationally ignoring the stark reality that he hadn't a hope of being allowed to board a plane.

During his spare time on Death Row, by way of relaxation, Gacy painted endless portraits of clowns. Possibly revealing that, subconsciously, this was really how he saw himself in the final analysis: a frenetic, perhaps tragic figure of absurdity, reaching for the impossible.

Should such a suggestion seem unlikely, I point out that it is not uncommon for notorious criminals to take a far less serious view of themselves and their actions than society does. It may further offend some zealots to learn that a great many murderers believe their actions to have been absolutely natural and fully justified, and are quite frankly puzzled by what all the commotion is about — soldiers feel no remorse, so why should they, is a frequent reaction.

Imprisonment confirms, rather than denies, their beliefs. Mindless punishment hones the spirit of revenge. They regard 'rehabilitation' as something that exists only in the vain imagination of the authorities, a public-relations device invented by officials for their own personal and public self-esteem.

Gacy's legal arguments finally ran out and he was put to death by injection, while crowds cheered and jeered outside the prison.

An exhibition was held of his paintings of clowns — no doubt due more to his notoriety than artistic merit. Nevertheless, one painting sold for $33,000.

So perhaps Pogo the Clown had the last laugh after all.

> The hope I dreamed of was a dream.
> Was but a dream; and now I wake,
> Exceeding comfortless, and worn, and old,
> For a dream's sake.
>
> — Christina Rossetti

Chapter Ten
Graham Young

Man, false man, smiling, destructive man.

Nathaniel Lee (1653-1692)

During a stay in London, I had the opportunity to interview some prominent English serial killers, most of whom — with notable exceptions such as Peter Sutcliffe, the 'Yorkshire Ripper' — seemed to prefer quality to quantity.

But, then again, in a small country with a low crime rate it is obviously much easier to track down a serial killer. So, conceivably, their careers were cut short prematurely through no great fault of their own. Nor any special forensic ability on the part of the English police who, by American standards of forensic science, are comparatively primitive.

The English forces of law and order rely more on projecting an empirically unjustified Sherlock Holmes/Scotland Yard foggy mystique to deter the less-informed types of criminal. It did not have any effect on Graham Young.

St Albans, a small, respectable market town in the south of England with a thousand year history, had approximately 54,000 inhabitants when a black-haired young man, with saturnine features and piercing dark eyes, descended upon it and, in his studious manner, almost immediately began to 'decrease the surplus population.'

Graham Young, a psychotic manic depressive from an early age, was a disorganised killer, destined to become known as the St Alban's Poisoner.

Highly intelligent and articulate, he could converse on a wide range of subjects, though his favourite, obsessional topics were toxicology and Nazi Germany. He owned a sharp sense of humour combined with a ready, acid wit. Dapper in appearance, black hair combed flat, Young had the practised affectations of a medical consultant, but lacked any of the qualifications. An enthusiastic amateur, he was nevertheless expert in his voluminous knowledge of poisons and their symptoms.

Young was an ardent admirer of Dr Josef Mengele, the German concentration camp doctor known as 'The Angel of Death,' and had his boyishly handsome looks.

Emulating another idol, Young sometimes grew a Hitler moustache, fastidiously trimming it with a razor until the skin around it was red raw and the prison staff had to stop him.

An inveterate but excitable chess player, he rather foolishly favoured the black pieces, likening their potency to the Nazi SS. His daily opponent on the board for years was the author of this book, against whom Young always failed to win a match.

Graham Young would probably be regarded by some as — to use a recently fashionable term — a 'natural born killer.'

I personally do not believe in such socially convenient theories as genetic/hereditary determinism, except at the crudest, most obvious level, in that we are what we experience and ingest, be it knowledge, food, drink or drugs; a definition which pretty well covers all schools of psychology from psychophysical to psychoanalytical.

The truth is, in the Western hemisphere in particular, society is atavistically opposed to accepting medical evidence as an explanation for criminal behaviour. This is a curious anomaly, Western countries being the most sophisticated and technologically advanced.

The general population willingly accepts all the comforts science and technology provide, yet remains constitutionally resistant to accepting psychiatric or physiological evidence which mitigates criminal behaviour, as such findings confound accepted moral and ethical standards.

This ethical fudging threatens to deprive them of the primal satisfaction of unqualified vengeance, a bloodlust which appears to persevere no matter how cosmetically civilised and educated a society wishes to present itself in a geopolitical context. Thus the instincts of the majority reflect man's true, unalterable nature, essentially that of an ephemerally higher form of animal.

If the scientific analysis of violence were generally accepted, scientific, rehabilitative methods for the treatment of violent offenders would be given more emphasis within penal systems.

To sentence a mentally disordered patient to prison is tantamount to punishing a blind man for jay-walking.

However, if the traditional practice of bowing to the desires of the uninformed majority — who generally can see no further than their own nose — is given precedence over expert psychiatric evidence, then the majority should axiomatically be prepared to suffer the consequences. Namely, the vengeance of the released mentally ill criminals temporarily caged rather than committed to the hospital indefinitely for remedial treatment.

In my experience, the insane have a more inexorable and inspired appetite for revenge, chiefly because they care less about the consequences to themselves. What goes around comes around.

Graham Young was as enthralled as the mob with the aesthetics of reciprocatory revenge.

His first and only ardent love was murder. Not the garish public variety, rather more a secret, intimate relationship or fleeting liaison of which only he knew the details and fatal result.

His covert, slow destruction of another human being by poison was in fact a form of absorption; as he watched the spirit, energy and vitality of his victims decrease so did his rise. A psychic process of vampirism.

Those he embraced with his art died without knowing how or why, perhaps suspecting bad food, bad karma or simply awfully bad luck, before giving up the ghost and dropping off the twig. Graham may have had a fatal lack of good taste as far as others were concerned but he certainly possessed exquisite good manners.

He always took pains to attend the funeral of those he had lovingly relieved of all the world's travails. A truly professional mourner — unique, in that he could, with absolute certainty, rehearse his condolences with some exactitude far in advance of the actual expiration.

At the tender age of fourteen, Graham Young was committed to Broadmoor, a top-security hospital for the criminally insane, for attempting to poison: (a) his stepmother, whom he hated not only for attempting to take the place of his mother but also for being the restrictive bane of his existence and high ambition; (b) his father, ironically because he shared his love with the stepmother; (c) his sister, who doubtless further depleted his share of paternal affection, and finally; (d) a schoolfriend, who apparently fell from grace for failing to appreciate Graham's superior intellect and fatal enthusiasms.

Graham spent the next nine years in captivity at Broadmoor, surrounded by inadequates and intellectual inferiors who further exacerbated his seething resentment for those who stood in his light.

Displaying a farcical degree of incompetence, records show that the hospital authorities saw *nothing remarkable* in the fact that Graham habitually carried a textbook on toxicology under his arm wherever he went, even to compulsory church services.

It is also documented that mysterious bouts of food poisoning occurred amongst the hospital inmates during the period of Graham's incarceration.

Despite these ominous facts, he was eventually pronounced sane in 1971 and released upon the unsuspecting public, where he hastened to make up for enforced inactivity and lost time.

———————•◆•——————

Graham obtained a menial job in the stores department of a photographic company, Hadlands. An astute choice, considering that many poisons, including various decoctions of cyanide, are used in some photography processing.

Ambitious as always, he assiduously began to climb his way to power rather like Richard the Third, murdering anyone who stood in his path to advancement.

The first victim was Bob Engle, his immediate superior in the stores department. Engle mysteriously fell ill and was treated for peripheral neuritis, to no effect. He eventually died in hospital, having enjoyed the company and fruit Graham brought on several convivial visits.

Young attended the funeral in his favourite garb, black.

With the death of Engle, Graham Young had the greater freedom he sought and began to take over the storeman's responsibilities as planned, which included making tea for the office staff!

Soon, as one would expect, other employees were falling victim to an esoteric series of illnesses, collectively referred to as 'the bug.'

———————•◆•——————

The next employee to be seriously hit was a Mr Fred Biggs. Again, Graham solicitously visited him in hospital, taking ample provisions of fruit, and showing a keen interest in the physiological symptoms of the patient.

After three weeks of intense suffering, his hair falling out in handfuls, Fred Biggs succumbed in hospital. Graham again dutifully attended the funeral.

The cemetery was by now becoming rather like his second home, or a precious piece of real estate to which he made regular contributions.

From a spiritual perspective, Graham greatly enjoyed casual strolls along the gravel paths of graveyards, pondering the literary sentiments on the tombstones with a judgmental, sombre eye. Like many people, it made him feel more alive and vital to be in close communion with the dead.

The 'bug' was now beginning to become widespread amongst other employees at Hadlands, who were also complaining that their tea had a bitter taste.

Medical inspectors were called in to thoroughly examine the storehouse and other premises for chemical leaks or other possible sources of contamination. They found nothing.

The doctor in charge of the inspection interviewed the employees and was impressed by Graham's knowledge and astute grasp of medical terminology. The fact that Young even suggested to the doctor that thalium poisoning had similar symptoms to that of the 'bug' appears to indicate either uncontrolled egotism, a craving for recognition, or a subconscious wish to be caught. But perhaps the fact that Young was also prey to cyclical psychotic fugues of chronic paranoia and delusions of grandeur more explains his reckless, erratic behaviour.

Graham's affective psychotic condition was also compounded and made more manically flagrant by a growing dependence on alcohol which, combined with the daily dosage of prescribed drugs he had to take as a condition of release from the mental hospital, demolished the final remnants of emotional and intellectual control, helping to nurture the delusion that he was invulnerable.

At any rate, luck was with Graham for the moment, as the investigating doctor paid no heed to his astonishing prognostications re: thalium poisoning. Graham managed to attract further attention to himself by airing to staff at the photographic company his medical expertise in the field of toxicology. It is more than likely that these additional dissertations by Graham finally prompted the upper management of Hadlands to bring in the police to investigate the increasingly dire situation.

The police, carrying out a routine preliminary check of all staff for anyone with a criminal record, came upon Young's past excursions into poisoning.

When detectives called at his house to arrest and question him, they discovered Graham blithely making tea and a sandwich in the kitchen. Upon searching him, a glass phial containing a lethal dose of thalium was found in his pocket.

Intensified police investigation soon uncovered that Graham had illegally obtained his supplies of the little-known metallic poison thalium from chemist shops by posing as a medical student.

Graham, bright enough to recognise the game was up, under questioning flamboyantly boasted that he had intended to swallow the lethal dose of thalium he carried to escape imprisonment. But that is unlikely, considering the agonizing, lingering form of death he knew it inflicted. Had he really intended to commit suicide if apprehended, he would have taken the trouble to obtain potassium cyanide, which kills within ten seconds.

Searching his house, the police found a notebook with, appropriately, the warning insignia of poison, a skull and crossbones, drawn on the front cover.

In the style of a diary, Graham had written accounts of his poisoning exploits, naming not only his past victims (some of whom did not die) but also his scheduled ones. He lamely claimed that the notebook was the outline of an intended novel.

Graham's morbid preoccupation with death reflected to some extent the nagging self-analysis which critically obsesses and drives many serial killers and lesser criminals: Am I a unique individual or simply a common insect? Do I possess the courage to act autonomously, against man and god?

Faith versus free will.

The serial killer unfortunately perceives that the only real way to distance himself from the banality and senility of the herd is to exercise free will of the most extreme kind — by killing others. Subconsciously, he began to regard others as little more than insignificant ciphers. Not unlike a general who, on the eve of a crucial battle, calmly calculates that the sacrifice of tens of thousands of his own men is quite acceptable.

The serial killer, essentially conceiving life as meaningless and death as nothingness, is consequently not afraid to die or kill in a final vainglorious attempt to introduce some degree of design.

In 1972, at court in St Alban's, Graham Young, dressed in his habitual black, pleaded not guilty to all charges and then dexterously bested the crown prosecutor in verbal duels from the witness box.

Had his loyalties been Churchillian, Graham would have regarded this courtroom triumph as his 'finest hour.' However, as a fervent admirer of Nazism, he probably likened himself more to Reichsmarschall Hermann

Goering, routing the Allied prosecutors and dominating the proceedings at the Nuremberg Trials.

Inevitably, Graham was found guilty on all charges and sentenced to life imprisonment.

He served fifteen years in horrendous conditions of incarceration before dying mysteriously in the crumbling red brick hospital of Parkhurst Prison on the Isle of Wight. Possibly, as some speculated, he commended 'the poisoned chalice' to his own lips, in a final gesture of triumphant contempt.

> Bloody instructions, which, being taught, return to plague the inventor.
>
> — *Macbeth*, Shakespeare

It was difficult not to empathise with Graham Young.

If his excellent intellect had not been tragically flawed at such an early age by emotional and environmental factors which led to psychosis, I am sure that, having disciplined his mind properly, he would have risen to prominence in a more healthy profession than the one he chose.

However, fate knows no distance. We all like to appear what we are not, be something we are yet to be. Some fellow said all aristocrats want to die.

Graham's one compulsive ambition was to become 'the greatest poisoner of all time.' An aspiration bound to fail in competition with so many more romantic, historical figures as the Borgias and several of the more notorious Caesars.

Yet in many ways Graham was at least possessed by the sane insane drive for god-like absolutism that possessed those tyrants — an insatiable thirst for supreme power, of life and death over all they surveyed.

There is no question that, in microcosmic terms, he enjoyed and savoured above all that false sense of omnipotence given when dispensing death almost in the same manner as the Caesars with a whimsical flick of the thumb, investing himself with the aesthetic powers of divinity.

He viewed his destiny in Wagnerian terms and would sit in his miserable, almost bare cell as though it were the Berlin Bunker, listening rapturously to *Gotterdammerung*, a doomed figure with his grandiose dreams in ruins.

When depressed, or in the throes of a schizophrenic fugue, he had the dejected stoop of Hitler in the final days. An air of general abandonment, hair prematurely grey, features jaundiced and drawn, his frame physically shaking, wrecked by the daily high dosages of prescribed drugs.

Graham, like Hitler, unable to bear fools gladly, occasionally flew into violent, maniacal rages which further depleted his reserves of nervous energy and kept him thin and gaunt. In physical appearance he actually more resembled another Nazi leader, Dr Josef Goebbels, the diminutive, fiery Minister of Propaganda.

Envisaging his own death to be imminent during these psychotic episodes, he would repeatedly write his final testament and intone a solemn, ominous warning to all within hearing: 'I shall return.'

The only pieces of popular music he liked were the double album 'War of the Worlds,' based on the novel by H.G. Wells and narrated by Richard Burton, about the Martians invading Earth, and, incongruously, the 1950s single 'Hit the Road Jack.'

Like many psychotics, in periods of lucidity his fantasies were not always maladjustive. He was still capable of creative thought and methodical, strategic planning. Significantly, he relaxed daily in his cell by reading the obituary columns in *The Times* newspaper; deaths of the high and mighty greatly lifted his spirits and tickled his morbid sense of humour. 'Better to be a live dog than a dead lion.'

Graham was greatly impressed by the sentiment expressed in a passage from a play I quoted to him by heart, and asked me to write it down for him. The play was *Death's Jest Book*, by Thomas Lovell Beddoes, an English 19th century scholar, poet and playwright who descended to insanity and committed suicide.

> The look of the world's a lie, a face made up
> O'er graves and fiery depths; and nothing's true
> But what is horrible. If man could see
> The perils and diseases that he elbows
> Each day he walks a mile; which catch at him,
> Which fall behind and graze him as he passes;
> Then would he know that life's a single pilgrim,
> Fighting unarmed amongst a thousand soldiers.
> It is this infinite invisible
> Which we must learn to know, and yet to scorn,
> And, from scorn of that, regard the world
> As from the edge of a far star.

On a second occasion, I quoted the complete opening, defining soliloquy from Shakespeare's *Richard the Third*, watching to see whether he marked the parallel of homicidal will and ambitious intent extant between that royal murderer and himself. He did not, so I pointed out the similarity to him. He rocked with delighted laughter and again asked me to copy the passage down for him.

———•◆•———

It was clear, that Graham, in his bouts of deep melancholia, repressed a great deal and had developed an acute anxiety neurosis.

Highly aware that his peers were shrewdly suspicious of him and in constant fear of being poisoned, he nevertheless genuinely yearned for their approval and trust. Failure to achieve this emotional goal compounded his frustration and anxiety.

Once the repugnant deed is done, and the treacherous character revealed, it is of course far too late to seek the approval and love of those you once contemptuously treated as inferiors, your enemies or your victims. This is a ubiquitous dilemma, but is perhaps more poignant in the captured criminal, who has forever lost the opportunity to attempt a fresh beginning.

Surprisingly, Graham had never read Machiavelli's *The Prince*, but I believe he would have agreed with a maxim in it by natural inclination: 'It is safer to be feared than loved.' But perhaps he would not have fully appreciated the antithesis. Having engendered fear, he unreasonably wanted to be loved as well.

———•◆•———

Graham was genuinely asexual, finding even discussion of sexual matters not only uninteresting but also distinctly distasteful. It was not an affectation; relatives confirmed that he had always possessed a natural attitude of boredom in regard to sex. Power and death were his aphrodisiacs and *raisons d'etre*.

His celibacy, in a sexually permissive society, probably exerted a subconscious influence, channelling untapped energies into an alternative course of satisfaction that would prove fatal to others. It might be sardonically argued that Graham Young, partly from lack of a misspent youth, virtuously entered the annals of English criminal history.

A final scientific note: Graham's relatively unambitious and modest use of the metallic poison thalium was improved upon during the Gulf War by the American forces, who bombarded and poisoned the enemy with thalium-tipped shells.

Had Graham lived to see it, this would have brought a cynical smile to his thin pale lips and a mischievous sparkle to his dark eyes.

> There was in him a vital scorn of all:
> As if the worst had fall
> In which could befall,
> He stood a stranger in this breathing world,
> An erring spirit from another hurl'd . . .
>
> — 'Childe Harold,' Lord Byron

Chapter Eleven
Dean Corll

> The next greatest misfortune to losing
> a battle is to gain such a victory as
> this.
>
> **The Duke of Wellington (1769–1852)**

We now return to the Lone Star State of Texas (where Henry Lee Lucas met his particular nemesis) to yet another prolific serial killer, who received surprisingly little notoriety compared to others, such as Lucas and John Wayne Gacy, whose case bears some striking similarities and surprising coincidences with that of Dean Arnold Corll.

Those who knew him called Dean Arnold Corll 'The Candy Man.' In Houston he owned an extremely profitable candy shop, with a small factory at the back that manufactured the product, and was liberal in handing out samples of his wares to the local children, with whom he was naturally popular.

Corll was generally regarded by his close neighbours as a pleasant, successful business man and a credit to the neighbourhood. But on the morning of 8 August 1973, a garbled phone call to Pasadena police headquarters was to alter that misconception dramatically.

The distraught call was from a seventeen-year-old youth named Elmer Wayne Henley. When police cars screeched to the given address, 2020 Lamar Drive, there were three teenagers sitting dejectedly on the front steps of the house. One youth was the aforementioned Henley, another was sixteen-year-old Timothy Kerley, and the other was a fifteen-year-old girl named Rhonda Williams.

Henley gestured to the door of the house behind him, and casually stated, 'The body's in there.'

When the police entered the house they discovered the naked body of Dean Corll lying in a lake of blood in the hallway with no less than six .22 calibre bullet holes in him. Somebody had taken no chances.

Elmer Wayne Henley, suddenly more animated than he had at first appeared, anxiously confessed to the police that Corll had tried to kill him and that he had shot him in self-defence. Piece by piece the story was repeated and embellished in more detail by Henley.

Apparently, it emerged, Corll had invited Henley to a drugs- and glue-sniffing orgy of some sort, requesting Henley to bring a boy along with him. But when Henley arrived with a handsome sixteen-year-old, Timothy Kerley, who was accompanied by the teenage girl, Rhonda Williams, Corll had become agitated, annoyed and threatening towards Henley over the presence of the girl. Corll only liked young boys.

Henley, eyes downcast, hesitantly and with understandable reluctance explained to the police that the original arrangement had been for Corll and Henley to rape and kill Timothy Kerley. Therefore Corll's anger had stemmed from the fact that the unexpected presence of the girl threatened the plan and disrupted the whole criminal scenario. Had Corll but known it would also lead indirectly to his own violent death.

When the police searched the apartment they discovered a 'torture room,' the floors and walls covered with sheets of plastic, and the main item of furniture being a blood-stained wooden board, approximately seven feet square, with handcuffs and strong cords attached to each of its four corners. By the side of the board lay a large vibrator, a tin of Vaseline, a sharp sheath knife, some four feet canes and a leather whip.

They also found piles of pornographic books and magazines. But the most shocking find of all was a collection of Polaroid photographs of naked boys being sexually abused and tortured. Almost immediately the police recognised the faces of boys who had long since been reported as having mysteriously gone missing in Houston, Dallas and other parts of the state.

Next they discovered a long, coffin-like wooden box with a padlock attached. Airholes had been drilled at the top. Inside they found traces of blood. A similar box was found in the back of a van with covered windows outside the house. Chains and other bondage equipment had been welded to the sides and roof of the vehicle; a bloodstained carpet covered the floor.

The police now turned their attention more vigorously to the three dejected teenagers, concentrating on Elmer Wayne Henley, who had first confessed on the telephone to having killed Corll.

Henley reiterated that Dean Corll had exploded with insane anger when Henley and Timothy Kerley had arrived with Rhonda Williams for the glue-sniffing session. But then Corll's mood had suddenly altered — this probably marked the point when he reached an innovative decision to go ahead with the original plan and add the intrusive girl to the list of victims, and the glue-sniffing commenced. It continued until all were unconscious — all, that is, except Corll.

When the three teenagers slowly swam back to consciousness, they found themselves all securely trussed up hand and foot with handcuffs and ropes. They could see Corll was busy in the bedroom setting up a large plywood board. But only Henley, his intended accomplice, knew the dreadful significance of the contraption and began frantically struggling to get free.

As Corll went about his business, fastidiously arranging all the implements he was about to use ready at hand, he casually explained to the three bound victims that he intended to torture and kill all of them. He obviously enjoyed the fearful anticipation reflected in their eyes.

Henley was now slick with sweat and becoming desperate. He began to plead and flirt with Corll in a last-ditch effort to capitalise upon their past complicity and save himself. Consequently, having already participated eagerly in previous tortures, rapes and murders with Corll, it was not difficult for him to persuade Corll that he wanted to take part in the rape and murder of Timothy Kerley and Rhonda Williams.

Henley said he would rape Rhonda while Corll raped Timothy Kerley. Corll eventually agreed, probably rather relieved that he was no longer faced with the logistical problem of having to dispose of three bodies by himself. He released Henley from his bonds.

Corll stripped himself and carried both Timothy Kerley and Rhonda Williams into the bedroom. He gagged and stripped Timothy Kerley, cutting his clothes off with the sheath knife, and bound him onto the torture board. He then handed the sheath knife to Henley, telling him to strip Rhonda Williams, and began applying Vaseline to the squirming Timothy Kerley.

While Corll raped Timothy Kerley, Henley began to strip Rhonda Williams, but in reality his mind was on other things. He was highly aware that, despite their previous close relationship, Corll had been ready to kill him as casually as anyone else and that only his glib tongue had saved him from death. Instinct also warned him that Corll, having betrayed his readiness to kill him, would now always regard him as a potential danger. Corll would never forgive Henley for knowing that he (Corll) had been prepared to murder him.

Henley, shaken by his narrow escape from the grave, would also have realised that, after he helped Corll dispose of the bodies of Timothy Kerley and Rhonda Williams, there would be nothing to stop Corll from eradicating all threatening dangers by killing him and tossing him into the grave beside them.

In the often paranoid realm of self-survival in a criminal context, there are few apprehensions more psychically potent than expectation of betrayal, especially by someone trusted and confided in. Even in the best of circumstances, the conviction of having attributed discretionary power to those who have consequently done us ill compounds the degree of resentment and craving for retribution, whereas from an enemy we would accept the injury as natural for being anticipated.

So much more is the sense of injury when, as in this case, the dominant partner has become to expect loyalty not only as a right but also a duty. Corll's sudden intention to kill Henley reflected that he had detected incipient treachery or weakness.

Under such psychological pressure, Henley must have sighed with relief when he saw Corll's .22 pistol lying on a table within easy reach in the bedroom. By killing Corll, Henley would not only be saving himself from the present danger of being murdered but also from the possibility that Corll, if ever apprehended by the police, might reveal that Henley had been a more than willing accomplice in multiple rapes and murders. Henley grabbed the pistol and pointed it at Corll, who was so completely immersed in the rape of Timothy Kerley that he did not immediately notice the threat.

According to Henley, he ordered Corll to stop raping Timothy Kerley. Why should Henley have done that, when he had not only witnessed but participated in such scenes many times before? The most logical explanation is that he had already decided to kill Corll, to protect himself from present and future dangers and, at the same time, was obliquely conditioning Timothy Kerley and Rhonda Williams to testify that he had killed Corll mainly to save them rather than himself.

Corll, in amazement, withdrew from Timothy Kerley and ran at Henley.

Henley's first shot hit Corll in the head. As Corll, mortally wounded from the small calibre bullet, staggered about blindly, Henley pumped the next five bullets into his back. Corll eventually slumped to the floor in the hallway dead.

Henley then released Timothy Kerley and Rhonda Williams from their handcuffs and bonds. As the two teenagers put the remnants of their slashed clothes back on, Henley telephoned the Pasadena police headquarters.

In the course of police interrogation of Henley and Kerley, certain discrepancies began to surface in their two versions of what had happened. But, more important, in their eagerness to provide the police with damaging background material against Corll, both youths made some extraordinarily self-incriminating ad lib comments.

Kerley claimed that Henley, after the latter had telephoned the Pasadena police, had casually stated to him that Corll would have paid a thousand dollars for him (Kerley). Kerley stated this in a matter-of-fact tone of voice, which implied he saw nothing surprising in this and knew precisely what Henley was getting at.

Even more sensational, Henley told the police that Corll had been regularly paying him several hundred dollars a time to bring boys and youths to Corll's various flats and houses, where Corll had raped, tortured and murdered them, then buried their bodies under the earthen floor of a corrugated iron shed some miles away.

News of what was developing at Pasadena police headquarters was inevitably leaked to the mass media, and a milling crowd of reporters and TV crews began to assemble outside the building. Incoming telephone calls clogged the switchboard. By sunset, the police station was under state-of-siege conditions, as the coast-to-coast American networks flew their anchormen and crews into Houston. Foreign journalists were also arriving and adding to the chaos.

Whether the two youths being interrogated were aware of just how much media coverage was being devoted to them is a matter of conjecture. However, one must assume that their professional inquisitors had a good grasp of criminal psychology and the mechanics of the teenage psyche. In which case they would have deliberately fed the two youths news of their instant fame, either overtly or obliquely (based on personal assessment of the individual's intelligence and personality), the simple object being to transmute the inner glow of self-importance into a chain reaction of self-confidence, verbosity and self-incrimination.

Whatever the methodology being employed — probably sympathetic and ostensibly collusive — detectives were extracting a fast, steady flow of detailed information from the two youths. This technique would have been followed until the interrogators were satisfied that the two youths were in fact not only witnesses against Corll but also willing accomplices. Aggressive questioning would then be resorted to.

A third team of detectives was frantically delving as deep as it could into the murky past of thirty-five-year-old Dean Arnold Corll, and sorting out police files on reported missing boys and youths in and around Houston over recent years.

Politicians who had never previously shown the least concern or interest in the high rate of boys and youths disappearing in Houston, particularly in a working-class area known as the Heights, were now queuing in front of the floodlit television cameras to display their synthetic sympathy to gullible voters.

The police had achieved their first major priority the following day by persuading Henley to lead them to the boat shed where he alleged Corll had buried most of his victims under the floor.

For self-preserving, tactical purposes, Henley had pretended to be rather vague about the precise location of the boat shed, and the police played along with the crude deception.

Their next problem would be to drive Henley out of police headquarters without the horde of reporters tagging along behind. This proved to be an impossible task, and the cavalcade of police and reporters' cars proceeded through the busy, sun-baked streets of Houston in accordance with Henley's directions, heading southwest. On the outskirts of the city, Henley indicated a group of corrugated iron sheds, where a faded sign proclaimed 'Southwest Boat Storage.' He then led the police to the shed Corll rented.

Breaking the padlock, detectives let in the light of day and surveyed the dismal interior. The place contained mostly junk iron, bits and pieces of cars and bicycles. It was difficult to imagine that this squalid dumping ground could be the site of a mass grave.

Thoughtfully, the police had brought along a few trustee convicts to do the hard work. The convicts first cleared out all the domestic junk from the shed, then commenced to dig up the earthen floor where the police directed.

Soon the stench of rotting flesh clogged the throats and nostrils of those crowded in the hot confined space, momentarily bringing the digging operations to a halt while police chiefs sent for sterile face-masks and gas-masks.

Meanwhile, reporters were sniffing the air like nervous bloodhounds and furiously scribbling in their notebooks, while television cameras zoomed in on operations around the shed. There's nothing like death to make the media lively.

Digging resumed and the first carcass was delicately unearthed by a squad of forensic scientists — the naked body of a boy, aged about thirteen, wrapped inside plastic sheeting. After that, victims were being uncovered at regular intervals and carried out in body bags to waiting ambulance crews, for conveyance to the mortuary and detailed examination by forensic teams.

Parents of missing children were arriving at the crime scene; others were frantically phoning police headquarters for information, hoping not to hear what they feared.

The small, innocuous shed had taken on the dimensions of a disaster area. As daylight faded, a total of ten bodies had so far been discovered. Digging operations were halted till the next day.

Henley, as evidence and pressure mounted, now helpfully admitted that he had not only procured victims for Corll but had been present when they were raped, tortured and murdered.

It was too late for Henley to straddle the fence. The police had already concluded that Henley must have played a more active part in the murderous events, in order to have become so intimate with Corll and survived. Having procured so many victims and willingly witnessed their rape and murder, Henley obviously had enjoyed the whole experience, developed a liking for it. That being the case, he would have been drawn to participate physically in the stimulating tableaus with Corll.

This theory was reinforced when it was discovered that Henley had also been Corll's lover.

Realising that his sense of self-importance had led him into a tangled mesh of implicit confessions from which he could not extricate himself, Henley finally confessed in the course of the following months in captivity that he himself had raped and killed some of the boys, allegedly under duress, and that many of those he lured had been trusting, personal friends of his. Henley's admissions also implicated another eighteen-year-old youth, David Brooks, who was immediately arrested and interrogated.

Brooks broke down and admitted that he, in addition to Henley, had also been Corll's lover since the age of fourteen, and had been procuring victims for him, some of them his friends, before Henley had joined in and started doing likewise.

Brooks stated he had subsequently become jealous and tried to persuade Corll to kill Henley. But by that period Corll had come to rely heavily on Henley for a non-stop supply of victims. Brooks, as it were, had practically run out of friends to feed Corll.

———•◆•———

Astonished detectives were having difficulty in keeping up with the fluctuating scenario, and the seemingly endless list of victims both Henley and Brooks were naming or identifying from photographs in police files of missing boys and youths.

Even harder to comprehend was the seemingly natural manner in which both Henley and Brooks had not only accepted but also heartily participated in Corll's homicidal orgies.

This perplexity on the part of the detectives seems to suggest their unawareness of a psychological mechanism known as *folie à deux* — a delusional system or insanity shared by two or more individuals, the weaker of which accepts without question the stronger's philosophy, code of ethics and values.

Some might say that the manner in which Hitler cast a whole nation under his spell is a supreme example of the *folie à deux* principle. I do not believe Henley or Brooks were conscious of this psychological mechanism, merely victims of it. Artificial inhibitions are naturally far easier to break than abide by.

Viewed in this pragmatic light, where whole nations can fall prey to the same delusion, there is nothing at all extraordinary or terrible in the conversion of Henley and Brooks to comparatively limited barbarism. Except to those of a suburban mentality not versed in moral relativism. I trust the observation does not lack civility.

There are countless circumstances in which the natural inclinations of people are deceived (by social conditioning and other control devices) into believing in moral and ethical expediencies. Murder lurks in even the most outwardly civilised bosom, as I've already instanced.

Those of a religious bent who invariably perceive the vicarious enjoyment of others as crimes should note that the venerated Italian theologian and scholar, Saint Thomas Aquinas, maintained that, in the eyes of God, a crime committed in *thought* is as sinful as commission of the crime itself. In an implicit or aphoristic mode, similar sentiments are to be found in Nietzsche's *Also Sprach Zarathustra* and the works of other universally respected classical writers.

All in all the police unearthed from the corrugated iron shed a total of twenty-six bodies of youths and boys. All had been physically tortured before death, some castrated, with their sexual organs separately wrapped in plastic and buried beside them.

Henley had also led the police to a sandy beach at High Island, where they discovered two more bodies, and to parts of the shoreline of a lake where, Henley stated, additional young boys had been buried.

A growing storm of criticism against the Houston police, for having paid scant regard when parents had reported their children missing over the years, resulted in the counterproductive effect of making the police reluctant to widen their searches for more bodies, the discovery of which would further underline their protracted negligence.

So the total number of deaths Corll, Henley and Brooks were responsible for will never now be known for certain.

———•••———

It is unfortunate that only second and third-hand accounts of Corll are now available from which to compile a more detailed psychological profile. Yet, despite this, some classic 'personality prints' are to be found in his past, his method of killing and in his choice of victims.

Born in Indiana, Corll is said to have had an unhappy childhood relationship with his parents, and this was perhaps exacerbated by physical ailments such as rheumatic fever, glandular dysfunction and a heart condition. At an early age he exhibited classic anti-authority traits, regularly playing truant from school, indulging in petty pilfering, and showing hypersensitivity to any form of criticism.

Trivial and harmless traits are found in any young boy of spirit, you may agree, but which become more significant if the boy remains emotionally undeveloped and extends such immature characteristics into adult life. The childhood teddy bear which Corll remained sentimentally attached to and was photographed embracing somehow takes on a sinister dimension being cuddled in the arms of the adult Corll, as though it exerted an occult or unnatural sway over him. But perhaps there was a scientific physical reason for this emotional immaturity.

It is a medically accepted fact that the endocrine glands have a comprehensive effect on a person's temperament. Glandular deficiencies can distort the whole personality, causing unreasonable bouts of emotional irritability and a low attention span, generating feelings of frustration and inadequacy which would naturally influence emotional development. If such glandular deficiencies occur during the most formative years of a child, the more likely its effect on the natural evolution of personality. Detrimental feedback from social interaction would also be a contributing factor in possible malformation of emotions and intellect.

To what extent Corll was affected would naturally have depended upon how constitutionally resilient or moral his inclinations were in the first place. If there was in Corll a natural propensity towards the perverse, it is reasonable to assume his will to resist would have been to some extent eroded by physical/mental dysfunction, perhaps causing him to rationalise and reinforce his abnormal sexual drives and sadistic fantasies.

Even innocent fantasies can transform themselves into fixed delusions. If subconscious imprinting of morbid delusional fantasies is allowed to go unchecked it is likely to develop into psychosis, affectively diminishing powers of discretion and discrimination.

Without the development of a normal conscience, the unquestioning human mind, being impure by nature and naturally bewitched by the exciting dark side of life, would be inclined to transform obsessive sexual fantasies into action, and there would be no reason to exclude murder, the most fascinating crime of all, from the agenda.

It goes without saying that there are of course many people who suffer debilitating illnesses in childhood and do not develop into serial killers. But, impartially, is that argument supposed to diminish the possible factor of mitigation re: those that it does turn into killers? We are examining possible cause and effect in an individual and factual context, not idealistic abstractions and random variables.

Army records show that Corll became an overt homosexual while in the service, deliberately flaunting his propensities but not sufficiently so as to be dishonourably discharged — which, considering his antagonism towards authority, was perhaps his real strategic aim. It is intriguing to speculate that he might have started playing the role of homosexual simply to get out of the army, then, finding the experience sexually or emotionally satisfying, ended up actually becoming the role. At any rate, he was discharged from the army after less than a year, on medical grounds, and returned to Houston.

Curiously, only then did he suddenly begin trying to hide the fact that he was homosexual. In fact, after Corll was dead and his crimes known to all, none of his neighbours or the parents of boys he murdered who knew him had a bad word to say about him, describing him as a 'kind and generous man.'

When his mother got a divorce and went to live in Dallas, Corll was quite literally a kid alone in a candy shop; all his appetites and secret fantasies could now be hedonistically indulged. There was no one to check or censure him, pry into his affairs. Psychologically, we can reasonably assume this was a pivotal factor, where dark obsessions could be turned into reality. The factory would become his personal, private kingdom where he ruled supreme.

Corll was finally coming to life, a life suddenly full of energy and vitality, sexual fantasies flourishing like exotic mushrooms in his inner darkness.

A new order of creative destruction was about to be brought into being. His whole existence now had purpose and meaning. He had never felt more alive now that he was actively planning the destruction of others. By taking lives he would enrich his own, making up for wasted time in the wilderness of other people's moral delusions and legal impositions.

Approaching the age of thirty, Corll now sought to surround himself almost exclusively with groups of youths and young boys, seeming to shine in their company. It is entirely possible that his motive in doing so was not entirely sexual. Most normal adults find the company of the young a refreshing change from the far too serious adult world. It invigorates and reminds one of happier golden days. We draw raw energy, spiritual stimulation and delight from the relative innocence and spontaneity of the young. So I perceive this tendency as evidence of a distinct dichotomy in Corll's personality.

As I suggested in my chapter on John Wayne Gacy, the majority of ordinary people often fail to realise that crime is no more a full-time occupation than any other profession, but simply another means to an end. The law-abiding, or socially engineered, choose to bask in the happy delusion that they are morally superior to the criminal, yet these same paragons, apparently innocently enjoying the lithe movements of a pretty girl walking past, are of course vicariously stripping and pillaging her simultaneously. In short, we are all voyeurs and surreptitious criminals at heart.

It is human nature to long for the forbidden then resentfully and jealously punish those who have actually sampled it.

Should you question the truth or validity of this general proposition, official statistics show that 95% of murders and sexual abuse crimes are committed by *members of the victim's own family,* or *relatives and friends of the family.* Only 5% of victims are murdered or sexually abused by strangers.

The popular mass media, primarily for commercial reasons, understandably gives scant coverage to such embarrassing analytical statistics. It would make their readers or viewers feel morally uncomfortable, guiltily glancing at one another in the sanctity of the home, and blaming the media for their dilemma. That is bad for business! Much more profitable to divert, expediently and sensationally, all public attention on to the 5%, especially the small fraction of that 5% who are serial killers.

This lucrative, selective social engineering by the media industry, especially the tabloids, enables the general public to indulge itself ritualistically in ostentatious paroxysms of self-righteous indignation. So perhaps Oscar Wilde was in error when opining that the only thing lower than a prostitute is a prison warder. Tabloid reporters must surely be in the running.

More often than not it is foolish to try to kid a kidder. There are no saints in this world, only liars, lunatics and journalists.

However, to say that all people possess this dual personality, the Mr Hyde within, does not posit that they all have the capacity to translate their criminal inclinations into *action*. That incapacity is where the crucial disparity between them and the criminal almost exclusively lies, not in moral integrity or superior intellect.

The realm of *absolute possibility* is desired by all but sought out only by the few, who grow to accept it as the norm, leaving the others to dream on.

While a part of Corll spontaneously enjoyed youthful company, another part was actively savouring this realm of absolute possibility, in his case their sexual abuse and torture. The two perceptions running parallel, each complementing and heightening enjoyment of the other.

It often feels good to feel bad, most honest people will admit. The remaining dispute is simply one of degree, personal taste and interpretation.

Corll, when exercising his criminal side, allowed morality and legality to enter the equation — not only as obstacles to be circumvented and guarded against, but also as appetizers to the criminal main course. Censorship and prohibition delight the senses, as apparently all but would-be protectors of public morality are aware. Such people exercise public probity chiefly to advance their own spurious claims to moral superiority.

I believe there is ample evidence that Corll was capable of love.

He was devoted to his mother, and formed an emotional and sexual relationship with fourteen-year-old David Brooks — who more than returned his love and affection, treating Corll almost as an idol. The affair continued for more than three years.

When David Brooks eventually discovered that Corll was a killer, it did not diminish his affection one bit, and the idea of betraying Corll never entered his head. In fact, as evidenced, David Brooks not only began to adopt the same beliefs and views as Corll, but also shared and enjoyed the stimulation and sensuality of the new world Corll had to offer him: a heady mixture of unconditional eroticism and the will to power which, once tasted, is probably far more addictive than any drug.

There is no doubt in my mind that Corll was a psychotic killer, not a psychopath.

Obvious traumatic changes took place as he gradually lost contact with the real world and a dual personality evolved. Normal adjustive mechanisms failed and his behaviour became progressively more extreme and polarised — the insane sadist on one side, the 'kind and generous man' on the other.

To compensate for this schizophrenic lack of equilibrium, he sought out younger, less discerning company in which his dangerous personality defects would not be so noticeable, and his criminal tendencies would more readily be acceptable to the chosen few he risked revealing himself to. Chosen ones he could control and would not hesitate to destroy if they proved disloyal, or were of no further use to him.

Instinct and caution would have warned him not to reveal, even to those he transiently trusted, the darkest compulsions of frenzied sadism which drove him to savagely mutilate and castrate some of his victims. Controlled application of fear has its uses, but to inspire blind terror in a confederate or enemy is dangerous, leading to unpredictable reaction. All minds have their limits. It was therefore politic that his accomplices should not know his full capabilities, — the horrors he was capable of only in total privacy. Certain powers should be held in reserve. Better to play the weakling, his other self, 'the kind and generous man,' and be underestimated.

The ridiculously dangerous method of paying others to lure and bring him victims is further evidence of Corll's dual personality, the psychotic schism. This is also reinforced by the spontaneous and reckless way he killed victims whom he knew and who could easily be traced back to him. Ruthless intent was openly compromised by brash recklessness.

The minimal signs of stress Corll evinced during the crimes, his obvious depersonalisation of the victims, and the innovative but absurdly ingenuous chaos of the final scenario leading to his almost suicidal death, also bear the maladjusted personality print of the florid psychotic.

The method of transfixing his victims by all four limbs to the torture board suggests further inadequacy, lack of self-confidence in general and a pathological obsession to achieve no less than absolute control.

Cutting off the sexual organs of his living victims — in effect turning them into sexless oddities — obviously served to compensate for his own feelings of homosexual guilt and his incompetence in normal sexual relationships. The more degradation he heaped upon his victims, the more superior he felt . . . an additional compensatory mechanism.

In murdering the victims, Corll, as with many serial killers, was, in a psychological context, symbolically killing his own guilty lust, at least for a short period. As stated, in some killers, consciously or subconsciously, the act of murder serves to slow down the cycle of homicidal compulsion.

This aspect of self-deterrence is a partial factor in most serial killings. The killer yearns for a period of rest, wishing to enjoy the ordinary things of life like other people. However, in some cases the opposite effect is achieved and the homicides accelerate in resentful reaction.

The pattern of dualism surfaces again in Corll's compulsion to sodomise the victims for days, deliberately and methodically conditioning sexual ambivalence in them, loss of sexual identity, and inevitably provoking their reluctant, pleasurable arousal.

Thus, in attempting to *destroy* and simultaneously *re-create* a new psyche in the victim, it could reasonably be contended that Corll was, probably subconsciously, transcending the boundaries of mere sadism and vainly reaching for delusive omnipotence. Arguably the ultimate, impossible ambition of all serial killers.

At their trial, both Henley and Brooks were found guilty of murder and sentenced to multiple terms of life imprisonment. Ironically, after both were repeatedly sexually abused by other prisoners, they asked to be segregated from the main prison population.

Detectives found documents and pornographic material in Corll's house that led them to investigate a Dallas organisation called the Odyssey Foundation, which had a membership of 50,000. Its function was to supply its members with young boys for sexual purposes. The files contained nude photographs of the boys along with personal details.

Some good did emerge indirectly from the Houston murders. It spurred United States law enforcement bodies into a less casual attitude towards cases of young people being reported as missing.

Statistics released by the National Committee for the Prevention of Child Abuse showed that, in America, around 70,000 children were being killed annually by sexual/violent abuse, mostly perpetrated by members of their family, relatives or friends.

In 1975, this led to the FBI National Crime Information Center setting up a computerised national index of missing persons to assist and supply information to state and local police forces. At a later date, the FBI national data bank was expanded to include the fingerprints of missing persons. Dualism sometimes works to good purpose.

> Experience is never limited, and it is never complete; it is an immense sensibility, a kind of huge spiderweb of the finest silken threads suspended in the chamber of consciousness . . .
>
> — Henry James (1843–1916)

Chapter Twelve
Peter Sutcliffe

> He did not wear his scarlet coat,
>
> For blood and wine are red,
>
> And blood and wine were on his
> hands
>
> When they found him with the dead.

Oscar Wilde

It is a curious fact that, in England, a murderer, or series of murders, tends to be quickly forgotten by the public unless a title is bestowed by the media — 'The Black Panther' (Donald Nielson), 'The Acid Bath Murders' (John George Haig), 'The Moors Murders' (Ian Brady and Myra Hindley), 'The Ten Rillington Place Murders' (John Reginald Halliday Christie), 'The Cannock Chase Murders' (Raymond Leslie Morris), etc.

Most serial killers are quickly forgotten, and relegated to a cursory mention or perhaps only a small footnote in anthologies of murder. Others, exploited regularly by the media for profit, attain the status of folk devils in the public mind, become icons of their era, their names written large in the milestones of homicidal history.

'Jack the Ripper,' attributed only with five murders, remains fresh in the public's memory after over a century. An independent survey commissioned by an English national newspaper, *The Guardian*, revealed that, even after thirty years, the English newspapers continue to print articles about the 'Moors Murders' an average of 154 times a year, simply because it guarantees immediate increased circulation. 'The Yorkshire Ripper,' after fifteen years, came second in the poll with only thirty-four mentions a year.

So what is the common factor in these cases that so enthrall the English public?

The answer is 'gestalt.' Atmosphere. The mystical and sometimes almost romantic evocation of a memorable era or ethos. Plus a theatrical, dramatic setting in keeping with murder or, better still, enhancing its spine-chilling qualities.

The mention of 'Jack the Ripper' immediately conjures up streets congested with horse-drawn carriages; men sporting top hats, capes and canes;

women wearing decorative bonnets, ankle-length dresses and twirling fringed parasols. Whitechapel, the sordid slum district in London frequented by prostitutes, where all the Ripper's murders were committed, its cobbled narrow alleys swirling with fog and lit only by bleary gas lamps, offered a perfect dramatic setting for the horrendous, savage murders. The public loves being 'horrified.'

The 'Moors Murders,' committed during 'the swinging Sixties' to background music of the Beatles and the Rolling Stones, was the permissive era of mini-skirts for girls and long hair for men, and had a memorable enough setting, one would think. But it was insufficient in itself to pleasurably thrill and chill the English public. For that task, it took the brooding, desolate Yorkshire moors, treacherous with bogs and shrouded in deathly mist, to provide the amorphous, cathartic ingredient necessary to penetrate the public psyche and generate enduring, even endearing, morbid fascination.

In the case of Peter Sutcliffe, 'The Yorkshire Ripper,' as soon as the media bestowed him with the appellation 'Ripper,' with its connotations of the legendary 'Jack,' his lasting infamy was assured. The fact that Sutcliffe did not rip his prostitute victims or carry off parts of their bodies in the manner of his illustrious namesake did not deter the newspapers from cashing in on a good eye-catching title.

I had the opportunity to interview Sutcliffe at length when I was passing through the south of England. He had a mild and pleasant mien, his tone of voice quiet and deferential throughout. The overall impression was one of ordinariness, a lack of personal charisma.

He spoke of the murders he committed in a matter-of-fact, humdrum manner, sometimes quite humorously, perfectly convinced that he had done the right thing in carrying out a mission given to him by God (a phrase which comically reminded me of the Blues Brothers!) and that there was no need for him to justify his actions further than that.

This mundane attitude reduced the conception and enactment of his crimes to the mere commonplace, as though discussing adverse variations in the weather. A paradox, considering he was simultaneously claiming his eminent accomplice to be no less than God himself (then, many years later, changed it to that perfect gentleman, the Devil).

Sutcliffe said that he first received his mission from God while working as a gravedigger in a Catholic cemetery in Bingley, Yorkshire. Although he was speaking of a supernatural experience, his voice maintained the same flat-vowel drone you hear a northern English radio commentator employ when describing play in probably the most boring game in the world, cricket.

Perhaps this routine quality of tedious recital was due to the fact that he had probably described the experience already so many times to psychiatrists that he, in course of time, practically knew it by heart.

According to him, he had been casually digging a grave in pretty hard ground and had suddenly begun to feel hot and tired, so he stopped and sat down in the grave to have a rest. Could anything be more natural?

Without warning, and apparently issuing from nowhere in particular, he thought he heard a voice, which at first he took to be human but with a sort of weird echoing quality to it; he attributed it to some defect in his own hearing. He stood up to have a look around. The graveyard was totally deserted, not a person even distantly in sight. As he was standing almost up to his neck in the grave, he didn't have a very good view, and began to suspect that possibly some of his workmates were concealing themselves nearby and playing a joke on him, perhaps trying to frighten him by speaking deeply into a funeral vase or something to create the ghostly echoing effect. He shouted out sarcastically a few times but no one answered.

After a brief period he again heard the indistinct echoing voice. Becoming annoyed by what he was firmly convinced was a morbid practical joke, he climbed angrily out of the grave to see what was what. He searched around furiously, expecting someone to pop up and run for it, but the immediate vicinity of the grave offered no surprise appearance or solution. Deciding that whoever it was that had been fooling around had probably pre-empted him and nipped out of sight over the other side of a slope, Sutcliffe trudged uphill. Still not a soul in sight.

Again he heard the voice. Sutcliffe stated that he still couldn't make out the meaning, as the sound-distorted words seemed to be jumbled up, like echoes on top of other echoes or a multi-track reproduction. However, by now he had sensed the direction from which the sounds seemed to be coming and, still curious and suspicious, he went walking towards the source, a certain gravestone.

As he slowly realised that there was no reasonable place for a joker to hide in that particular area, he began to feel wary and genuinely frightened as the sounds continued to emanate. It could not have soothed his jangled nerves much then to realise that the voice was coming out of gravestone!

As he described this, I, unfortunately in the clinical circumstances, had visions of the hilarious scene in a Mel Brooks film where some biblical character played by a comedian is having a heated argument with the Burning Bush, so I had trouble maintaining a suitably serious demeanour.

Sutcliffe, having ascertained that a tombstone was talking to him, said he had a good look at it and found it to be Polish! Whether or not it had been speaking to him in Polish — or, indeed, in any other foreign or arcane language — Sutcliffe did not elucidate. I found this omission curious, as Sutcliffe kept insisting that he had received a divine message by personal delivery from God or Jesus in person. I asked him if the voice had spoken to him in Hebrew. But Sutcliffe seemed not to hear the question and was gazing into space as though psychically back in the cemetery reliving the experience.

Finally he broke the reverie. 'The name on the grave was Zipolski,' he said. I nodded solemnly, eyes downcast, waiting for something I could insightfully interpret or put some additional psychological flesh to, over and above the hallucinatory and delusional explanations I had already reached. But again he lapsed into self-absorbed cogitation.

Eventually he resurfaced, describing how he just stood there in the by-then pouring rain looking out over the valley, like some modern-day John the Baptist, with a feeling of religious exaltation. He had been chosen, given a divine mission. At last he was someone, a person of unique importance, his dull life had ended and he was galvanised with a sense of steadfastness and portentous purpose, an instrument of divine will.

'The mission I'd been given was to kill all prostitutes. I was under God's protection,' he resolutely concluded.

———————

As many people equate religious belief with moral right, it is not uncommon for captured criminals to plead religious conviction in mitigation of their offence. Similarly, many prisoners are wont to adopt religious beliefs as an ostensible signal to the authorities of moral improvement and, more pragmatically, early parole.

Religion is the *deus ex machina* of the misfortunate and oppressed.

I was not quite sure whether or not some past misfortune Sutcliffe had experienced with a prostitute was at the root of the psychosis . . . his subconscious had obviously projected into that tombstone the message of revenge he craved to hear.

I then tried a wide variety of approaches to elicit or invoke a hint of the injurious catalyst buried and, in all probability blocked off, deep in his psyche, but with no success. This eventually led me to conclude that probably nothing short of drug-induced hypnosis would be able to extract the fatal secret, if indeed there was one.

———— • • ————

In captivity Sutcliffe spent most of his leisure periods in his cell obsessively reading the King James version of the bible.

His physical appearance had changed from being slim to positively podgy — a mesomorphic side-effect of the daily medication he was forced to take to maintain mental equilibrium.

There was no intellectual capacity in his conversation, no philosophical or even theological structure in discourse. Most surprising of all was his lack of urge to proselytize, a turgid characteristic of most religious maniacs. Instead, there was simply that calm, almost prim self-righteousness. Yet in stark contrast to this air of sanctity, medical evidence showed that Sutcliffe had performed sexual assaults upon the victims.

According to police evidence, the instrument of divine will used had sometimes been a screwdriver, serving as a penis substitute to violate the victims. There was further evidence that he indulged in oral sex before murdering some of the prostitutes for their mortal sins.

Religious fanaticism — with its fascist assumption of moral superiority and concomitant intolerance — invariably postulates a systematised rationale of inherent sadism and victimisation of one degree or another.

It salves the conscience to perpetrate evil perceived as good.

The use to which he put the screwdriver clearly indicated sexual inadequacy, leading to self-contempt which, perhaps, comprised at least part of the root cause of his psychosis, and the eventual schizophrenic descent into homicidal religious mania.

But although Sutcliffe denied the hypothesis that he had in some way, at some period of his life, suffered a real or imaginary injury at the hands of a prostitute, I remain unconvinced. He was rather too glib and defensive when the possibility was raised. Whatever the truth of the matter, by periodically destroying the object of his mania, he was simultaneously attempting to eradicate his guilt, the homicidal urge and unclean desires.

In most serial killers it is the psychic ritual itself that gradually becomes paramount. The search for power, controlled power. But, instead, what they actually are laden with, paradoxically by their total freedom of action, is an energy beyond their control. Homicidal addiction.

Normal life becomes insipid by comparison, once the adrenaline-charged high has been experienced, driving them insatiably, in a futile effort to capture and retain the god-like charge of omnipotence, the ambience of divinity, the lofty gestalt of Olympus — but some forget to take their oxygen masks before attempting such heights.

———•·•———

To normal sensitivities, it may sound unbelievably callous to remind you of the fact that the actual killing itself is usually only an afterthought, an irksome necessity, the conclusion of a ritual, a logical precautionary measure not only to elude capture but also to erase the only witness who has seen and been subjected to the killer's true nature.

However, in Sutcliffe's case, killing was actually an integral part of the ritual or, if you like, his mission from God.

It is yet once more paradoxical that, on the one hand, the serial killer often wishes to demonstrate his contempt for society, yet still feels compelled to maintain his good name, as it were. A second, more extreme example, of how maintaining a good name can be a most corrupting preoccupation.

The inner knowledge that he is a house divided slowly corrodes the artificial boundary the killer has tried to build within to separate his two selves, his dual personality. The inevitable collapse of this edifice will almost certainly result in psychotic chaos and, probably, the total destruction of the weaker of the two polarised psyches.

In my experience, this process is most likely to begin shortly before the killer is captured, the predominant part of the psyche subconsciously betraying the weaker yet homicidal. This process, I believe, accounts for the expressed feelings of relief many killers experience immediately after being caught, the strenuous internal battle within the divided psyche being over at last. There have been instances where serial killers have actually left messages at the scene of the crime asking to be caught before they kill again. Rather an insult to the police, when they can't catch a killer who is begging to be captured.

Sutcliffe struck me as a classic example of this adjustive mechanism, with one crucial difference. After arrest he continued to delude himself and shun personal responsibility for the crimes.

When, after some years in prison, he eventually saw the light, it was with one eye shut. Through a glass darkly. He shifted responsibility for his crimes from God to the Devil. Having used God as a balm to conscience during the murders he now used the Devil to same effect. This of course greatly diminishes the nature of his repentance and strength of moral commitment. A question of simply passing the buck from one myth to another.

Meanwhile, as already posited, the serial killer at large must continue to murder his victims not only because of the wrong he knows he has done to them, consciously or subconsciously, but also in order to preserve his perilous balance of self-esteem. The victim is, so to speak, always in double jeopardy.

In the serial killer a more extreme form of this emotionally debilitating self-knowledge makes him hate the victim even more, as though the victim were to blame for the whole predicament. He actually resents the moral imposition or discomfort they are causing *him*! Thus the killer progressively rationalises until he regards the victims as mortal enemies and is able to demote and depersonalise them to the level of objects which have served their purpose. Troublesome obstacles in his existential path, embarrassing reminders of his own treachery — a treachery which, in a more relativistic frame of mind, the killer might actually be proud of, as a physical extension of his intellectual superiority or concrete evidence of having advanced beyond the trivial confines of good and evil.

In Sutcliffe's particular case, the resulting guilt-complex was so severe that he pushed all the responsibility onto God and the Devil.

Sutcliffe was in the disorganized, psychotic killer bracket: of average intelligence; socially introverted; unskilled worker; frenzy during the crime; delusionary and hallucinatory psychotic episodes; victims randomly selected and easy to approach; depersonalisation of the victim; minimal conversation prior to surprise, violent attack as talking would confer human value, impeding or endangering the depersonalisation process; no restraints used; chosen crime scene haphazard and dangerous; sexual acts sometimes committed after death; body left unhidden at crime scene.

Towards the end, he killed two victims he wrongly believed were prostitutes, and expressed at least a modicum of remorse to me over them.

I tend to believe that the remorse in these particular cases was genuine, incongruous though it might seem to others. But by that stage of his murderous career Sutcliffe had descended into such an advanced delusional state of psychotic maladjustment that a woman only had to *look* like a prostitute in order to qualify as a victim. In his eagerness to find a *sacrifice*, he had subconsciously begun to transpose the qualities of prostitutes onto any female he found remotely within the province of a red-light district.

It is my opinion that Sutcliffe was in the sub-category of schizophrenia. In the grip of schizo-affective psychosis, and suffering from paranoid delusions of grandeur and persecution. His mission direct from God in actuality being symbiotic revenge for some real or imaginary injury at the hands of a prostitute, or a female he retroactively deemed a prostitute or to be immoral in some way. His paranoid condition, in the early stages, was probably exacerbated by involutional psychosis or abuse of alcohol, which served as a catalyst to homicidal urges. The satisfying of those urges helped to substantiate and neutralise the threat posed by psychic schism. He needed a sense of commitment. Immediacy. Escape.

On one occasion when Sutcliffe was driving in broad daylight with a male companion, he suddenly stopped the car and got out, making a hasty apology and stating that he would not be long. He then walked briskly into a red light district and, in the street, struck a strolling prostitute on the head with a stone, badly injuring her. He then made his way back through the streets to the car. This spontaneous, extrapunitive act indicates his incipient psychosis was as yet episodic rather than systematized. That he was not unduly depressed and could still distinguish, to a significant extent, between his inner world and the realities of the external.

This hypothesis is reinforced by the loving relationship he was still able to maintain with his wife, Sonja, his parents, relations and close friends, despite the fact that the dualism had obviously started to take root in his personality. Had he been caught and hospitalised at this violent but non-homicidal juncture, there was every likelihood that he might have responded to treatment and escaped his eventual fate.

Whether or not he has responded to treatment since his capture is now of no earthly consequence. He will never be released. Politicians serve the mob, not the individual.

The fact that Sutcliffe managed to evade capture for five years was not due to his intelligence but rather to an astounding lack of it on the part of the police. Had the killer left a photograph of himself, posing with a foot on each victim, English police chiefs of such outstanding quality might have caught him eventually. In any event, they didn't, but two ordinary coppers on the beat accidentally did.

Sutcliffe had not only killed thirteen victims but had also attempted to kill seven others, who gave a detailed description of him to detectives. In addition, Sutcliffe most considerately shortened the odds by making no attempt whatsoever to change his appearance.

During our conversation, he described in a jocular manner one of the many occasions on which his lorry was stopped at a police road-block.

A detective with a clipboard in his hand had approached the lorry. Sutcliffe leaned over and obligingly opened the left-hand door and, in doing so, by reflex moved his left foot forward so that one deep-tread boot dangled unwittingly over the rim of the high cab. Looking down at the clipboard the detective was holding, Sutcliffe saw on it a photocopy of a boot-print he had left in soft mud next to the body of a victim he had killed in Manchester.

He casually confided to me that the situation had presented him with a quandary: should he draw his foot back into the cab and risk the furtive movement being spotted by the detective? Or should he leave it precisely where it was with the sole of the boot right in front of the detective's face?

He decided to leave it. The 'detective' didn't even give it a second glance, Sutcliffe laughed.

Even more amazing was the fact that detectives had questioned Sutcliffe at his home several times during the five-year hunt as, with his black beard, he fitted almost identically the police artist's portrait of the killer drawn from the descriptions of victims who survived. Why the police never even thought to put him in a line-up for the surviving victims to identify defies comprehension. After each interview, the police were apparently satisfied with Sutcliffe's explanations and suspected nothing.

However, to be fair to the lesser ranks, a bad calculation by police chiefs was really the main cause of Sutcliffe's apparent invulnerability. During police investigations in June 1979 they had received a tape recording sent to them by a man claiming to be the Yorkshire Ripper. The man had a 'Geordie' accent (Northeast England). Police forensic experts even managed to identify the precise local district of the particular dialect, narrowing the field further to that of Wearside.

Two prostitutes had been killed in the Northeast. This and other facts convinced the police chiefs that the tape was genuine. They had parts of the tape broadcast on television and radio, hoping someone would identify the voice.

Quarter of a million people were interviewed, forty thousand statements were taken and almost six million car registrations were checked. All to no avail, as the police chiefs had instructed their forces to look for a man with a Wearside accent. Sutcliffe, with his broad Yorkshire dialect, was therefore ruled out as a suspect.

To this day, long after Sutcliffe's arrest and conviction, police are still hunting for the man with the Wearside accent.

As related, in speaking to me, Sutcliffe was passionately adamant that the two prostitutes in the Northeast were not his victims. That vehement denial, from a man who had committed thirteen murders and seven attempted and therefore had nothing to gain by lying, rang true. In which case it almost certainly indicates that a copycat killer, a second Ripper, sprang into being, and is still at large probably somewhere in the northeast of England.

It was therefore ironic, and poetic justice in view of the errors made by police chiefs, that it took two ordinary patrol-car policemen to finally capture Sutcliffe during a routine check-up.

The historic event occurred on 2nd January, 1981, on a drizzly, bitter-cold night in Sheffield — a city world-famous for its stainless steel cutlery and surgical instruments.

Raucous singing, stale smoke and beer fumes spilt out of the dingy backstreet pubs in the red-light area. High-heeled drabs clicked their way along the wet stone slabs of the pavement, touting for custom from passing cars, unaware that the Ripper's was amongst them.

But two policemen in their patrol car did happen to notice a vehicle almost hidden in the shadows of a dark driveway. They decided to investigate purely out of idle curiosity. Police forces in the northern cities the Ripper haunted had been instructed to note the registration of every car seen in the red-light districts. Sutcliffe's car registration had been noted in prostitute areas, which had led to the several times he had been questioned at home by detectives.

When the two policemen walked up to the car, they saw the occupants were a man and a woman. The man had a black beard, and they recognised the coloured woman as a local prostitute. Asked for his name, the man replied, "Peter Williams" — why this name was chosen by Sutcliffe is not recorded.

Meanwhile, the other policeman, who was checking the registration of the car noticed that one set of number plates had been taped over the real ones.

Sutcliffe and the woman were told they were being taken in for further questioning. Sutcliffe immediately expressed the need to urinate and was allowed to walk to a clump of bushes in the dark driveway.

At the police station it took surprisingly little questioning before Sutcliffe stated, 'I'm the one you're looking for. I'm the Ripper.' Police chiefs converged on the station from all points of the compass.

Sutcliffe's car was searched but no weapons were found. This was perplexing. The Ripper's *modus operandi* was first to batter the victim unconscious with a hammer, then stab her to death with a knife or screwdriver.

One of the arresting policemen suddenly remembered allowing Sutcliffe to urinate. Detectives raced back to the spot and discovered a hammer and a knife which Sutcliffe had hurriedly thrown into the bushes. The police chiefs, who had so ineptly misdirected the hunt for the Ripper, were now celebrating, jockeying with each other to grab the limelight in front of the assembled mass-media.

The junketing became more subdued when they discovered the many times detectives had previously questioned Sutcliffe and let him go.

When the police searched Sutcliffe's lorry, they found a card taped to the window:

'In this truck is a man whose latent genius if unleashed would rock the nation, whose dynamic energy would overpower those around him. Better let him sleep?'

———◆———

At his trial, as already evidenced, Sutcliffe's defence was that he had received instructions from God to kill all prostitutes.

Both the defence and prosecution psychiatrists who had examined him had agreed he was insane. But the trial judge was not going to be cheated of his personal moment of glory. He decided that the medically unqualified jury should decide whether Sutcliffe was mad or not, and the trial went ahead.

Predictably, Sutcliffe was found guilty and sentenced to life imprisonment.

He was sent to the psychiatric wing in Wormwood Scrubs Prison, where he had long conversations with this author, the 'Moors Murderer.' The press got wind of this and falsely reported that the two notorious killers had played chess together. 'Brady Checkmates the Ripper' took up the whole front page. Sutcliffe stated that Brady had simply asked whether he, Sutcliffe, could play chess and, as he had replied, 'Not very well,' no game had taken place and they had simply talked all the time, mostly about cities in the north of England they had both visited and left their mark upon. The chess gambit had simply been a good story for the newspapers to concoct, as previous press reports on file had accurately stated that Brady had played John Stonehouse (a former British government minister convicted of embezzlement) in the chess final at Wormwood Scrubs in 1979.

After five years in prison, where he was attacked by other inmates and suffered facial scars, Sutcliffe was transferred to Broadmoor, a hospital in the south of England for the criminally insane.

There is no prospect of him ever being released. The fact did not perturb him. The Devil was to blame. He was a martyr.

———◆———

Despite the larger body count, in the public eye Sutcliffe's case holds none of the quixotic, shrouded intrigue which still surrounds his infamous, anonymous predecessor more than a hundred years after he prowled the decaying, foggy byways of Whitechapel.

> I hope you have not been leading a double life, pretending to be wicked and being really good all the time. That would be hypocrisy.
>
> — Oscar Wilde

Chapter Thirteen
Richard Ramirez

They are no members of the common throng;
They are all noblemen who have gone wrong.

W.S. Gilbert (1836–1911)

He was to become known as 'The Night Stalker.' His will to power and revenge would peak in the summer heat of 1985 Los Angeles, culling victims from amid the professional, middle-class milieu for whom he harboured an unqualified, pathological hatred.

Conflicting, polarised motivations made him a disorganised psychotic killer with secondary psychopathic symptoms, perpetrating random homicides, rapes and other unnecessary acts of violence ostensibly in the furtherance of theft.

Here was yet another killer who, like Dostoevsky's Raskolnikov, deluded himself into believing that his main motive was financial gain, when in fact it was really the satisfaction to dominate self and others. The will to dare, the resolve to inflict whatever punishment he chose on a class of society he despised, and which drove him to commit one savage excess after another. The middle class were his 'chosen people,' as it were. He would teach them the meaning of loss.

Over and above the 'Napoleonic complex,' the bisexual rapes committed by Ramirez betoken what I have dubbed the 'Alexander complex,' the sexual urge to conquer all he surveyed, not only half the sexual world but male and female, adding a further dimension to the degradation he felt compelled to inflict.

That Ramirez had some awareness of these internal personal struggles is evident from his third-person hallucinations, indicating a paranoid and probably schizophrenic cycle, in which he perceived himself as an emissary of Lucifer, a demonic secular instrument of occult will.

In his particular case, this probably served as a release/defence mechanism to lessen the impact of conditioned guilt and concomitant, almost certainly constant, melancholia.

Physically in the ectomorph category, restrained and introverted in episodic cooling-off phases, he was psychologically pent-up and primed, by schizo-affective-paranoid-psychosis, to commit homicides and violent, extra-punitive sexual assaults with savage, hate-filled enthusiasm, which afterwards left him drained, withdrawn and melancholic.

Perhaps this *partly* reveals why he allowed some victims of the assaults to live. The other, less altruistic and far more aesthetically satisfying prime motive will be dealt with in due course.

Any passing moral insights Ramirez may have experienced whilst under the delusional influence of his paranoid convictions would not have been likely to influence him to any significant extent.

The nature of his crimes indicated that Ramirez had progressed very rapidly from the episodic stage to the chronic schizo-affective, prone to settle all problems by violence. This rapid progression was probably accelerated by an increased bilateral, abrasive interaction between his paranoid delusions and confirmatory or negative social events in the external world.

———•◦•———

Citizens of the respectable residential areas of Los Angeles, districts once considered relatively safe and secure, were so shocked by 'The Night Stalker' that they began to arm themselves with pistols and baseball bats in a state of panic and siege. Was nothing sacred?

Ramirez' *modus operandi* was first to crack his way into the chosen house, then stealthily check the occupants of each bedroom. If there was an adult male in residence, Ramirez would immediately neutralise him with a shot through the head. He then had the house to himself, all other occupants being completely under his control, and would rape the females and sodomise the male members of the family.

He apparently derived sadistic, exhibitionist satisfaction from carrying out these humiliating sexual assaults in front of the other members of the family, ensuring profound traumatic effects on the family unit as a whole. This was probably an integral part the revenge-fantasy he was pursuing, The other part we will come to presently.

———•◦•———

The police already knew from surviving witnesses that "The Night Stalker" was a tall, young, lean Hispanic. According to FBI profilers, serial killers usually select victims of their own race, but Ramirez did not conform to this pattern. He was choosing mainly Caucasians (also, curiously, a few Asians) and this probably reflected the general element of deep-seated racial hatred or revenge behind more than a score of his attacks and homicides.

Witnesses stated that the teeth of 'The Night Stalker' were badly decayed; again, whether the police thought to question all L.A. dentists, particularly in the Hispanic districts of the city, is not recorded, but it seems likely that they would have done so. Again, if so, it produced no results. At any rate, the attacks in Los Angeles suddenly stopped.

Had 'The Night Stalker' forsaken his vendetta, or had he become bored by unsatisfying repetition? Perhaps he was just lying low until the high state of readiness among those in the white residential areas of the city relaxed?

For whatever motive, Ramirez had moved his operations to San Francisco. Los Angeles police were alerted when, thanks to a new computerised filing network, a murder bearing all the hallmarks of 'The Night Stalker' was reported in San Francisco. Los Angeles detectives moved in swiftly to assist the San Francisco police department. Some good, routine detective work yielded results. Checking the cheap hotels for an occupant fitting the description of Ramirez, they discovered that just such a person had been using a particular hotel spasmodically over a period of several months, and that his last date of departure from the hotel had been the day prior to the attack in San Francisco.

The police obtained a very detailed description of Ramirez from the owner of the hotel, but were not able to lift any fingerprints from the vacated room, as it had been used by many people after Ramirez' departure.

The location of the next attack bearing the *modus operandi* of the Night Stalker indicated that he was moving back towards his familiar hunting grounds in Los Angeles. This is an error many serial killers make, as previously stated, feeling safer and more confident in the territory of their past initial successes. The Los Angeles police were put on full alert. As deduced and projected, Ramirez staged his next attack in an outlying district of Los Angeles, shooting the husband through the head and raping the wife repeatedly before leaving her. Alive.

That act of clemency was his fatal mistake. She managed to see the car's licence plate as he drove away. Detectives speedily discovered that the car had been stolen in the Chinatown district of Los Angeles. Now every policeman in the city was looking for the car. Several days later it was found hidden away in the corner of a car park in Los Angeles.

This time the police were in luck — they managed to lift some fingerprints from the interior of the car. Feeding the prints into the newly installed digitized computer, they soon knew the identity of 'The Night Stalker': Ricardo Ramirez. He had a criminal record for small-time burglary. The photograph was immediately given to the mass media for widespread circulation.

The general public takes true crime all too seriously. By that I mean they seem oblivious to the fact that, even in the commission of the gravest and — that word all judges love to use — most 'heinous' crimes, an element of total absurdity or slapstick comedy can impishly intrude. The following example will serve to illustrate my point.

Apparently the only person in Los Angeles who did not know that the rest of the city was searching for him was Ramirez himself.

Without a care, he strolled leisurely through the sunny, thronged streets of early morning Los Angeles and entered a shop to buy some provisions. As he stood at the counter waiting to be served, he failed to notice that all the other customers were eyeing him intensely. It was only when he let his gaze drop to the newspapers on display that he saw his own visage staring back up at him from the front pages.

Too late, he fled from the shop and raced along the streets with the alerted, shouting and gesticulating customers in full pursuit. Adrenaline pumped super-energy into his thin legs, keeping him ahead of the howling pack.

By ironic serendipity, he found that his panicked flight had taken him into the Hispanic district of the city. Not that he gained advantage from it.

Trying to pull a Hispanic woman out of her car to commandeer the vehicle, he attracted the attention of yet another mob of pursuers, this time of his own ethnicity. The hectic gaggle of hunters continued to career along the busy streets at a madcap pace.

Next, Ramirez jumped through the open door of a parked car, not knowing that the owner of the vehicle was lying under it doing some repairs. When Ramirez started the engine, the portly owner rolled out hastily from underneath the car in fear and indignation. Ramirez glared with some genuine surprise at the sudden, dishevelled apparition and began to drive away regardless.

But by this time the owner had managed to grab hold of him and was running frantically alongside the moving car, legs a thrashing blur. Ramirez, trying to shake himself loose from the tenacious citizen, put the car into fast reverse and crashed through the owner's garage wall. Still the increasingly unfortunate man clung on to Ramirez. A prolonged struggle took place amid the general wreckage of the garage until Ramirez at last succeeded in tearing himself free.

He next high-jumped over a garden wall, rampaging his way through foliage and flowers. In order to regain the road and faster speed, Ramirez raced without ceremony through the open back door of a house, crashed through the rooms and out of the front door, with the outraged occupants running after him.

Again he tried to bundle a woman driver from her car and, during the tussle, the woman's husband came out of the house and began to pummel Ramirez around the head with a length of wood.

Ramirez, understandably by now in a dazed state, took to his heels again, but this time was caught and dragged to earth by the crowd, who held him down until the police arrived.

After a series of lengthy trials, Ramirez was found guilty of multiple murder and sentenced to death. Since then his legal arguments have kept him alive on Death Row to this day.

He did make one interesting statement in court: 'I don't believe in the hypocritical, moralistic dogma of this so-called civilized society. I need not look beyond this room to see all the liars, the haters, the killers, the crooks, the paranoid cowards — truly the *nematodes* of the earth, each one in his own legal profession. You maggots make me sick — hypocrites one and all. I am beyond your experience. I am beyond good and evil [presumably he had read Nietzsche at some period in his life], legions of the night, night breed, repeat not the errors of the Night Stalker and show no mercy. I will be avenged. Lucifer dwells within us all. That's it.'

One friend who knew Ramirez in his childhood days said that Ramirez had once been profoundly religious and that bible classes had turned him to Satanism! There, in my opinion, lies the crucial psychological key to Ricardo Ramirez: childhood or youthful disenchantment rooted in the yawning gap between Christian theory and practice in the secular world.

Like Captain Ahab, Ramirez had found his Moby Dick, his white phantom, in the form of the WASPs, whose religious/ethical corruption he saw as having been designed to cripple and weaken him at an early age, robbing him of hope.

Had Ahab managed to destroy Moby Dick, the dumb creature who had grown to embody his blind, malignant fate and mock his pursuit, he would have experienced the same hollow sense of achievement that Ramirez must have felt after raping and murdering his victims. That the killing had solved nothing, and that he continued to breathe without hope or faith in a world for which he still had only contempt.

With each successive killing Ramirez was really sacrificing himself and gaining no human advantage. Even if he killed all those he hated there would still be a craving to discover something that made sense of life, transforming it to an experience worth enduring.

> Naught's had, all's spent, where our desire is got without content: 'Tis safer to be that which we destroy than by destruction dwell in doubtful joy.
>
> — *Macbeth*, Shakespeare

The manner in which Ramirez, without hesitation, cursorily shot through the head the adult male of all the households he raided, shows not the least degree of concern for human life. So why did he not also kill the remaining women and children after he raped them, especially as they were witnesses to murder and could provide the police with a detailed description of him?

In shooting the adult male of each household, was he ritually killing a symbolic father figure? There was nothing in Ramirez' family history to indicate he had been mistreated by his father or that he harboured hatred for him. Killing the adult male of the household would therefore appear to have been simply a pragmatic act of caution. Leaving the other members of the family alive could have ministered to some selfish purpose, some fantasy fulfilment. Or perhaps it was due to a weakness, a subconscious residue of sentiment from the far past.

We have, in a previous chapter, already touched upon another possible motive as being the common sadistic wish to leave the other members of the family alive to suffer their degradation for the remainder of their lives. Was attainment of that relatively modest object sufficiently important to justify allowing such dangerous witnesses to live?

No, in my opinion.

This distinctly limited theory of revenge neither fits in with Ramirez' pathological cunning nor, more significantly, his anti-Christ, grandiose conception of himself in the scheme of things. And most acts of revenge are based on the necessity of surviving the victim to savour the triumph. Therefore, I believe Ramirez must have been grasping for something more ambitious, more enduring, something unique — perhaps a form of immortality other than that which public recognition of his crimes would earn him. Some motivating goal that sufficiently merited apparent acts of dangerous mercy.

What if his hidden agenda were not only to inflict traumatic damage on his immediate victims but also, by chain reaction, on their future children, and their children's children, ad infinitum?

To envisage and cherish in the mind the reality of his malignant, vengeful influence spreading, imperceptively and implacably, from generation to generation beyond estimate, could indeed be viewed as having achieved, as near as any human can hope to expect, god-like powers. Immortality.

Conscious deliberation and calculation would distinguish his acts of destructive creation from the imponderables and coincidences of mere chance, making him a Shakespeare of homicide in terms of hereditary or psychological effect. Here was an ambition befitting his metaphysical stature, something that be might consider worth the risk of allowing his victims to survive. For, even in the event of capture, nothing could stop the grand vision from evolving and becoming reality.

A divination he could dream upon, draw vitality from, even behind bars.

———

I am convinced that variations of such lines of thought — or a strong sense of personal destiny — are shared by most serial killers, but are seldom voiced.

Serial killers are, in that particular respect, very much like writers, pursuing the quest for a measure of immortality in similar solitary fashion, using a knife rather than a pen, skin rather than paper. In metaphysical terms, they would regard anything less a medium than human material as too insubstantial, lacking in existential satisfaction and durability, no substitute for the actual experience of *writing* on living and breathing pages.

In which case, retroactive metaphysical pondering of the long-term consequences of the act would be paramount to the act itself. Especially as experience soon teaches that nothing is quite what one expected or imagined and that, paradoxically, as previously evidenced, perpetration of the act itself invariably distracts and detracts, lessening immediate existential appreciation. The novelty dulled by concomitant confusion of the senses. This is resented.

It seems to them that nothing less than challenging God or the indifferent universe will satisfy. A form of reversed hope, as it were: 'Show me your power, your existence, by stopping me.'

Naturally no response is elicited. So their acts, their crimes, become increasingly outrageous and nihilistic to prove to *themselves* that *they themselves* exist! That *their* acts have some meaning. By their rationale, if they do nothing, they might as well be dead. They demand *acknowledgement*, at any price.

To be ignored is to be deprived of human dignity and meaning.

Deep within the child part of Ramirez, as in us all, there would still have existed a small but sinewy remnant of faith or idealistic longing he could not completely destroy even if he tried. Patiently waiting there like the Ghost of Christmas Past.

The vehemence inherent in the killer's actions betrays the weakness which he most wishes to conceal. Not even serial killers are entirely what you expect. Sometimes they can actually be the rope across the spiritual abyss, between man and his failed aspirations.

From the standpoint of Ramirez, this poor member of a minority group, possessor of an undisciplined intellect and an indisputably strong will, the doctrines of organised religion had eventually been perceived as a scornful deception, a conscience devised 'to keep the strong in awe' (Shakespeare, *Richard the Third*).

To his eyes such altruistic doctrines had become a system of counterfeit, absolute and obsolete morality, preaching abnegation of, and contempt for, the real world of the senses, by urging a death-wish on the basis of a better life to come. A despicable rejection of perhaps the only worthwhile values of life — aesthetic.

Existence as an exquisite art, rather than a grotesque moral penance.

This deeply vengeful schism appears to have almost certainly generated psychosis within Ramirez and given birth to schizo-paranoid delusions of grandeur/persecution. Which, in turn, had probably led to an over-compensatory appraisal of his superiority, particularly over those he saw as having deliberately deceived him with false teachings.

This would have fermented a burgeoning, perhaps delusive awareness of his intellectual and amoral virtuosity, at having seen through the evil deception of a society exploiting mythical ethics to keep him meek and deprived.

It is common that very often people with an inferiority complex adopt this line of reasoning and related action. They over-develop a skill, trait or degree of contemptuous reaction to compensate for their actual or imaginary deficiencies in other fields.

In extreme cases of upward-spiralling psychotic paranoia, if this blinkered approach flounders and eventually proves to be unsuccessful, the individual will perceive himself as a victim and cast about for scapegoats of his own.

The transference of hatred or revenge is usually concentrated upon individuals or established authorities which most symbolise the source of obstruction/frustration initially experienced. In some cases not only the object of hatred can be symbolised or connoted, but also the original target. In other words, instead of persevering in the attempt to achieve what he really desired, an attempt which he subconsciously believed would lead to failure and loss of self-esteem, he perversely sets out to degrade or destroy the object of desire. But the subconscious truth goads him to escalating excesses, by which he vainly hopes to convince himself both superior and impervious to the previous attraction.

It is doubtful whether Ramirez had any profound knowledge of existential philosophy, with the exception of my previous deduction that he had read Nietzsche. But I believe he must have experienced a Thomastic leap of faithlessness, an atavistic grasp of hedonistic reality. His sudden, dramatic conversion to the world of the senses — in modern parlance, sex, drugs and rock and roll — appears to augment this hypothesis. On his revelational journey along a personal road to Sodom and Gomorrah, Ramirez' baleful eye would have searched eagerly for those *responsible* for his past misery, deprivation of his vitality and, perhaps above all, for simply wasting his precious time!

That darkly analytical glance, zealous with jealousy and vengeance, would then have sought those who merited death or punishment for that mistake. Those who had gained most from the enfeebling fable indoctrinated and now had most to lose — the aforementioned WASPs.

He would teach them the meaning of misery, of existential accounting. The enemy identified, the attack began, and the result is criminal history. So, when Ramirez sneered, 'I am beyond your experience,' he was to some extent perfectly right. We are all beyond one another's experience. But not so far beyond as the law-abiding would piously prefer to pretend. One fine day the dispossessed become the possessed. Beware the wrath of the disillusioned idealist; it knows no bounds. To seriously paraphrase Groucho Marx, such people end up declaiming they would never join any club that would accept them as a member.

In the modern inferno of crumbling inner cities, such militant outsiders now grow in number by the hour. With a little help and instruction from their friends.

Be in not the least doubt that they are coming to confront some of you. Read tomorrow's newspapers — if mercy or accident has left you alive after encountering one of this number — for you may be featured in them. Ponder, like Scrooge, that it is never too late to change direction. Or buy a gun. For all the prisons in the world shall not increase your vain hopes of safety one jot, only lessen them.

> In our course through life we shall meet the people who are coming to meet us, from many strange places and by many strange roads, and what it is set to us to do to them, and what it is set to them to do to us, will all be done.
>
> — *Little Dorrit*, Charles Dickens

Chapter Fourteen
The Mad Butcher

> Finally, there is an imperative which
> commands a certain conduct immedi-
> ately, without having as its condition
> any other purpose to be attained by it.
> This imperative is Categorical.
>
> **Immanuel Kant (1724-1804)**

You may agree with my estimation that the forensic facts of this case are much more complex and intriguing, and certainly more savage and horrific, than those surrounding the enigmatic Jack the Ripper (excepting the treatment of Jack's final victim, Mary Kelly, who, some say, was the one he was hunting for all along, and consequently literally hacked to pieces).

Yet 'The Mad Butcher of Kingsbury Run' is practically forgotten, rating hardly a mention in the annals of criminal history. I am now helping to rectify this curious oversight.

As the 'Mad Butcher,' like Jack the Ripper, was never captured, the question as to whether he was clinically mad or not is open to dispute. As is also the sex of the killer/killers — both the police and some commentators conjectured as to gender and the possibility that there might have been more than one killer involved.

I believe the forensic evidence indicates clearly that there was only one male killer at work.

In the 1930s, the port of Cleveland, on the shores of Lake Erie in northeast Ohio, was already a centre of major heavy industries. Its network of main railway tracks ran through a mile-long, soot-blackened gulley in the middle of Cleveland known as Kingsbury Run. Makeshift shacks and huts housed a fluctuating population of hoboes and vagrants.

It was at night that the Run and its environs took on the most sinister, foreboding cast, like a visual projection of Blake's dark satanic mills. Gaunt, high smoke-stacks of factories, where the night-shifts toiled and sweated, raggedly broke the brooding sky on both sides of the Run, looming in the murk like the decayed teeth of some gigantic beast. Spasmodic tongues of flame belched from the mouths of blast furnaces, occasionally slanting their reflected light even into the dark depths of the Run, where only the bleary flicker of hobo campfires and the dim glow of steam-engines being stoked both broke the darkness and added to it with more soot and smoke.

There was no sense of space in that murk, nothing of breathing room. Seen from above, the Run had a hemmed-in air of suffocation, of hidden rot and stagnation, reminiscent of the slum burial ground described by Dickens in *Bleak House*. An netherworld subsisting in a metaphor of coiling black fog, channelled sluggishly along the steep gulley of the Run like the river Styx.

Those derelict denizens forced to inhabit the Run huddled close to their campfires, trying to draw what comfort they could from the vestiges of confined warm light, their rheumy eyes seeking visions of better times past in the flames. Other bundles of rags swigged their dreams from bottles. Some more fortunate enjoyed the solitary solace of sleep, huddled like corpses in whatever crevices they could mould their forms to in uneasy oblivion.

This was indeed an environment tailor-made to accommodate horrific murder, a stage fit for the dramatic entry of the homicidal phantom who was about to appear and disappear at will, unseen in the acrid haze as though part of it.

The Run was not only a dumping ground for living refuse but also old cars, sofas, bedsteads and other general detritus of modern civilisation. Therefore, during the hours of daylight, the Run was naturally a favourite haunt for scavenging children to play and escape from boring, bothersome adults.

So it was quite natural that, in the chilly autumn of 1935, frolicking slum children were the ones to discover the first two victims of the Mad Butcher, thus becoming a footnote in criminal history.

This childhood discovery would probably be the only mark of modest fame or achievement their drab existence would ever afford, there being no just apportionment of happiness or pain in these infernal environs, only the like arbitrary selection process of the holocaust and an absurd, indifferent Creator.

It would be left to the Mad Butcher to brighten the lives of these children a little, provide a compensatory spark of fascinating interest, as it were, the relating of which would widen the eyes of their own children-to-be. Even the Mad Butcher was not as merciless and condemnatory as their imaginary God.

The killer's unwitting generosity would long be treasured by them.

———•◦•———

Both victims found were adult males. Both were nude and had been castrated and decapitated by their killer.

Police conducting a wider search of the area eventually found the missing sexual organs a good distance away along the foot of the craggy side of the gulley, as though casually discarded by the departing killer as he prepared to climb back up to the normal world.

Eventually the heads of both men were found by the detectives in separate shallow graves some distance from the bodies. Both bodies had been ritualistically arranged by the killer in an orderly manner, lying on their backs, arms straight by their sides, legs also straight and heels together. At attention to meet their maker.

Although both victims had been drained of blood, there was no trace of blood under or anywhere in the vicinity of the bodies, obviously denoting that both men had been killed elsewhere and conveyed to Kingsbury Run.

It also became obvious that both bodies had been very thoroughly washed, neither bearing even a smudge of blood.

The first victim was a stocky man, estimated to be in his late forties or early fifties. The state of decomposition indicated he had been dead for quite some time. The skin of this man had a curiously hard texture, as though it had been tanned or preserved by some chemical process. The second body was that of a much younger man who was estimated to have been dead only a matter of days. Incongruously, his sole apparel was a pair of socks.

Checking fingerprint files, the detectives soon managed to identify this body as being that of Edward Andrassy, a twenty-eight-year-old small-time thief with a criminal record including sexual deviance. Rope-burns on his wrists indicated that he had struggled ferociously for his life.

The police pathologist later deduced from the retracted neck muscles that both men had been decapitated while alive and, perhaps, fully conscious.

The body of the older man eluded all attempts at identification due to decomposition. The pathologist deduced that the strange leathery texture of this man's skin had been brought about by the body having been preserved, for a lengthy period of time, in chloride of lime (more commonly known as bleaching powder).

Another interesting connection was found.

A year earlier, in September 1934, half of a headless female torso had been washed up on Cleveland's Euclid Beach, and a search discovered the other half several miles away. The skin of the victim had the same peculiar texture denoting preservation in chloride of lime. The arms had been cut off; there was no way to identify her.

Detectives painstakingly examined the scene where the two male victims had been found, and meticulously reconstructed the methodology the killer must have used to convey the two bodies to where they had been carefully deposited in the Run. First, according to police conclusions, it was believed that the killer would have had to carry the bodies down the steep slope of the Run in total darkness, as the local topography dictated that he would have been immediately spotted during daylight hours. Next, after a thorough inspection of the craggy line of descent, they decided that the two bodies had not been rolled or thrown down into the Run but actually carried there by the killer for seventy-odd precipitous feet.

Why had the killer been so apparently considerate and respectful of the dead?

The superhuman strength the murderer would have had to possess to twice perform such a task, chilled the detectives. Presumably the killer would then have had to carry down the severed heads and sexual organs separately.

Again, the unavoidable question: why had a man with so little regard for the living ostensibly taken so much trouble over the butchered remains?

Personally, I do not believe he did; the contemptuous manner in which he dumped his other dismembered corpses, and their severed parts, demonstrates that such humane consideration would have been out of character, reinforcing my theory that the police misinterpreted as *respect* certain actions that the killer had daily performed simply from *habit*, mere reflex, thus subconsciously leaving, by his *orderly* conduct, very significant clues. I shall explain more fully in due course.

Another find the detectives made near the rail-tracks is worth a mention, as it demonstrates the rather basic forensic methodology the police employed in those days, and their inability to read a crime scene both clinically and psychologically, charting every action the killer must have made, and the reasons why.

The item found was a rusty old bucket half-filled with dirty oil, in which the police discovered small traces of blood and human hair — though no allusion is made as to whether either the blood group or the hair matched that of either of the two victims, it is reasonable to assume that they did, the coincidence being too great.

The expressed police theory was that the killer had brought the bucket of oil with him to burn the two bodies. Neither of the bodies bore any traces of attempted destruction by fire or any other method, so why the police chose that hypothesis is entirely a mystery. There is no reference as to whether or not the police found any fingerprints on the bucket.

Here is my theory and explanation:

1. The killer would not have thoroughly washed the bodies had he intended to burn them, and would not have bothered to bury the heads either.
2. Half a bucket of dirty oil would have been entirely useless for burning the two bodies or the heads, even in the unlikely event of the killer being able to ignite the oil at all with a match or lighter.
3. Even if it had been petrol instead, the perfect fuel for such a grisly task, that small amount would only have slightly charred the surface flesh.
4. There was no trace of oil on either of the two bodies or the heads. It is unlikely the killer would have made an extra arduous journey, down into the Run in the darkness, with half a bucket of oil and then not have at least tried to use it.
5. Such an obviously meticulous murderer would hardly have left the bucket at the scene of the crime had it belonged to him and perhaps bore forensic evidence or could be traced to him.
6. The bucket was rusty, which means it had been out in the open for weeks, more probably months, whereas the younger victim had been dead only a matter of days.

From these facts I interpret the scenario as follows:

The killer, having placed the two bodies where they were found and buried the heads, peered around in the darkness for something or somewhere to clean or wipe his soiled hands. Searching in the darkness he stumbled across the rusting bucket. In the moonlight its contents gleamed like water. Not until he had immersed his hands and begun to clean them did he identify the slippery substance as oil. No matter. It served just as well to rid his hands of evidence such as blood and hair.

Afterwards, he probably wiped the oil from his hands with grass or a handkerchief, putting the latter back into his pocket.

In January 1936, the Mad Butcher delivered another victim. The dismembered body of a woman was discovered, piecemeal, in a sack dumped openly in a snow-covered street above Kingsbury Run. The head was missing, but again the tell-tale retracted muscles of the neck indicated that she had been alive when beheaded.

Fingerprint records identified her as a prostitute, Florence Genevieve Portillo. This raises self-evident questions.

If this murder, which bore the same killing MO used on his previous victims, was committed by The Butcher, why had he this time also cut the body into pieces? To make it easier to transport to the Run? If so, why had he then dumped the dismembered body in a public street? Had someone seen him and forced him to make a hurried retreat? If so, why had no witness come forward? Alternatively, had he been running behind schedule and simply ditched the body at the nearest convenient spot?

A pattern had begun to develop. Two of the three victims of the Mad Butcher had criminal records in Cleveland, so perhaps the third, the decomposed man, had a criminal record in another city or state. This line of inquiry, if it was followed at all, provided no fresh clues.

The famed Eliot Ness, founder of 'The Untouchables' who caged Al Capone, had become Cleveland's Public Safety Director. However, for the time being, he was keeping himself aloof from such a sordid murder investigation. The public hue and cry over the murders had not yet reached its peak, and Ness was otherwise fully occupied investigating the more politically sensitive problem of corruption in Cleveland's Police Department.

In the sweltering summer of 1936, the body of another beheaded, castrated male was found by two more slum children amongst the junk in Kingsbury Run.

The retracted neck muscles and lack of blood at the murder scene again related their legend.

Police were unable to identify the body. The victim had the appearance of having been a hobo, so perhaps he had been riding the rails from Pittsburgh and, unfortunately for him, jumped from the freight cars at Kingsbury Run only to meet his murderer there.

Police inquiries were leading nowhere, and yellow press sensationalism was frantically whipping up public hysteria.

At night people were now walking in pairs or in groups and keeping well away from Kingsbury Run, irrationally ignoring the strong indication that the

Mad Butcher did his slaughtering elsewhere in the city and simply used the Run as a convenient area in which to dispose of the bodies.

But perhaps this purblind, atavistic reaction by the public was subconsciously justified to some degree.

The fact that the severed heads were discovered at some distance from the bodies in Kingsbury Run, and that all the victims so far were itinerant tramps and prostitutes, could well mean that the murders had been committed in some of the thousands of freight cars travelling through the Run every night.

Significantly, as already mentioned, there were no signs that the bodies had been dragged to their final resting places but carefully carried in dark, dangerous terrain. So either the killer possessed abnormal strength or two men were involved — the fact that victims of both sexes were chosen could well support a theory that two killers with different sexual preferences, or fixations, were working together.

The travelling freight-car theory would also explain the absence of blood at the sites where the bodies were found. Could one man or two have then tossed the bodies a good distance from the freight-car? That would not explain the ritualistic neatness in which most of the bodies had been found, nor the fact that some victims had been chemically preserved for an extended period.

Only a map of the 1930s rail network through Kingsbury Run, and the precise locations of where some of the bodies and matching heads were discovered, could provide an answer to the possibility that some of the murders themselves had been committed in a rail-truck, the bodies drained of blood, then washed and carried into the Run.

But unless the trucks were used for cattle or slaughtered meat, surely some railway worker would have reported a truck extensively stained with blood? There were no such reports on record.

All sorts of theories were broached by police and public. Could The Mad Butcher have been a uniformed policeman, a railway worker or a woman, as was speculated by some? Definitely not a woman. I personally believe, from the forensic evidence, that it is extremely unlikely the killer was a policeman or railway worker. And, as evidenced earlier, I am firmly convinced that the Mad Butcher was one man, not two.

The ritualistic beheading and methodical dismemberment of the victims characterises a single pair of strong, skilled hands and a solitary, obsessive mind at work.

Decapitation was probably the killer's ultimate method of depersonalising the victim, and he then logically extended the pathological compulsion by carrying the severed heads some distance from the bodies before burying them. The element of sadistic contempt involved in this practice is reinforced by the way he castrated his male victims and pitched the organs aside like scrag-meat.

The use of restraints, namely the severe rope-burns on one of the male bodies suggests that he castrated him while he was alive and conscious. The theory that this particular victim had been struggling against being decapitated is medically erroneous — in the process of beheading, the unavoidable, immediate severing of the carotid artery in the neck, halting the flow of blood to the brain, renders the victim unconscious almost instantly.

The Mad Butcher, according to forensic evidence, had the curious habit of washing his victims before conveying them to the Run. The most logical explanation for this cleansing ritual would be that he intended the victims to be discovered, and therefore went to great pains to cleanse them of all forensic evidence.

One promising line of thought that did occur to me was that the killer, having lured a vagrant to his house or place of business with promises of a hot meal, then also offered (in reality to erase traceable forensic clues or evidence of sexual assault) the opportunity of a bath — either before or after a meal — autopsy reports having shown that undigested food was found in the stomachs of some of the victims.

If the killer did use this method, the bathroom door would obviously have had no lock or bolt, which would hinder a quick, surprise entry and attack. As the victim bathed, the killer would have entered swiftly and, with the heavy, sharp knife forensic experts said he employed, sliced deeply through the carotid artery of the neck rendering the victim immediately unconscious. This method of killing the victim in a bath would also offer a possible explanation as to how the Butcher was able to deal with the immediate deluge of pumping blood with which such an incision would present him.

But would his women victims have accepted the offer of a bath in a stranger's house? And, in the unlikely event that they did accept, would they have not taken the precaution to find, or ask for, some means to keep the bathroom door closed? If any victim, male or female, politely declined the offer of a bath, what would the killer do then? Cut their throat and flood his house with blood? Or knock them unconscious (which, in practice, can be a protracted, bloody business in itself), then carry them into the bathroom, undress them and put them into the bath to kill them?

Such cumbersome, uncertain methodology does not fit in with the personality-print of the cautious, cunning psychopath the Butcher had undoubtedly shown himself to be. Forensic examination of the bodies revealed that the heads and organs had been removed with considerable dexterity, suggesting that the person wielding the sharp instrument had the skill and anatomical knowledge of a butcher or surgeon.

Once again, those were precisely the same speculations which had surrounded Jack the Ripper.

In July 1936, a young hiker stumbled upon the naked, beheaded body of a man in the city park. This time there was blood where the victim lay. No head was found. His ragged, blood-soaked clothing lying nearby indicated (a) it had been a surprise attack, probably while he was sleeping, and (b) that he was another vagrant.

Why was the killer now taking the heads away with him instead of burying them? Being a killer of some intelligence, one must assume he had quite consciously decided to change his method, which also means he had brought some bag or other receptacle with him in which to carry off the severed head.

Next, in September 1936, a hobo in Kingsbury Run discovered a beheaded, armless torso of a man. The police found the lower, legless half some distance away. The way the remains were widely scattered suggests the victim could have been killed in a moving freight wagon, dismembered and, eventually, thrown out one section at a time. The head was missing, and the distinctive sure-handed dissection was the crime-signature of the Mad Butcher. Investigations identified the victim as a tramp.

Examining the verifiable facts up till then, it would be reasonable to conclude that the Mad Butcher had himself at some stage been a vagrant and was now perhaps posing as one, thus explaining how he was able to approach his down-and-out victims without arousing suspicion. But other evidence — including the scrupulous washing of the bodies, and the preservation of some in chloride of lime, in my estimation, pretty well disposes of this theory, as it indicates that he had moved up in life and owned a house or premises in which to conduct his slaughtering.

Nevertheless, I shall briefly return to these aspects later on when dealing with three additional murders in Pittsburgh which, I am convinced, were definitely committed by the Mad Butcher. It is entirely possible that he was expediently disguising himself as a vagrant, both to lull his victims into a false sense of security and to enter and leave the Run without attracting attention. As a tramp amongst tramps, he would have been as good as invisible to the police, appearing to be a potential victim rather than a hunter.

On the other hand, an offer of charity from a respectable man of wealthy appearance would appear more genuine to most vagrants, opportunists who would readily follow a well-heeled mark they hoped to dupe for all they could get. But, of course, a man of such appearance in the Run would attract beggars (and witnesses) like flies.

<hr />

Eliot Ness finally decided to act as public uproar mounted.

The police in Kingsbury Run were instructed to prevent more hoboes from jumping off the passing freight-cars. This policy — helped along by the fact that many hoboes were leaving the Run of their own volition in fear of the Butcher — appeared to produce results. Months passed without further murders.

But, in February 1937, another headless, female torso was found on the shores of Lake Erie. The victim was estimated to be in her twenties. Police efforts failed to identify her.

The next find, by a strolling teenager in June 1937, was a skull under a bridge spanning the Cuyahoga River, a tributary of which flowed through Kingsbury Run. Police found further human remains in a sack some distance up the river. The checking of dental records led to the woman being identified as a local prostitute, Rose Wallace.

A month later, the headless torso of a man was discovered drifting down the Cuyahoga River. His severed legs and arms were later fished out, but not the head. The victim was around thirty years of age. He had been gutted and the heart was missing; it appeared the Butcher was literally beginning to follow his trade. Was cannibalism starting to enter into the equation? If so, he did not develop a taste for it, and never took any organs or offal again. But apparent surgical skill was once more noted.

April 1938 produced a woman's leg from the Cuyahoga River. Other dismembered sections of the same body were later taken from the river. Only the head was missing. Within a period of twenty-four hours another two bodies were uncovered in the city rubbish dump. The first was the torso of a female in her thirties. Searches failed to recover the remainder of the body. Then the head of a man was found neatly packaged in a box.

Eliot Ness was again forced into action. Police raided the shacks in Kingsbury Run, arresting every hobo they could lay hands upon. Fire engines were then called out to supervise the burning down of the shanty town in Kingsbury Run. As all the victims of the Mad Butcher had been itinerant vagrants and prostitutes, it was Ness' strategy to deprive the Butcher of further prey from this class of society. The scheme worked. Having claimed a total of twelve victims, the 'Mad Butcher' stopped slaughtering.

Or did he?

———————

The main railtracks from Kingsbury Run led directly to Pittsburgh, Pennsylvania, another busy city with a dense manufacturing industry.

In May 1940, shortly after the Kingsbury Run murders ceased, the beheaded, naked body of a man was found in a freight-car in Pittsburgh. Further searches discovered the naked, decapitated and dismembered body of a woman in another freight-car. Then yet another naked and decapitated man was uncovered in a third freight-car. All three murders bore the personality-print of the Mad Butcher. It was as though the Butcher, having been forced by police action to cap his homicidal compulsions for a comparatively lengthy period, had eventually lost control and exploded into a final, bloody spree.

Had the train, on its way to Pittsburgh, halted for a period in Kingsbury Run, or had the Mad Butcher, starved of victims, moved his base of operations to Pittsburgh?

Even more fascinating a speculation, to my mind, had the freight cars in question been scheduled to depart from Pittsburgh to Kingsbury Run? In which case, as previously touched upon, perhaps the killer had perpetrated many of his classic-style killings in Pittsburgh and travelled with the bodies in freight cars to dump them in Kingsbury Run, in a systematic attempt to decoy the police from his home territory. This would certainly help to clarify the mystery of how he was able to enter and depart from the Run so easily without detection.

But such a theory leaves unexplained the puzzle of how he was able to wash some of the bodies before disposing of them. There is the possibility that he could have utilised the railyard's large water tanks, with their attached rubber pipes for filling the steam locomotives, to sluice the blood and forensic evidence from the bodies. And, if the Butcher conducted his messy business in the nude, he could have showered by the same method — but this highly visible use of railway water facilities could only have been employed in the Pittsburgh yards, not in the hobo colony of Kingsbury Run with so many nocturnal witnesses wandering around haphazardly.

Whatever the case, the three Pittsburgh murders also remain unsolved.

———————

In attempting to build a psychological profile of the Mad Butcher, the ferocious, eccentric nature of the murders first inclined me to classify him as psychotic. But study of the case as a whole persuades me he was primarily an organised psychopath of above-average intelligence, perhaps suffering secondary symptoms of incipient psychosis not sufficiently affective to distort his 'normal' thought processes or detach him from reality.

The abnormal physical strength and mature, strategic planning that the crimes necessarily involved, suggest he was a large, physically fit man in his prime, aged between thirty-five to forty-five. It is more than likely that he conducted his indoor dismemberments in a small business or detached house in close proximity to Kingsbury Run, significantly the scene of his first two (known) murders and, therefore, an area he was highly familiar with and confident to operate in, thus fitting the psychological pattern of most serial killers. He most probably owned a functional vehicle, such as a small van, which he used to transport bodies and dismembered parts to the vicinity of the chosen disposal area.

For ease in beguiling victims to accompany him, he would have deliberately cultivated genial mannerisms and persuasive verbal techniques, casually adopted to lure his victims to the killing place. His use of restraints in one of his first known murders indicates (at this particular stage of the discussion, and according to the principles of psychological profiling) excess caution or lack of personal confidence, as does also the preserving of some of his first probable victims in chloride of lime, and then waiting patiently for the hunt to die down before choosing an opportune moment to dispose of the corpses, whole or in dismembered sections.

It is only when one comes to the castrations, and particularly his obsessive compulsion to depersonalise all his victims by beheading them and then, as already stated, logically extending the principle by distancing the heads further from the body, that a secondary psychotic symptom becomes apparent.

This element strongly suggests he had a verifiable history of mental illness and probably a police record for violence of some description. Which would also explain his obvious familiarity, and necessary easy manner, in the company of the petty criminals which mostly comprise the down-and-outs of society he was preying upon.

Thus the nature of the chosen victims not only partly reveals the personality of the killer, but also suggests a facet of his probable past.

That he exhibited apparent knowledge of human anatomy does not necessarily postulate that he was of the medical profession. He could well have read books on the subject, either in prison or in a mental hospital, or simply borrowed from a public library. Even experience as a common butcher would have taught him the simple methodology of dismemberment. Castration of the male victims, as stated, indicates further psychotic symptoms and strongly suggests repressed homosexual tendencies, sexual inadequacy and a concomitant guilt complex sufficiently severe to induce manic depression and suicidal tendencies. The fact that he meticulously washed some of the naked bodies points to the strong possibility of an additional, abnormal sexual practice being involved, most likely necrophilic in nature.

As the police never discovered a weapon, his compulsive retention of the incriminating cutting implement, despite the obvious dangers of doing so, intimates an emotional, psychotic attachment to it, perhaps subconsciously as a penis substitute, or as an instrument believed to be invested with some occult power; a lucky charm.

He would have taken a keen, pragmatic interest in media accounts of his crimes and police tactics to outwit and capture him.

In studying the case, I concentrated upon obtaining from outside contacts as much forensic information as possible about the first two certain victims of the Mad Butcher, the two males found decapitated and castrated near the bottom of the steep descent into Kingsbury Run.

As already alluded to, most serial killers, consciously or subconsciously, make small mistakes, or leave significant aspects of their personality/crime-scene-print, during their first killings.

At the beginner stage, they have not yet been mentally equipped by practice to condition their conscience or subconscious mind to cope logically and coldly with the consequences of their drastic decision to break from humanity, leaving all programmed human values behind. Brought up from childhood to expect punishment for wrong-doing, a deeply rooted, albeit small, part of their socially-conditioned conscience actually still *desires* some external sanction to be applied, almost as a mark of distinction and recognition that they have value and that somebody cares about their welfare.

Therefore, that selfsame subconscious urge may even coerce them into leaving some little clue to their identity at the scene of the crime. Conscience has in consequence become their enemy, a psychosomatic symptom of illness, as it were, gnawing insidiously at the will to self-survival. Distorting their judgment, it causes them to become 'accident prone' by implying that punishment will somehow bring them relief and end all future suffering. A subtle variation of the pain-pleasure principle.

I now wish to clearly state my analysis of the case which, if closer investigation of the official records I am about to refer to yields what I expect, shall belatedly lead to the identity of the 'Mad Butcher.'

First a brief resumé of the pertinent facts re: the first two bodies discovered. Facts which, as you shall see, provide the building blocks of my theory.

Body number one was that of an elderly man in a decomposed condition, despite the body having been preserved with chloride of lime. Body number two was that of twenty-eight-year-old Edward Andrassy, a petty criminal, who had been dead only two or three days. His wrists bore severe rope-burns. Both naked victims had been decapitated and castrated, their heads buried separately a considerable distance from the bodies, and their severed sexual organs thrown casually aside. Both had been drained of blood and thoroughly washed. No blood was found around or under the bodies. Both bodies had been neatly arranged on the ground by the killer in precisely the same manner — their arms straight by their sides, their legs straight with heels together.

Police were of the opinion that both bodies had been carefully carried, one at a time, down the seventy-feet precipitous slope of the Run, by the killer.

The initial, puzzling questions I sought some explanation for were: why did such a savage killer not simply toss both bodies down into the Run, instead of so considerately carrying them down at great personal risk ?

Why did he then so respectfully and charitably arrange their bodies on the ground in precisely the same manner?

Why had he benevolently washed both bodies?

What *common* factor connected all three of these curious patterns of behaviour?

What kind of person would perform, consciously or subconsciously, all three of these acts, from common usage and force of habit?

An undertaker? He would have washed the bodies and carried them with respect, but he would have most probably folded their arms on their chest in an attitude of eternal rest or prayer, not put them straight by their sides.

A male nurse, hospital orderly or mortuary attendant? Yes, any of these would have automatically washed the dead bodies, treated them with respect and arranged them neatly with their arms by their sides, legs straight, ready for inspection on the mortuary slab.

Next I looked for an *uncommon* factor amongst all the Butcher's victims. One significant fact stood out prominently: none of the victims except Edward

Andrassy had shown any signs of rope-burns, or other physical marks that would have indicated they had been bound in some way.

So why had this powerfully-built killer decided to tie Andrassy's wrists with rope? Andrassy had been thin, weighing under eleven stone. Puny. What had made Andrassy struggle so fiercely that the killer bound him with rope, rope that had torn deeply into his wrists as he manically fought to get free?

What had he fought so desperately to prevent? Did he know he was going to die? How did he know?

If this meticulous killer was in the habit of warning his victims in advance of death, surely he would have adopted the same practice of binding them as he had done with Andrassy?

His treatment of all the other victims clearly demonstrated that the Mad Butcher was not a sadist; he killed swiftly and efficiently without preamble. The retracted neck muscles and the heart pumped dry of blood medically testified to the fact that he sliced deeply into the carotid artery of the neck. The castrations had taken place after death. So, the question as to why Andrassy alone had been bound with rope and struggled so violently had to have a logical, convincing answer.

----•◦•----

Based on my *own* empirical experience and judgment, the severity of the rope-burns spoke for themselves. It had been a struggle against death. Andrassy must have known he was going to die.

Q: How could he have known if not told so by the killer?
A: Andrassy not only knew the killer but also what he was capable of doing.
Q: Where/how did he first get to know the Butcher and possibly learn of his highly dangerous or homicidal tendencies?
A: Problematic till further evidence.

Supposing that Andrassy had known the dangerous killer he was dealing with, what other strong motive had overridden Andrassy's understandable apprehension, caution and instinct for survival? What had lured him into such an obviously perilous situation? Monetary gain?

I believe it is quite likely that he did try blackmail. By all accounts, he was just cocky enough and greedy enough to make such a stupid error of judgment. No doubt his self-confidence was bolstered by the fact that he had successfully blackmailed many of the elderly homosexuals he had supplied with boys and to whom he had sold his own personal favours.

————•◆•————

The Butcher himself being a silent phantom, the only possible way to get answers to some of these pertinent questions was to research Andrassy's past as thoroughly as possible, looking for some obscure clue linking him with the Butcher.

For this I had to get information and documentation from outside contacts, who delved back over three-quarters of a century to before Andrassy's death on 23rd September, 1935. Obtaining details of Andrassy's criminal record was a comparatively simple matter, his file still being in existence due to the fact that he was the victim in an unsolved murder. In 1931 Andrassy had served thirty days for carrying a concealed weapon. He had lived at home with his mother and father until his death, and had a younger brother named John, who had no police record. Andrassy had been in and out of police custody for a variety of other petty offences — street brawling, drunk and disorderly, etc., and was known to have been a procurer for homosexuals, a trader in pornography, a practitioner of small-time frauds and con-tricks. All these criminal activities provided fertile grounds for blackmail and a natural aptitude for same.

His parents had last seen him four days before he was found dead. The police investigations discovered no previous link between Andrassy and the elderly second victim he was eventually found lying dead with in the Run.

Andrassy had frequented criminal haunts in the slum districts of the city, smoking 'reefers' and mixing freely with gamblers, hoods and prostitutes. Further confirmatory evidence of homosexuality surfaced. It was now certain that he had sometimes made money as a prostitute himself.

Detectives investigating his murder found a book in his room containing the names and addresses of homosexuals known to the police. All the leads were checked but produced nothing.

It was only when I checked back further, to the mid-1920s, when Andrassy had been honestly employed, for a change, that some astonishing facts came to light.

————•◆•————

For four years Andrassy had worked as an *orderly* — in a *mental hospital*, Cleveland City Hospital. As I conjectured previously, the nature of the

Butcher's savage crimes, combined with his secondary psychotic symptoms, strongly indicated that he probably had a history of mental illness and a record for violent behaviour.

The obvious question was: Had the Butcher been a patient at the hospital during the period Andrassy had worked there? This would explain how Andrassy had come to know him and, perhaps from reading his medical record, learned of his savage capabilities.

The hospital records of those four years appear not to have been checked by police and searched specifically for any or all of the following:

(a) Any record of a physically large patient who had evinced signs of abnormal or maniacal strength?

(b) Any record of such a patient with psychopathic tendencies, incipient symptoms of psychosis, fixation, manic depressive illness, a fantasy or delusional/hallucinatory pattern which, upon retrospective analysis, bore some relationship to the bizarre methodology and rituals employed by the Butcher?

(c) Any patient with a particularly violent reaction to active/latent homosexuality?

(d) Any patient with a past history as a convict or vagrant?

(e) Any patient with a past history of having been employed, in any capacity, in a hospital or mortuary?

(f) Any patient or member of hospital staff shown by the medical records to have had a close association with the medical orderly Edward Andrassy?

The killer would be a man who, so horrified by his inner visions, was probably much more afraid of himself than he was of other people — unless he projected his own faults or savage capabilities onto others, which would cause him to be morbidly suspicious of everybody. Paranoid. Self-defensively homicidal. Which would reinforce his lack of remorse and guilt — even the law concedes that to injure or kill someone in defence of one's safety is both legally and morally justifiable.

Next, detectives should have thoroughly checked every member of the hospital staff, looking for anyone with a police record.

They also should have closely examined hospital staff records — those of doctors, nurses and menials — searching for any suspicion of criminal behaviour or brutality towards patients. The Butcher could just as well have been a member of hospital staff. Naturally, particular attention should have been paid to staff who had not only worked in the hospital during the four years Andrassy was there, but also had still been working there in the years the Butcher had murdered his victims. The hospital mortuary would have provided the ideal facilities required by the Butcher — marble slabs with drainage channels for the deluge of blood, and water taps to wash the slabs and bodies.

Another interesting fact emerged.

Andrassy, in 1928, married a nurse who worked at the same mental hospital, then obtained a divorce just over a month later. It was said that Andrassy was the father of the child she eventually had.

Astonishingly, there is no record of the police having bothered to question her when Andrassy was murdered seven years later. In view of the presumably abrasive circumstances in which Andrassy and his wife had so hastily parted company, surely she would have been a readily compliable source of indiscreet information about Andrassy, perhaps yielding confidential, incriminating facts nobody else knew about. Facts that might have provided the police with some clue or lead to the identity of the 'Mad Butcher.' There is an outside possibility that she could still be alive today, though in her nineties.

Given that public interest in, or even knowledge of, the murders committed by 'The Mad Butcher of Kingsbury Run' is now practically non-extant, one could reasonably argue against the likelihood of the killer ever being identified.

Unfortunately, absorbing though the case is, even in these modern days of recreational mass murder, the gruesome deeds of the Mad Butcher apparently do not afford the public that salacious frisson which still enthuses an army of amateur sleuths to pursue the identity of Jack the Ripper.

But it is still not too late to reach back into the gloom of Kingsbury Run and catch the devil by his tail, when all other methods have obviously failed.

The detailed medical and other records of the mental hospital where Andrassy worked, Cleveland City Hospital, should certainly still be in existence, possibly tucked away in some dusty store-room, or perhaps transferred onto microfilm. Access to such files is not made readily available to private individuals, of course, unless they have managed to obtain official, written permission of some sort beforehand.

The police could access the files at will, given that the Mad Butcher's murders are unsolved and still *remain open* to further investigation. But perhaps the Cleveland Police Department would be reluctant to prove my theory correct, possibly on the grounds that it would make them appear incompetent.

I do not agree that it would necessarily give rise to such criticism, considering that, seventy years ago, forensic science was still in its infancy, and the art of sophisticated psychological profiling had not yet been developed. However, if the

Cleveland Police Department are reluctant to resume the investigation, perhaps the FBI Behavioral Science Unit of the National Center for the Analysis of Violent Crime (NCAVC), at Quantico, Virginia, could be persuaded to gain access to the said medical files and test my theory, just for the fun of it. After all, the Mad Butcher is, beyond doubt, long dead by now, so no expensive manhunt would ensue as a result of the findings — an important factor in these modern days when cost-efficiency seems to be the paramount concern in law enforcement. It would at least be a fascinating academic experiment in retrospective investigation by modern profiling techniques. Perhaps even an historical event, if proof positive were found.

Even if my theory should prove wrong, possibly the FBI, in course of the exercise, might stumble upon the correct solution, or discover evidence for an alternative theory. At any rate, I have thrown down the gauntlet.

This has been a purely clinical, psychological assessment of the Mad Butcher of Kingsbury Run murders, based upon the known, albeit comparatively limited, forensic facts placed at my disposal in the close confinement of a prison cell.

The anonymity of the Mad Butcher still leaves him an elusive, fantastical figure to comprehensively catalogue and analyse. Was he some demoniacal, taunting psychotic playing hide-and-seek in the fog of a lost era? Or a melancholic solitary, perplexed by his demanding compulsions, obscurely stalking amid the acrid outpourings of furnaces and chimney-stacks gravitating into Kingsbury Run? Or perhaps a religious maniac, walking through the gulley of death, devoutly delivering the despised and rejected of society to salvation in heaven? Or a cold, vampiric psychopath, gliding through the murk, goaded by blood-lust?

The Mad Butcher could have been any one of these, or a composite persona of them all. But I have already categorised him as a psychopath with probably non-affective psychotic symptoms.

I have briefly resurrected him to the best of my ability for others to ponder, and his spectral figure may yet be invoked to stride posthumously into the light.

> We stand on earth, among our rages and our boredoms. We raise our heads; see passing in the stormy skies the banners of ecstasy. Is it God or Satan who paints such skies, so fabulous — and false?
>
> — Rimbaud

Chapter Fifteen
Ted Bundy

Ever let the fancy roam,
Pleasure never is at home.

John Keats (1795–1821)

The irrevocable reversal of one's fate, one's being, can hinge upon such inconsequential considerations as a single betrayal, an unanswered prayer or an unthoughtful slight, subconsciously resulting in the sardonic, paradoxical conversion not only to a diametrically opposite theology/philosophy but also to facets of the very one loathed in the first instance.

Milton's 'Evil be thou my Good' can just as easily be transmuted to 'Virtue be thou my Evil' — the longer virtue slumbers, the more fanatic when it awakes.

The avenging Virtue of Robespierre, the 'Incorruptible,' unconditional and unswerving, logically extending the enemy's own espousals of morality and ethics to destroy them; self-righteous in the certainty that there is no one worthy to cast the first stone and, therefore, no one is exempt from punishment.

The least infraction of this new order of virtue being a capital offence, a world of potential victims is created, and the creator of this paradoxical counter-culture becomes a Rastignac, coldly examining the alien city from the heights, viewing the despised inhabitants as antagonists to whom one owes no nercy. By this tortuous route we can perhaps comprehend the intellectual/atavistic conversion and, at the risk of understatement, the over-reaction of Ted Bundy and many other highly intelligent serial killers.

Essentially this category of resentful, vengeful beings, *creative* architects of reaction and ruin, feel neither the desire nor the need to justify their 'crimes,' but rather regard them as meritorious in themselves. Such absolute self-certainty is, as already evidenced, beyond the intellectual scope, imagination and experience of most ordinary people, who remain transfixed in a cultural stasis of conditioned social sensibility and moral decorum.

It is so much easier to be nice. The majority fear the *unconditional*, the embracing of comparatively demoniacal, tumultuous fields of mental and physical energy. Their dread is, as previously inferred, a fortunate state of affairs for the remaining predatory minority, who eagerly inhabit the kaleidoscopic realms of moral and legal relativism without the least ethical turpitude or aesthetic discomfort.

———— · ◆ · ————

The first wavering steps in Ted Bundy's decline and fall began with the childhood discovery that he was illegitimate — a born reject sired by Bible Belt bigotry and prejudice, not a born killer.

Natural resentment at the aberrant social stigma inexorably bred in Bundy an inferiority complex, which he fought to overcome and, in the end, over-compensated for. His futile struggle to defy the intolerant self-fulfilling prophecy of his birthright naturally served only to confirm it, tightening the warp of the net. The law of reversed effort then compounded this innate damage to the psyche, permanently curtailing and retarding emotional development in his early teens.

This self-fulfilling prophecy also nurtured in Bundy an immature hypersensitivity to any form of criticism or mark of low achievement. The classic secondary pattern of attention-seeking criminal behaviour soon began to manifest itself in acts of petty theft, vain mendacity and other forms of aggressive peer-group rivalry.

In setting himself too high a standard in studies he consistently fell below his own expectations, which inevitably exacerbated an increasing lack of self-esteem and dearth of future prospects.

But high ambition was pragmatically schooling Bundy how to bend the rules, shape the world to his own advantage and get what he wanted despite his conscious failings. Why stick to the rules made by others, especially religious precepts which branded you an outcast from the day of conception, when you can make more favourable ones of your own? There is no monopoly in the making of rules.

Bundy shrewdly plotted his course. He would defeat them all; style a crown from his bastardy, bear it silently as a badge of merit, fashion derogation into a rod for their self-righteous backs. Before he was through, they would regret the concept of illegitimacy to the roots of their soul and the anguish of their misbegotten hearts. Bastard? They had not yet met one as rancorous as he.

———— · ◆ · ————

Whether Bundy knew it or not, he was drifting towards moral relativism.

Life was too short to be restricted and deformed by the selfish designs of the already privileged. He would thoroughly enjoy giving them a lesson in idiosyncratic 'justice,' and lead them a dance worthy of Zarathustra, 'lover of leaps and tangents,' monster of divine laughter! A Dionysiac demon was rising from the abyss of his subconscious, eager to take flight, sink talons and teeth into living flesh, savour the blood, rip out the soul.

How much more fascinating and vital the world had suddenly become in this new shade of vision. There's nothing like resolve to lighten the step.

He would study their law, use his dark good looks and glib tongue to personal advantage as ruthlessly as any conniving politician. Become a player in this hustling, bustling world or die in the attempt. Let all those of servile stamp slide to perdition on a prayer mat and rot there!

But some things did not work out as planned.

His engagement to a fellow student, Stephanie Brooks, who had the attributes he most envied — a wealthy family and high social connections — was broken off by her when she discovered he was emotionally shallow.

This crushing public setback and humiliation struck deep, and was probably another significant factor in the eventual launching of his murderous career. No more Mr Nice Guy. The rich bitch could afford the luxury of emotional pretensions. Patronise him, would she? She would pay the price at a future date. Her and her kind. He would see to that. Meanwhile, he had more important matters to tend to. Places to go. People to meet. Powers to exercise. Revenge to exact.

He left university and failure behind to gain practical experience in the ways of the world, particularly the criminal subculture. He mixed with easy dexterity in both high and low circles, in the company of drug addicts, thieves and aspiring politicians.

He proved a quick learner. Ambition continued to spur him on. He went back to university to study psychology, obtained a degree and attended law school, then, eventually, with an exquisitely ironic sense of the absurd, went to work with the Crime Commission and the Office of Justice Planning. Here he would get to know the enemy and how to circumvent the law like its creators. Prominent legal circles aptly generated in him an ardent taste for pornography and drugs and a high-flying lifestyle, completing his social education and skills.

At this point, some might say that Bundy, having acquired the fruits of honest effort, could have consolidated his base and become a reasonably successful, dishonest member of the bourgeoisie.

Too late for that. He had much higher things in mind. There were still far too many people above him. Dull and smug people he still had to bow and scrape to. They were blind to his potential. He would soar despite and smite and spite them.

———◆———

Psychosis and incipient schizophrenia, in his case doubtless aggravated by the tedious company he was forced to bear to get ahead, were implacably delving and quarrying into his psyche. The 'hunchback' (the name he gave his criminal persona) was inexorably taking up permanent residence.

In Bundy's rationale, society had branded him a failure in advance. He was committed to mastering the stacked game and balancing accounts. Higher education does not postulate higher humanism; he was clever enough to note that. Intelligent people start wars. And so would he, in his own hedonistic and comparatively simple fashion. You have to break eggs to make omelettes, and all that. At any rate, humanism wasn't all it was cracked up to be.

For good deeds to be effective, they must be highly selective. Humanists make the basic error of spreading their benevolent butter so widely and thinly that it leaves no taste and has no nutritious effect. Serial killers avoid that mistake by using selectivity to spread anguish to maximum effect.

Bundy should have joined politics. He would have been that common variety of politician who, out to screw the voters for every cent they've got, when asked why they had been attracted to politics in the first instance, solemnly declare, 'I believe I have a contribution to make to society' — presumably referring to their cynical sense of humour.

Bundy was about ready to make his 'contributions.' The start of the body count was fast approaching.

———◆———

Voyeuristically, he began to prowl the streets at night in search of erotic serendipity. Through a window he saw a girl undressing, and this seems to have fuelled his sexual fantasies to the point of psychotic obsession.

On a trial and error basis, first reinforcing his fantasies with alcohol, Bundy practised methods of attack.

On a summer night in 1973, he stalked a young woman through the streets and, cave-man style, hit her on the head with a wooden club. She screamed and he ran off.

Undeterred, he used the same tactic on several more female victims with similar lack of success. Failure would have served to exacerbate his violent tendencies and increase their ferocity.

As previously stated, it is invariably the case that actions bright and exciting in the imagination are, unfortunately, often disappointing or farcical in practice, more so when they have not been thought through thoroughly. Deep thinking gives people a headache.

They think they are thinking when in fact they are merely day-dreaming. For instance, if you were to ask them what they thought of 'adventure,' they would express a vague, undefined pro-adventure attitude, as practically everyone does, albeit from the comfort of an easy-chair. They equate, or confuse, their liking for the idea of adventure with an ability to possibly participate in the real thing. Whereas, in practice, they might immediately discover that real adventure — of the neck-on-the-line variety — is unsettling, like entering a fourth dimension where the comfortable laws and rules they take for granted in normal life no longer apply; adrenaline speeds the pumping blood and distorts the faculties; immersion in the immediacy of action obviates wider appreciation. Riding the whirlwind is an acquired taste. The psyche aspires to accommodate the new perspective of both inner and external vision. The more times you act as supreme architect, the more you become one.

Again, like our student Raskolnikov, Bundy had badly overestimated his own ruthlessness. Whatever the truth, he was soon to overcome such weakness as he progressed and routinely transgressed every obstructive icon of decency.

By instinctive design or lack of control, Bundy eventually discovered a successful method of attack which also satisfied his psychological needs.

He gained access to the bedroom of a sleeping eighteen-year-old girl, Sharon Clarke, and, without hesitation or compunction, battered her unconscious with an iron bar. Not much finesse or panache, but it worked.

Bundy must have then realised that this was what he had sought all along, a totally inert, compliant victim completely under his control. No more need for the infuriating frustration of social niceties, courting rituals and such, he could now just get straight down to the main course.

Apart from the obvious overtones of necrophilia involved, this drastic method also revealed aspects of sexual inadequacy. Only absolute power over the victim could surmount this, acting on him as a potent aphrodisiac. This in addition indicates that, at this stage in his career, he still retained some remnant of conscience and could only function by first depersonalising the victim, turning her into an inert object of his passions, a mistress bereft of any form of reproach.

Understandably dazed by the novelty of his first success, he remained sexually inhibited and simply introduced objects (penis substitutes) into the vagina of the first victim. He then departed, leaving her alive. Her life probably saved by the lucky fact that she had not seen his face.

His next victim, Lynda Healy, a twenty-one-year-old student, was not so fortunate. Bundy again used what was to become his modus operandi, entering the bedroom of the sleeping victim and hammering her senseless. But this time he carried the unconscious body out to his car.

This additional act is significant. It shows that Bundy not only still felt sexually repressed and possibly morally uncomfortable in the victim's bedroom, but that he was also seeking a higher degree of power by taking her from her familiar surroundings to a place of alien isolation dictated by him. This isolating technique — control by environment rather than a weapon — psychologically empowered him to extend depersonalisation and power over the victim even further. In which case, if psychologically satisfying, he would repeat the technique. Which he did.

His choice of location was Taylor Mountain, twenty miles away, where he stripped and raped her and, as she had resumed consciousness in the course of the ordeal long enough to see his face, he then killed her.

In the next few months, using the same hit and rape tactics, Bundy murdered five more female victims, three of whom were taken to Taylor Mountain. The other two were driven to a house near Lake Sammanish — a more elaborate, time-consuming and risk-taking method.

After he conveyed the first girl, Janice Ott, to the house and raped her, he tied her up and drove back to kidnap a second girl, Denise Naslund. Returning with her to the house, he raped her in front of the first girl, then killed both of them. He then drove both bodies to a deserted location several miles away and simply discarded them, making no attempt to conceal the bodies — the classic hallmark of the psychotic, disorganised killer, but not entirely valid in Bundy's case, as I will eventually explain.

———•◆•———

Although Bundy had found a system of raping and killing which satisfied psychological needs, the sudden escalation in his rate of victims betrays an equally rapid deceleration of sexual satisfaction, a progressive stimulus-deficiency.

With Bundy, novelty obviously soon paled. He was, in effect, chasing a psychosexual will-o'-the-wisp, a higher degree of stimulation and satisfaction which would always be just beyond his grasp. The concomitant, ever-increasing sexual frustration was predictably goading him on to greater outrages. The 'hunchback' side of him had rapidly run out of control against his better judgment. But, yet again, this was not entirely so, as you will discover.

———•◆•———

As Bundy, for strategic purposes, moved his homicidal activities from one city to another, he no longer seemed to care about his well-being at all, openly picking up victims in front of numerous witnesses who could later identify him, and even introducing himself by his real first name.

Again, all apparent symptoms of psychosis. He had, I'm sure, insight enough to identify the cause of the weariness and boredom building up within himself, namely, the certainty that his search for the unholy grail was doomed to failure, and that his life, even by his own standards, was becoming increasingly tiresome and repetitious. Another aspect of the tragedy was that, knowing he was in pursuit of the impossible, he still could not give up the quest.

Contrary to socially-engineered public opinion, even 'criminals' have more than sufficient virtues in their character to qualify as tragic figures. Which, in view of the fact that, as earlier opined, professional criminals have a surer and more pragmatic understanding of morality than the majority of the public, should not be surprising.

The thinking criminal shrewdly observes and accurately reads society, notes the characteristics of those who benefit most under its rules, and emulates their invariable deceit, greed and self-absorption.

Bundy had enjoyed the advantage of experiencing both polarised cultures, first the legal profession and then the criminal, both of which apparently did not offer the satisfaction he was seeking. He had run out of alternatives, but had obviously decided that he would keep running the least tedious of the two courses, probably hoping against all odds to be pleasantly surprised at some juncture.

———•◦•———

Striving for elusive originality, fresh excitement and novelty, Bundy clashed his two experienced worlds together by abducting and murdering the daughter of a police chief! Naturally this would have given the particular crime an additional esoteric piquancy and verve in Bundy's mind. But the axiom 'Once tried, soon forgotten,' would doubtless still hold sway.

What next? The daughter of a priest, a judge, a politician? The principle would be much the same, and so would the victims. So no point in flogging a dead horse. This possibly inescapable ennui and spiritual lethargy which seem to creep up on many serial killers, an antecedent to increasing carelessness and indifference especially towards the end of their career, obviously contribute towards their capture, as detailed previously.

Is it the lack of drive and energy, the constitutional inability to take risks, the high threshold of boredom, the plodding capacity to perform the same monotonous job daily year in, year out, that differentiates the bovine conformist from the criminal? Is it merely a case of 'what you've never had, you'll never miss?' Or, less praiseworthy, 'what you've never done, you can dream of doing?'

If the latter applies, the number of vicarious criminals must far outnumber the active. Not so much the silent majority, more the licentious. This of course implies that the law-abiding, by not satisfying their secret criminal desires, could well end up being more morally corrupt than the criminal who does and is quickly disillusioned by them.

Just as I previously assured you that you are rubbing shoulders with socially acceptable psychopaths daily without even knowing it, you can also be assured that there are more aspiring serial killers walking the streets of your cities at this very moment than there will ever be in prisons. I believe the public's obsessive fascination with serial killers reinforces the premise.

———•◦•———

Bundy next moved to Salt Lake City, then on to Colorado, casually raping and murdering on his travels, nihilistically disregarding the host of eyewitnesses building up against him.

He also displayed a suicidal underestimation of the pursuing police who, by this time, not only knew the man they were looking for but also the old

beat-up Volkswagen he insisted on retaining. Bundy, the
years old, was obviously already riding the black crest of a

On the 16th of August, 1975, after a police car chas
through the dark, dusty streets of Salt Lake City, Bundy w
was found to be full of incriminating but mainly circu
linking him with several murders.

Paradoxically, capture seemed to revive Bundy's spirit
with a new venue and exciting challenge. The game was not
one to speculate whether Bundy, had he concentrated upon
nal lawyer, perhaps would have discovered that field to be i
lating and fulfilling enough in itself. I am sure he would have t
himself. In gladiatorial style, taking arms against the justice sy
successfully using trickery and amorality to defend his obviou
set them free. In short, the exercise of a legal form of criminal
his guilty clients re-offended, Bundy would, in effect, be re
crimes by proxy and could enjoy vicariously savouring them.

The irony and public play-acting involved would have a
they do to politicians and other socially-acceptable criminal

In court to face charges, Bundy was the picture of res
tive, polite, plausible and charming, putting up a brillian
natural air of sweet reason and injured innocence. For the m
by expediency, his good side had wrested control away from
and Bundy probably half-believed some of the arguments he
express his innocence. He bore the stamp of a good lawyer, b
and a deft relativist. His performance certainly impressed m
courtroom.

But the judge was less susceptible to smooth persuasion.
too clever by half. He sentenced him to one to fifteen year
The Colorado police then stepped in and arraigned Bund
murder, that of Caryn Campbell.

When he appeared in a courtroom in Aspen to face the
Bundy, incredibly, was allowed to stroll into the library durir
proceedings, and promptly escaped by jumping out of an u
and making off on foot!

He remained at liberty for eight days, then was again
chase in a stolen car — another Volkswagen.

The American system of justice being what it is, Bundy managed to ng proceeding over a period of months, simply on arguments re: the nissibility of certain strands of evidence against him.

Jnbelievably, on 30th December 1977, Bundy managed to escape from n yet again by breaking out of his cell through a ventilation shaft. He for Florida.

t is a matter of record that Bundy had once inquired as to which state the penalty still existed, and was told Florida. So, in Bundy being drawn there, iously or subconsciously, we see once again the death-wish operating in His conscious realities were obviously becoming unbearable and he could scape them, or himself; in prison, he had twice been compelled to escape edom; in freedom, he was equally induced to 'escape' back to prison.

Like a satellite falling out of orbit, Bundy was burning himself out tering the dual realities each time, and would attain his final incandes- in the electric chair in Starke State Prison, Florida.

———◆———

Meanwhile, in freedom, he had more recreational killing to do before ing his ultimate goal.

Ie broke into the Florida State University in Tallahassee and bludgeoned students unconscious, raping and strangling one. A second died being to hospital. Bundy's anguished psychic dilemma and suicidal spiral had him more reactionally sadistic; he bit off the nipples of one of the s. A third student suffered a crushed skull but survived. A month later, e City, Florida, Bundy abducted, raped and murdered twelve-year-old erley Leach, throwing her body into the Suwannee River.

he fact that Bundy chose to remain in Florida, despite the widespread or him, and then actually returned to Tallahassee, where he had attacked ur students, is further stark evidence of his tenacious death-wish. This inal resolution of despair exemplified what Pascal wrote:

Ve run carelessly to the precipice, after we have put something before prevent our seeing it.'

———◆———

the cold, small hours of 15th February, 1978, Bundy, significantly again g another stolen Volkswagen, was chased and captured after a violent le with the police.

When a check of records revealed to the police who he was, Bundy must have secretly felt a tremendous burden lift from his spirit, knowing that he would certainly not be allowed to escape from custody a third time, and that the great game was effectively nearing an end.

Bundy had committed between two to three-score of murders — he himself refused to give any definite body count. All that remained to him now was preparation of his final grand gesture against authority at the coming trial. Doubtless he applied himself to the challenge with buoyant enthusiasm, that uniquely paradoxical sensation of total liberty and panache one feels only when all is lost.

I myself experienced it. The Nietzschean dance of laughter and delight in confronting the abyss. Or the cold contempt of Balzac's Vautrin:

'They want us to repent, but refuse us pardon; they too have the instincts of wild beasts.'

But first, for his own psychological satisfaction, Bundy would try to explain himself — not excuse or incriminate himself — to some chosen academics who might understand. He picked a method of doing so which I myself once adopted and christened 'analysis by hypothesis.' This expedient method entailed his honestly answering questions on the basis that he was simply putting himself into the shoes of the *hypothetical* murderer, discussing the *probable* psychology and philosophy motivating the killer's actions. In some instances it can be a self-delusive state of mind — such as when John Wayne Gacy continued to protest his innocence, despite a mountain of physical evidence to the contrary, including twenty-eight bodies buried under his own house!

This expedient device obviously allows the killer to explain his actions without incriminating himself, and obliquely reflects his inability to confront those actions head-on and publicly define his true nature. He also avoids putting the success of his 'hidden agenda' at risk.

There is, as previously touched upon, a sado-masochistic element in all serial killings, a psychic swapping of persona between the murderer and victim, in which each becomes the other. On the killer's side, this occult element multiplies with each successive victim, cumulatively compressed with explosive force into the killer's psyche in montage form. For the killer ever to reveal comprehensively his personal, psychologically deepest experiences in this no-man's-land, this psycho-spiritual quagmire or force-field, is tantamount to psychic suicide; like blowing his brains out from the inside. Therefore, this territory stands solidly protected against all attack, all reason, all advice, all corrosive emotion.

This state of being can be comprehended more easily if one realises that the killer, once caught, is already rendered half-dead by capture itself, the cover on half his psyche having been blown, leaving him revealed, restricted and caged forever in the damaged half which remains, belatedly longing for anonymity.

But if all the captured killer has to fear is execution by the state, this gives him the advantage and initiative once again. For, all hope gone, he need not explain himself to anyone; or he can selectively choose that which he wishes to reveal or withhold for his own recondite purposes. Much better to have no hope than false hope. That is my expressed opinion also.

The captured killer's spirit feeds and regenerates itself on the hatred of the enemy. The will and intellect remain unbound. Men have died worse, been killed less kindly, in far-bloodier battlefields since time began. So there is nothing outlandish in the fact that the serial killer can summon up the last vestiges of the dignity and nobility he was born with, and die like, say, Gary Gilmore in Utah, or the Thane of Cawdor in *Macbeth*:

> Nothing in his life
> Became him like the leaving it; he died
> As one that had been studied in his death
> To throw away the dearest thing he ow'd,
> As 'twere a careless trifle.

Bundy was daily riding his rollercoaster emotions, veering between the extremes of exhilaration and despair, knowing he was facing certain defeat but enjoying the hedonistic exhilaration and challenge of the final courtroom confrontation.

He dismissed his lawyers and took over his own defence, a vainglorious action that led him to make a literally fatal legal error.

His lawyers had previously advised him to strike a deal with the prosecution through plea-bargaining; in return for confessing to certain murders and saving the time of the court, he would receive a sentence of life imprisonment.

Initially Bundy had agreed to accept this legal advice and cooperate. But then, for no apparent reason, he scorned to bargain and dismissed his lawyers. If memory serves me right, somebody or other once said, 'The man who elects to legally defend himself has a fool for a client.'

I personally believe Bundy's decision to defend himself in court was again influenced by the subconscious drive towards his own death. Preoccupation with death was fermenting an impatience with all such legal trivialities, and a contempt for the increasingly irrelevant, wearisome world he was in reality so eager to leave. He was too intelligent not to envisage the stultifying boredom and futility of spending the rest of his life behind bars.

Bundy was not the type of Dostoevskian figure who would choose to stand for eternity on a narrow cliff-edge in total darkness rather than accept death. Though not a pantheist like Wordsworth, Bundy would have by this time sided with the poet in one fatalistic sentiment, 'the world is too much with us.'

Only the final performance was left. The trial. A Bergman scenario, playing chess with Death.

Bundy gave a performance worthy of Cyrano de Bergerac — all was *panache!* He lied brilliantly, rationalised expertly when faced with concrete evidence, and conveyed by his clean-cut, all-American-boy air and delivery of speech that he was the soul of reason. Again, even the judge was impressed by Bundy's bravura, acting accomplishments and keen grasp of law.

But everyone in the court knew they were simply watching a gripping piece of theatre, a play the ending of which they already knew, as did Bundy. He was found guilty and sentenced to the electric chair.

Bundy left the stage. Reporters rushed to telephones. The audience shuffled homeward. And jaded, seen-it-all-before cleaners entered the silent courtroom, to sweep away the litter and dust of stale law in readiness for the next juggling act.

As death drew nearer, Bundy made some futile appeals against the sentence, doubtless motivated by just a few last-minute jitters coaxing him to avoid the death scene a little bit longer and eke out a few extra ad-lib performances.

All the appeals against sentence predictably failed and his date of execution was set for January, 1989.

Bundy played his last delaying gambit, proposing to trade confessions to almost twenty additional murders in exchange for life imprisonment. But the legal sell-by date for plea-bargaining was long gone; he should have plea-bargained at the trial, as his lawyers had advised.

On a cold January evening in Starke State Prison, Florida, the prison guards shaved Bundy's head and lower legs ready for the electrodes to be attached. They then smeared the shaved areas with a gelatine compound conducive to electricity. A wad of absorbent material was inserted into his rectum and a catheter was attached to his penis — the forty-odd selected witnesses, assembled beyond the glass inspection panel of the execution chamber, must not have their sensibilities outraged by the unseemly body functions occasioned by a mega-jolt of electricity on the human body.

Prison Chaplain and doctor stood by in attendance with the solaces of hypocrisy.

Bundy was escorted bare-footed to the execution chamber. Guards strapped his four limbs into the chair. Another strap was pulled tight across his chest. They attached a metal cap to his shaved head and electrodes to his legs. Before a black leather flap was placed over his face, Bundy gave the tiers of witnesses a cheerful grin; his troubles were about to end, and theirs would continue to multiply, not least from the sight they were about to witness.

Two trip-switches had already been thrown to build up the required electrical charge. When the second hand of the wall clock hit the hour, the executioner pulled the third and final switch.

Bundy's body suddenly arched up rigidly against the restraints as the massive electric fist hit; a wisp of acrid blue smoke curled up from beneath the metal cap as his skin sizzled and the blood in his brains boiled. The current was switched off, then on again, until the heart-monitor registered zero response.

Bundy's dead body relaxed into the hard contours of the chair as though he were settling to take a short nap.

He had successfully escaped it all at last.

Beyond the prison walls, grouped around charcoal braziers and waving 'Fry Bundy' placards, America's modern equivalent of a public-execution crowd was drinking, laughing and singing. Media crews and deep-toned anchormen bobbed about in a forest of parabolic microphones and cameras in a sea of steaming rednecks.

Bundy was to make a final public appearance. An enterprising prison guard with a concealed camera managed to snap a photo of Bundy's charred features as the prone body awaited burial. The ghoulish portrait was sold and syndicated throughout America and the world.

My final psychological assessment of Bundy is that he was a psychopath, but not a highly organised one, suffering from incipient psychosis, including an essentially non-affective form of paranoid/persecutory schizophrenia.

In short, his crimes were not committed as a result of any chronic mental illness. His schizophrenic, homicidal persona, the 'hunchback,' although steadily gaining in influence with each murder, was never beyond Bundy's psychic control. He was able to choose when to let it loose, or, put another way, periodically Bundy was able to make a conscious decision to go 'mad' and become homicidal.

He laid emphasis upon the influence of the 'hunchback' only at the end, obviously as a legal tactic to stave off the death sentence a little bit longer, despite his chronic death-wish.

The fact that Bundy, whilst in lengthy captivity and subject to no psychiatric treatment or medication, displayed no aggressive violence and was never prey to delusional or hallucinatory influences, is additional confirmatory proof that the 'hunchback' was always under his control, a servant.

Again, perhaps controversially, I perceive Bundy as a tragic figure. A highly intelligent man sliced in half by two opposing tensions — the inferiority complex bred by his illegitimate birth, and over-compensatory ambition designed to thwart perceived disadvantage. Not quite the same problem of indecision that tortured Hamlet, but in the early stages it had similar effect, leading Bundy to resolve the anguished dichotomy by embarking on the same course of action, multiple murder.

Had Bundy possessed Hamlet's talent for self-analysis, he might have solved his lesser problem more pragmatically by recognition of his own limitations. Instead, his inferiority complex goaded him to goals too high, drove him too hard to achieve them, and futilely challenged the law of reversed effort in his particular case. Then, not wishing to duplicate the dogging, depressing disappointment of failure, he tried too little or, perhaps more aptly, tried too hard not to try hard, and met failure once again. Double jeopardy. 'Catch-22.'

When I say Bundy 'failed,' I mean by his own perceived personal standards. By any normal measure, his academic achievements were well above average and highly commendable. But he was stuck on a psychic seesaw, forever thinking too highly or too lowly of himself, and ended up balancing in limbo between the two worlds. Had he achieved, even modestly, a more dexterous equilibrium, he would probably be practising as a reasonably successful lawyer today. Given his undoubted social and manipulative skills, innate ambition, amorality and ruthlessness, he might even have reached Congress or the Senate.

Is that all that life, fate, destiny, or whatever else you wish to call it, boils down to? That we are all born with certain talents and intellectual capacities and that our success or failure simply depends on what use we make of them, how well we can understand, control and channel them?

Your intellect, instinct and life experience may tell you that it takes only one short hop to get from philosophy to zoology. That's if you make any real distinction between them in the first place, of course, or deny that it is part of the human condition that the two shall ever walk hand-in-hand till humankind annihilates itself. Does anyone still believe that it will not?

Strip your leaders of sanctimonious verbiage and false sentiment. Construct a psychological profile of each. Examine their bank accounts and deeds. And you may then agree that they are much the same species tried and hanged in Nuremberg fifty years ago. Sociably-acceptable psychopaths, above national laws they legislate for others.

Can you distinguish amongst their number any saints or heroes, or even a genuinely honest individual? By merely directing attention to such glaring incongruities, it is not my intention to justify 'criminals,' more to define criminal action and analyse the behaviour of those who reach high office by criminal criteria.

In conclusion, it is only fair that I should point out — particularly to those readers exhibiting synthetic horror and disbelief — a significant fact that I have deliberately withheld up to this point.

Namely, that some leading psychiatrists *did* recently undertake a study of prominent politicians, militarists, financiers and other men of power, wealth and privilege (libel laws forbidding revelation of their names), and came to the firm conclusion that (a) most were suffering from affective forms of mental illness, and (b) many were found to be certifiably insane.

Observant readers among you can probably accurately surmise many of the prominent people who were on that list, and many more who should be.

A similar study, conducted by another team of psychiatrists fifteen years ago, reached almost precisely the same conclusions as the most recent. It's reassuring to know whose fingers are on the nuclear buttons.

Let those who speak of 'evil' first learn to recognise the genuine article and the most nefarious forms of disguise it assumes. In real terms you *will* learn to your cost eventually. Therefore, in that confident conviction, I am quite genuinely glad that my life is as good as over already, thank you, as the outside world suffocates slowly in pollution and corruption. Death is the balm of the hopeless.

However, *semantics* will be the death of you. Not Bundy and his like. We are mere passing amateurs.

> When a rich man is fallen, he hath many helpers; he speaketh
> things not to be spoken, and yet men justify him
> — Ecclesiasticus

Chapter Sixteen
The Green River Killer

A Christian is a man who feels

Repentance on a Sunday

For what he did on Saturday

And is going to do on Monday.

Thomas Russell Ybarra (1880)

In general we all begin life pretty well pristine and optimistic, believing that life is endlessly fascinating and exciting, and that it will only become more so as we grow older.

This, in fact, may actually turn out to be the case for some people; in the first instance, those fortunate few who are born with a superfluity of wealth or talent, and the leisure opportunities to enjoy and indulge same to a satisfactory extent. And even the less fortunate class of people, who are forced to work daily for a living, may be lucky enough to land a form of employment they actually enjoy performing, and which leaves them with at least sufficient time and energy to appreciate and relish their leisure pursuits to a more or less reasonable degree.

But what of the far greater majority of people who are reluctantly constrained, by lack of private means, to waste most of their lives toiling for the welfare and financial betterment of others far richer than themselves, performing repetitious daily employment that would madden a lower primate?

It is, to me, an *amazing* fact that most of that latter class, either from lack of intellect or will or spirit, in the course of time grow to accept their unenviable lot in life as the natural order of things, and settle down quite contentedly to entirely waste the next several decades of their brief existence in serf-like subservience.

The limit of their ambitions being apparently to marry, breed, further burden themselves by mortgage (significantly, the dictionary definition of 'mort' is 'a call blown on a hunting horn to signify the death of the animal hunted'), own a family car, and live in excruciating moderation and boredom till death do they depart.

This gives rise to apostrophe: 'Is there a life before death?' Some people, in my opinion, are to all intents and purposes born spiritually and intellectually dead in the first place.

———•———

Your average serial killer — if such a conflicting classification is valid — will have none of this social conditioning, consigning him to a lifetime performance of stultifying banality.

The very prospect and contemplation of such a bleak future are so contrary to the serial killer's psychic constitution that they have emetic effect. His beliefs, his philosophy and life ambition are firmly rooted in comprehensive hedonism. Whether it be considered immoral/illegal is not of the slightest ethical interest or concern to him.

His mind is governed and guided entirely by the precepts: whoever or whatever contributes pleasantly to my life is right and good; whoever or whatever opposes is wrong and evil. Those who obstruct court destruction.

Born alone, the serial killer is prepared to die alone.

They are predisposed to the universal concept of mutual indifference. Whatsoever they do is regarded as their concern and no one else's. Let those who attempt to oppose beware, for they shall receive no warning shot, be given no quarter for the presumption and impertinence of interference.

Those primal traits and characteristics form the remorseless remittance of the serial killer. He has, as it were, taken the American Constitution, in particular its sentiments on 'the pursuit of happiness,' very seriously indeed, much more so than the majority of the disaffected population, perhaps regarding it as literally custom-built to suit his own highly individualized and idiosyncratic view of life.

But — and this is important — when the lower-class criminal points to the far vaster and socially more damaging crimes of the upper class, he is accused of simply trying to justify himself. Whilst the upper class justify themselves by virtue of the power they hold.

Those members of the middle class who, either from mutual benefit or by omission, contribute to this socially-acceptable calibre of elitism, are, in my opinion, morally inferior to the working-class criminals who attempt to emulate the values of the upper class and invariably bear the brunt of penalty and guilt.

During President Richard Nixon's term of office, the Special Advisor to the President, Charles Colson, had a framed statement of personal belief mounted behind his desk in the White House:

'When you've got them by the balls, their hearts and minds will follow.'

———•◦•———

The serial killer largely perceives society as a jungle of corrupt power in which he has suffered a general defeat, or even as a personal affront to his originally optimistic expectations. Cumulative disillusionment and rancour in his case exacerbates the degree of post-traumatic stress, generating a fatalistic, unforgiving methodology of general revenge. The revenge of the conquered and disaffected. That of Milton's Satan in hell, fashioning his will and resentment to a personal quest of retaliation:

> What though the field be lost?
> All is not lost; the unconquerable will,
> And study of revenge, immortal hate,
> And courage never to submit or yield.
> And, what is else, never to be overcome . . .
> Here we may reign secure, and in my choice,
> To reign is worth ambition though in hell:
> Better to reign in hell, than serve in heaven.

———•◦•———

If a person is told enough times that he is honest and decent, or regards himself as such, he naturally feels *obliged* to live up to the image, be it real or fictitious.

It therefore follows that the same obligatory mechanism works if he is told or believes he has qualities opposite to those, again be they actual or imaginary. Perceived by other as a problem to be managed, he will react accordingly.

'A problem? Managed? I'll show you what a problem is! I'll show you managed!'

In addition, as indicated, even when people believe at a conscious level they are honest and fit to condemn the crimes of others, the taunting subconscious reminds them of their own dark fantasies, and guilt makes them more vociferous. Innocence is at best a myth or a form of self-delusion, at worst a paradigm of internal and external corruptive influence which inexorably incites or invites crime.

My point? People should be less dogmatic and pious when philosophically attributing *responsibility*, as they are usually quite purblind to their own share.

Responsibility is multi-motivational and multi-attributable, not some rudimentary political or legal calculation. An individual does not of course have to be a member of a committee in order to own committee-mentality, unctuously washing their hands like Pilate.

The category of serial killer who concentrates his thirst for vengeance upon prostitutes, like the Green River Killer did, is almost invariably suffering from a personal moral crisis or dilemma. In one sphere he perhaps self-righteously believes he has some form of mandate from God to punish transgressors in any manner he sees fit. In the second sphere, that of schizophrenic fugue, he may be unaware of the personal pleasure he derives from inflicting divine retribution, perhaps having rationalised the pleasure into an inescapable cross he must bear in devotion to a divine mission.

Most intelligent people have a strong sense of self-actualization but choose less harmless ways to achieve it.

In this psychically amorphous field of attributive endeavour, psychology has its obvious limitations. It strives to deal with the 'soul' by calling it the 'psyche,' predominantly because the psyche yields itself to principles of scientific analysis and interpretation. It therefore sanctifies the scientifically objective at the expense of the subjective.

The art of psychiatry is much more flexible in encompassing the mercurial spirit of mankind and its multi-polar affective disorders.

For instance, the person I once was, whilst in the pursuit of multifarious criminal activities in many cities, also enjoyed visiting their art galleries and historical/natural museums. The architectural qualities of cities also excited my interest and I would often relax in the ancient gestalt of old churches — existentially juxtaposing the sacred with the profane; the texture and tactile pleasure of polished wooden pews contrasting with the smooth gunmetal of the revolver under my arm; the contentment of sitting in mote-filled sunlight slanting through stained-glass windows while waiting for darkness to fall; the savouring of silence and tranquility before the storm; the pantheistic appreciation and communion with all forms of the animate and inanimate. Contrast is life. In this case what one could categorize as abnormal moral duality in tandem with dyslogistic spirituality.

———•◆•———

The sum total of murders the Green River Killer is said to have been responsible for — over forty in number by the last body count — in my opinion reflects officialdom's hasty expedience.

After examining all the forensic evidence, it seems plain as day to me that at least two or more separate serial killers were responsible for the Green River Murders. Therefore, if the police ever irresponsibly claim to have solved all the murders by arresting only one killer, that would amount to their criminally allowing the other killer/killers involved to remain free to kill again — as evidenced in the Henry Lee Lucas case.

Ironically, initial facts indicate that police investigating the Green River Murders were reluctant to admit that even one serial killer was responsible!

This dual expediency is understandable, as: (a) admission that a serial killer is at work generates public fear and hostility towards the police unable to capture him, and (b) when finally forced to admit the existence of a serial killer, it is officially convenient to attribute all the murders to one killer, rather than compound public panic by raising the spectre of two or more serial killers simultaneously prowling the city streets.

The first ostensible victim attributed by the police to the (using their non-plural sobriquet) 'Green Valley Killer' was sixteen-year-old Wendy Coffield, a convicted prostitute who specialised in decoying her clients into isolated areas where they could be 'rolled' by her male confederate or pimp.

On 7th July 1982, her body was found in the Green River. She had been strangled with her own jeans. The investigation was conducted by the King County Police, Seattle.

A month later, 12th August, the body of a second victim was discovered in the Green River, less than a mile away from where Wendy Coffield had been found. Again that of a convicted prostitute and part-time stripper, twenty-three-year-old Debra Lynn Bonner. The only relevant fact the King County Police apparently bothered to note was the completely irrelevant fact that both victims sported tattoos. They saw no other reason to connect the two killings.

A few days later, on 15th August, two more female bodies were discovered in the Green River, a quarter of a mile from where the body of Debra Lynn Bonner had been dragged out. The notable differences being that this time both victims were black, entirely naked and had been weighted down below the surface of the water with large rocks.

The King County Police managed to deduce, from forensic examination, that both of these bodies must have been there when they had searched the immediate area where Debra Lynn Bonner's corpse had been found three days earlier. So belatedly they spread their net farther afield in search of clues, only to find, almost immediately, yet another body, the fifth, this time not in the river but on the bank. Again the female victim was black and, significantly, had been strangled with her jeans, in the same manner as Wendy Coffield.

Please note at this juncture, for future reference, that I am of the opinion that a second killer, for his own purposes, deliberately copied the first killer's methodology and choice of dumping ground,

As already indicated, though the King County Police had initially been extremely tardy in coming to the conclusion that a serial killer was at work, this had been mainly due to their lack of thoroughness in not finding the other three bodies in the same locale. In view of events yet to unfold, I believe that it would not have made any difference, so far as catching the killer was concerned, had they found the three additional bodies earlier than they did. The three lost days were of little relevance as the killer had left no definitive traces to follow.

But if the King County Police had made a faster connection between the first victim found in the Green River, sixteen-year-old Wendy Coffield, and the second victim, Debra Lynn Bonner, both being convicted prostitutes, they would then presumably have placed that area of the Green River under close, round-the-clock surveillance. If they had done so, they would have captured the killer/killers within days, as shall be proven presently.

All five bodies having been found so close to one another conclusively signified (to the police) that they had all been murdered by a single serial killer, conforming to the classic pattern of killing and disposing of his victims in an area he was familiar with. As his easy-to-approach prostitute victims were transported to the carefully chosen isolated area in a vehicle, it seems at first glance reasonable to assume that the killer was a psychopath. But as some of the rocks (which 'weighted down' two of the four victims found in the water) had been rammed into their vaginas, it is questionable whether concealment of the bodies was his main motive, as in the case of a psychopath.

So secondary psychotic symptoms become apparent. Use of the rocks as penis substitutes and as a method of degrading the victim, reveals the killer's sexual inadequacy and his need to compensate, consciously or subconsciously. It also suggests the killer premeditates but does not fully prepare for the crime, using whatever objects come to hand, i.e., the use of the rocks and the strangling of two of the five victims with their jeans.

This reasonably indicated that the killer was physically powerful and confident, a deduction reinforced by his not having used restraints on the victims, street-hardened prostitutes who habitually carry some weapon for protection against possibly violent clients. Rather, the killer controlled his victims by choice of isolated killing-ground — 'microcosm-management' is the term I would coin for this particular method.

———————

The forensic scientists examining the latest three victims eventually came up with some startling findings.

One of the two black victims found in the Green River had been murdered only two days before discovery. And the body of the third black victim, who was found on the bank of the river, was still in a state of *rigor mortis*, thus indicating that she had been killed probably *less than a day* previous. Which signifies beyond question that, if you accept for present convenience that only one killer was involved, the murderer had returned three times to that area of the Green River with his additional victims, even after the police had found the bodies of Wendy Coffield and Debra Lynn Bonner there.

So, as already stated, if the King County Police had immediately connected the deaths of the first two prostitute victims and put that small section of the Green River under constant police guard, the killer would have walked straight into their waiting arms, not once but thrice! I must again add at this point that I personally believe they would have in fact captured two separate killers. I will explain why at the appropriate time.

The King County Police tried to rectify their oversight by belatedly setting up round-the-clock surveillance teams in that area of the Green River where all five bodies were discovered. Almost immediately, the sensationalist media leaked this information to the general public — and presumably to the killer, for he did not return to the scene of the crime this time.

———————

Meanwhile, the latest three black victims had been identified by Seattle detectives.

The first of the two found in the river itself was Marcia Faye Chapman, a thirty-year-old prostitute who had a family of three, and had gone missing on lst of August 1982.

The second victim was Cynthia Hinds, again a hooker, who had vanished on 11th August 1982.

The third victim, who had been found face down on the bank of the river, was sixteen-year-old Opal Mills, who had vanished a scant three days before her body was discovered. She had no criminal record for prostitution or any other offence. In brief, she was *respectable* and thus did not fit the pattern of the apparent prostitute killer.

Forensic experts concluded, from the scrapes and scratches on the body of Opal Mills, that the killer had dragged her corpse along the ground to the spot where it was found on the river bank. This suggests that she was *killed elsewhere* and *brought there* by vehicle. Another significant difference in the original pattern.

All of which raises further mystifying, psychological questions. A psychopathic serial killer, who takes a keen interest in media accounts of his crimes and police tactics, must have known that the police had found his first two victims and would not have returned three times to the selfsame area with further victims. So what was the explanation? That the killer was not the psychopath his methods indicated, but a psychotic who was not sufficiently alert to know that his first two victims had been found and who cared even less? Or was he a psychopath who believed in double-bluff? Or, perhaps more likely, one who was in a privileged position to know definitely that the police had not set up a trap to catch him there after the first two killings? Perhaps a policeman or a reporter with inside contacts?

Even if that were the case, the psychopath would have been intelligent and cautious enough to assume that the discovery of his first two victims had brought a highly dangerous amount of morbid public attention to that particular area of the Green River, and surely would not have risked immediately returning there three times with fresh victims.

———◦•◦———

The presence of the busy Seattle-Tacoma International Airport within a short distance from Green River prompts the outside possibility that the killer might have flown elsewhere on business for a couple of days, and missed the local news reports.

But that possibility is pretty much negated by the fact that he killed in the danger area on three separate further occasions in a matter of days, and was therefore in a position to know his previous two victims had been discovered.

If we accept the police theory that only one killer was involved, this apparently points to the killer being a pronounced psychotic in the grip of chronic delusions driving him to take foolhardy, monumental risks despite the odds. But such an assessment would have to ignore the strong psychological evidence to the contrary, essentially reflecting the personality print of a stealthy, intelligent psychopath with perhaps only secondary, non-affective psychotic symptoms. That profile is further reinforced by the significant determinant that he has been clever and self-controlled enough to evade capture to this very day.

If, as I believe, there were at this early stage two separate killers involved, the second copying the methods of the first for his own advantage, the second killer had made the pattern-breaking mistake of choosing his own preferred type of victim, i.e., Opal Mills, not a prostitute.

We must now progress to the forty-odd other murders the police have attributed to the so-called Green River Killer.

———•◦•———

The section of the Green River the killer had used as a dumping ground till then may have been small, but he stalked his prostitute victims in a much larger hunting radius, which stretched along the Pacific Highway from Seattle to Tacoma.

This long, broad highway is usually referred to as 'The Sea-Tac Strip,' as it runs past the sprawling Seattle-Tacoma International Airport which, like all large airports, has a multitude of bars, diners, hotels and motels studding its borders, including five-star Hilton and Holiday Inn, making the crowded, busy district a lucrative beat for hookers to sell their wares.

The city of Seattle itself, with its skyscrapers and neon pyrotechnics, is much like many others in North America. It is the largest city in the state, constituting a major port in West Washington, on an isthmus between Lake Washington and Puget Sound.

The city is generally regarded as the foremost commercial centre in the Northwest and has two excellent universities. In the fall it has a blustery atmosphere not too dissimilar to that of Chicago. The contrast between rich and poor is not quite so striking as in New York.

All in all, Seattle can be summed up as modest and respectable. The Town and Country Inn offers in neon: "A PILLOW FOR YOUR THOUGHTS."

Naturally the city has its districts of ill repute, where the hookers patrol the pavements in pants and bra, stand gossiping together on corners, smoking reefers and haggling prices with the johns in kerb-crawling cars.

Hookers are mostly a happy-go-lucky breed, and far more interesting than most of their sisters who walk the straight line.

The genteel look down their noses at hookers, never seeming to realise it takes a lot of hard courage to be one. Here the lights are not so bright, the doorways not so sweet. Here you meet stark reality, the quick and the dead. Here the killers come to prey.

***

With the monotonous foreboding of a production line, the flow of victims continued to mount.

A mere two days following the discovery of Wendy Coffield's corpse, another young prostitute, seventeen-year-old Giselle Lavvorn, mysteriously disappeared while strolling on the Sea-Tac Strip. The Seattle police searched around but could find no trace of her.

The next hooker to disappear was Kase Lee. She had not been seen since 28th August 1982.

On 29th August 1982, another prostitute, Terri Mulligan, vanished after being witnessed entering a car.

This was quickly followed by the disappearance of eighteen-year-old Mary Meehan, who had been seven months pregnant.

The tenth prostitute victim was fifteen-year-old Debra Estes. A curious, poignant piece of information about her was found in police files.

Three weeks before her disappearance, she had been driven to a deserted spot by a client in a pick-up truck. He had drawn a gun and forced her to strip and perform oral sex, then had robbed and tied her up. She had reported all of this to the Seattle police who, in a surprisingly short space of time, managed to trace and arrest the man. At first they were sure they had captured the Green River Killer. The suspect asked for and passed a lie-detector test, but that was not sufficient proof of innocence.

However, after the detectives made wider inquiries, it became clear that the man could not possibly be the Green River Killer. If further proof were needed, the aforementioned ninth victim, Mary Meehan, had disappeared while the man was in the police cells. But the young Debra Estes had taken no heed of the inherent warning in her lucky escape, and had chosen no new path or even another city, but had instead walked blithely on to her own annihilation.

Even serial killers can sometimes risk the self-destructive experience of introspective pathos and pity — but not too often, if they wish to survive in the solitary world they have chosen. To will their own death, they need only unlock those rusted, inner-sealed chambers where the imprisoned alter-ego waits to kill them with treacherous grief.

> No beast so fierce but knows some touch of pity.
> — *Richard the Third*, Shakespeare

As detailed in the explanatory opening chapters of this book, I will not devote a great deal of space to the names and biographies of the victims in various cases, except when I believe such details help to enhance the forensic exercise we are engaged in. I do this not out of any disrespect for the victims; the primary aim of this book, as explained, is to delve into the psychology of the serial killer.

In the remaining five months of 1982, another six victims were chalked up, bringing the total to sixteen. The Seattle police, patently and literally, did not have the slightest clue or insight to assist them in stemming the steady crop of corpses. Understandably, the detectives were becoming increasingly discouraged, their minds and spirits drained by the Green River, as it were. But, perhaps more to the point, as the police rely greatly on the help of the public, the public was by then actually becoming *bored with* the murders.

The killings were beginning to hold less interest than the synthetic drama of soap operas. The murders had no variety, no originality, no panache, no cathartic effect, just the same stale routine over and over.

The public's attitude to murder, whether they choose to admit it or not, is not dissimilar to that of a theatre critic. They are, as it were, always on the lookout for new, aspiring, homicidal talent to tickle the palate. But this killer seemed to have lost whatever *inspiration* he once possessed; he no longer shocked or surprised his audience, and they were silently booing him off the stage for lack of artistic creation and imagination.

Apparently the Green River Killer did not have critical acclaim at the forefront of his mind. He continued to kill with the same prodigious, unoriginal regularity.

March 1983, Alma Smith and Dolores Williams fell victim. The following month saw another five victims added to the total. Two of these actually disappeared on the same day, 17th April 1983. On 30th April, 1983, eighteen-year-old Marie Malvar was driven away by a man in a pick-up truck — her pimp took the trouble to follow in his car but lost them. Marie Malvar simply disappeared. However, 17th May, 1983, her driving licence was found in a room at the airport. Police did not even bother to retrieve the licence and examine it for prints, so it was eventually destroyed months later.

Another ten victims bumped up the overall total in May, June and July, 1983. By now the only visible function the Seattle police seemed to be serving was to keep score. There was no public outcry to spur them on to better efforts. Nobody seemed to care; after all, they were only prostitutes and it was about time somebody cleaned the streets up for 'respectable' citizens. That was the general attitude.

———— • •———

The Green River Killer, as the Seattle police still insisted on calling him, had long since stopped disposing of the victims in the Green River, and was now randomly using surrounding woods, lakes and other isolated locations. Some victims were skeletons before they were found, and defied attempts at identification. Many others simply eluded all searches by the police.

As 1983 drew to a close, over forty victims had been attributed by the Seattle police to the Green River Killer, no matter if many of the victims were dumped miles away from the Green River.

From a psychological viewpoint and public relations-wise, as already indicated, one can clearly discern the advantages to the police of putting all the murders down to one, diabolically clever psychopathic killer. If the public were informed that, since the original five victims were found in the Green River, another half-dozen budding serial killers had grasped the opportunity to get on the homicidal bandwagon in the sure knowledge that the police would credit all the murders to the invisible Green River Killer, the chaotic state of affairs would have inspired women to flee Seattle. It was much more acceptable and comfortable for the public to believe that there was only one perverted serial killer murdering at will.

Faced with a possible clutch of serial killers, the public would begin to wonder how many more serial killers were getting ready to join the queue to get their kicks. People would envisage Seattle evolving into a national or international hunting ground, or homicidal Disneyland, for 'tourist serial killers' who could fly in for a spot of sport, in a city where the chances of being caught by the police were non-extant.

After all, simple mental arithmetic by the Seattle public would have soon convinced them that there were only so many prostitute victims to go around and, at the present rate of fatality, that figure must be getting pretty low, and hookers with any sense would be packing their bags for the airport. Add to that the extremely alarming fact that several of the victims had no record of prostitution, other women would quickly appreciate the deadly logic of the situation.

Against all reason, the Seattle public continued to accept and believe what they were comfortingly told by the police. Such is human nature in general, unlike that of Sherlock Holmes:

> Detection is, or ought to be, an exact science, and should be treated in the same cold and unemotional manner. You have attempted to tinge it with romanticism, which produces much the same effect as if you worked a love-story or an elopement into the fifth proposition of Euclid.
>
> — *The Sign of Four*, Sir Arthur Conan Doyle

Instinct of danger slowly but surely began to penetrate the collective psyche of the Seattle public, sending influential waves of apprehension and dissatisfaction into police headquarters. For, in early January 1984, the Seattle police department took special measures by setting up a Green River Task Force. A development which, you might reasonably agree, should have taken place well before the number of victims rose to over forty.

The good citizens of Seattle were indeed beginning to think along mathematical lines, not only because prostitutes were becoming thin on the ground, but also as the killer/killers might be escalating activities from resentment at the lack of public interest and poor media reviews.

By far the most significant and important outside appointee to the new Task Force was Bob Keppel, seconded from the U.S. Attorney General's office.

Keppel had played a crucial part in the hunt for Ted Bundy — who, to help stave off his death sentence, had ironically offered his services in helping to track down the Green River Killer . . . initially on the premise that he had insight into the killer's mind and, eventually, on the suggestion that he himself had committed some of the murders. Keppel was one of the new breed of intelligent hunters impressed by the psychological methodology developed at the FBI Behavioral Science Unit at Quantico, Virginia.

The first practical moves of the Task Force included the setting up of surveillance teams and police decoys, in the Seattle red-light districts and along the Sea-Tac Strip, covertly monitoring and tabulating prostitutes and their clients.

The first pivotal break for the Task Force occurred in April 1984 when three skeletons were discovered in the vicinity of Star Lake, situated to the south of the Seattle-Tacoma International Airport. A fourth skeleton was found in some woods a mile or so from there. The latter skeleton was eventually identified as that of Amina Agisheff, who had disappeared on 7th July 1982. This meant that, according to the prevalent police theory that there was only one killer involved, Amina Agisheff displaced Wendy Coffield as being the first known victim of the Green River Killer. It also constituted an outstanding example of a victim who did not fit the expedient theory that there was only one serial killer involved.

Amina Agisheff had been a thirty-five-year-old housewife with two children and a thoroughly respectable background. She had been working as a waitress and had no criminal record, and had mysteriously disappeared when going to catch a bus after visiting the house of her mother.

As far as Bob Keppel was concerned, it should have been perfectly clear that there were at least two separate serial killers at work — the original Green River Killer who disposed of his victims in the river, and a second killer who discarded them on land.

In my opinion, sixteen-year-old Opal Mills, the only one of three black victims who was found on the river bank, was probably the victim of the second serial killer, after he read of Wendy Coffield and Debra Lynn Bonner having been dumped in that area of the river by the so-called Green River Killer.

Not before time, the fresh mind of Bob Keppel applied psychological profiling principles to the hunt. Working on the assumption that the first victim/victims of a serial killer are known to him even if only by sight, Keppel now concentrated the attention of the Task Force on thoroughly researching the background of Amina Agisheff, questioning those who knew her and those who lived in close proximity to her home.

Second, the large majority of serial killers do not suddenly start killing on a daily basis. The contrast between their fantasies and the reality of the first murder is often such a profound traumatic shock that they require a cooling-off period or, in some instances, actually commit suicide. With each murder, the cooling-off period becomes progressively shorter, reflecting the lessening effect on their psyche or the diminishing degree of satisfaction being obtained through repetition. Further, it is often the case that the incipient serial killer has a modest criminal record, or a history of mental illness, before he starts killing.

With these factors in mind, Keppel should have had the Task Force check through criminal records that preceded the first known murder by the so-called Green River Killer, searching for any other homicides which bore the same personality-print, or lesser crimes of assault that might represent some of the killer's first botched attempts (especially any involving kidnapping or efforts to strangle the victim in the vicinity of a river).

Intense police activity most likely made the other killer/killers more cautious. For, on 21st March 1984, after the skeleton of Cindy Ann Smith, a seventeen-year-old stripper and hooker was discovered in bushes near the Sea-Tac airport, the killings suddenly halted.

The Task Force did not realise this until months passed without any more prostitutes being killed or going missing. To me, this reinforces the deduction that the Task Force had brushed shoulders with one or more of the killers during its inquiries. The data obtained from these inquiries should have been very thoroughly re-examined for any clues of additional significance, in respect of the killings having *subsequently ceased*. Had any questioned male later died or left the Seattle area since? Whether or not the Task Force adopted these approaches I have no way of knowing.

After the passage of a year without any further killings, in April 1985 the head of the Task Force publicly stated that he was confident that the Green River murders had come to an end.

The first ominous computerised signal suggesting the contrary came from Portland, Oregon. Corpses of four hookers had been discovered on the outskirts there. Had the Green River Killer (or one of them) changed his base of operations?

Again, this should have prompted the Task Force to study their extant data for any male who had, within the preceding year, moved from Seattle to Oregon. Remembering that many psychopathic killers, for differing pragmatic, strategic or psychiatric reasons, frequently change their address or move to other cities. If that particular killer had moved from Seattle in 1985, he soon moved back again, perhaps in paranoid/narcissistic response to the Task Force having stated the killings had stopped. Two more skeletons were found in the vicinity of the Mountain View Cemetery.

Ironically, a 'trapper,' Ernest McLean, who worked in the area, was arrested on suspicion, but was released after detailed police inquiries and a lie-detector test cleared him.

Without any apparent reason the killings again halted, this time for two years, until September 1987, when the body of sixteen-year-old Rosie Curran was found in a drainage ditch. In quick succession, two more girls, Debbie Gonsales and Dorothea Prestleigh disappeared. This speedy rate of killing was a sure personality-print of the original Green River Killer, yet the Task Force did not attribute these killings to him.

Had the Task Force, too, interpreted the return of the Green River Killer as a paranoid/narcissistic reaction? Were they deliberately trying to provoke him by tactically not crediting him with the latest three victims? Or were they simply playing politics, hoping to make the Seattle public forget both the killer and their embarrassing inability to capture him?

Whatever the truth of the matter, no killer rose to the bait. Eventually, in October 1989, almost eight years having passed since the so-called Green River Killings had begun, the new head of the Task Force, Captain Bob Evans, announced that they were still no nearer to catching a killer than they had been at the beginning.

Over twelve million dollars had been spent in the futile hunt, and a total of 20,000 suspects had been interviewed. Finally, in January 1990, the defeated Task Force publicly announced that the hunt for the Green River Killer was now closed.

There is no doubt in my mind that there were two or more serial killers involved in the so-called Green River Killings.

The original killer had taken the trouble to hide the bodies in the Green River, indicating the cautious mind of a psychopath. The second killer had simply dumped his victims openly on the ground — the risk-taking personality-print of a psychotic.

However, many first-time killers usually panic and leave the body unhidden. So, there could have been any number of individual killers involved, psychically or emotionally or opportunistically infected by the increasing rate of murders and the apparent invincibility of the killer, or incompetence of the police.

It was a perfect scenario and ethos both for disturbed personalities and highly-educated aficionados of the art of homicide. Anyone already fascinated and excited by the very idea of murder would have been tempted to try it out for themselves. Seeing that all the killings were being attributed by the police to one killer, each successive killer would be both comforted and encouraged by the fact that, if apprehended, he could prove he was not the Green River Killer by providing a genuine alibi for when some of the other killings had occurred. A chaotic, convenient situation designed to attract aspiring killers, rapists and brutal muggers.

Even so-called 'ordinary' people have a morbid curiosity and atavistic urge to experience what it would be like actually to kill someone. The urge is buried inextricably within the human psyche.

If all the books that contain murder, rape and sexual perversion were to be burned, the bonfire would of course consist of most of the great classics, including the Bible. Books and films merely cater to crime. The catalyst to action lies not in the words or images, but in the individual psyche.

I have never experienced the need to corrupt anyone. I simply offered the opportunity to indulge extant natural urges. Innocence, once again, is the most corrupting influence of all. I am sure the collective perpetrators of the Green River Murders would heartily agree and concede the point.

> Where you thought me safely drowned
> In the depths I swim around.
> Thither when you too descend,
> With my claw I'll tear you, friend!
> — 'The Road to Sinodun,' George D. Painter

Chapter Seventeen
Carl Panzram

> When a liberal is abused, he says:
> Thank God they didn't beat me. When
> he is beaten, he thanks God they
> didn't kill him. When he is killed, he
> will thank God that his immortal soul
> has been delivered from its mortal
> clay.
>
> **The Government's falsification**
> **of the Duma and Tasks of**
> **the Social Democrats (1906)**

Those of you fortunate enough to have either been born with, or been inclined to have, a philosophical appreciation of the variegated splendour of life, must surely recognise that, in a perversely paradoxical fashion, some serial killers place a higher value on a human life than do many of their ostensibly more principled brethren.

As previously postulated, there are killers who, in order to annul their conscience or social-conditioning, feel compelled to depersonalise their victims rather than see them as people who possess, to a greater or lesser degree, the same feelings and rights as they themselves.

Soldiers wear uniforms both to identify their comrades and the enemy. They are trained to kill by reflex those who wear the enemy uniform in the same manner as bulls are conditioned to charge a red cape. This is simply a socially-acceptable, alternative method of depersonalisation to that used by the serial killer, but with precisely the same object: to kill without conscience or remorse.

Big business applies depersonalising criteria in the pursuit of profit. They distance themselves from general humanity, describing those who suffer from their exploitation as 'units' or 'consumers.'

Criminals are forever being told to think of the effect of their actions on society. The large corporations chopping down trees in the rain forests as fast as they can are not in the least interested that their actions are affecting the atmosphere to the extreme detriment of all who live on the planet. They actually employ gangs of murderers to get rid of the stone-age tribes in the forest who stand between them and profit. These gangs either simply shoot the whole tribe or drop 'gifts' of poisoned foodstuffs from helicopters for the ignorant savages to 'consume' and decompose.

When killing people, these respectable businessmen use precisely the same justification as the Mafia: 'It's business. Nothing personal.' And 'civilised' politicians and businessmen of the world, knowing these facts, expediently turn a blind eye, as their national economies rely on the wood supply — not least the tabloid newspapers, using it profligately to churn out synthetic indignation over comparatively petty murders, thefts, muggings, assaults, acts of hooliganism and vandalism, etc., fully aware the paper they are printing it on is soaked in blood more innocent than the 'civilised' blend.

Instead of indulging hypocrisy and ignorance by tendentiously arguing, *argumentum ad hominem*, that I only raise such facts to justify my own crimes or those of other criminals, rather ask why you yourself are willing to justify, on a much vaster scale, any capital crime so long as it indirectly provides you with a good job and a high standard of living.

Perhaps the more complacent amongst you are by now beginning to comprehend more profoundly what the philosophy of *moral* and *legal relativism* actually means, and, more important, that you and your good neighbours have been consciously or subconsciously adopting it all your life and still are, for your own personal comfort.

Now we come to the second category of serial killer I first mentioned, those who paradoxically kill because they place a great value on life. They deliberately personalise their victims not only to avoid the unpleasant exigencies of conscience but also to gain greater pleasure from the degradation and death they are inflicting. Their murders are perceived by them to be utterly senseless and without worth unless they attribute each victim with great spiritual value and metaphysical significance. There is no pleasure in killing someone who *does not* value life. No pleasure in killing unless you *value* life.

This type of killer's main motive may be to gain revenge upon society or humanity as a whole, for some real or imaginary injury resulting in post traumatic stress which, by degrees, has nurtured neurosis to full-blown psychosis or a psychopathic pattern of rationalisation. He is out for blood, and perhaps, ironically, places more actual spiritual value on it than some clergymen solemnly intoning merely from habit.

In effect, unlike the soldier or other government-sanctioned assassin, the serial killer regards the taking of each life as an act of *cosmic significance*. He perhaps even sees himself, in a polytheistic sense, as shouting defiance at the faceless gods, challenging and contemptuously daring them to intervene on behalf of his victims. Nothing less than divine intervention would have any meaning or importance to him. He is conceptually schizophrenic, in that he despises humanity as a whole yet is still able to invest the death of a single individual with great personal worth and metaphysical relevance.

You may or may not find it rather grotesque to suggest, as I now do, that the pivotal psychic ambivalence of such a killer is almost certain evidence that he is killing from despair and disgust rather than natural malevolence.

Like the 'Night Stalker,' Ricardo Ramirez, dealt with in an earlier chapter, this category of serial killer could be regarded as a disillusioned idealist, a moral perfectionist. A person who, so resentful of the zoological aspects of human existence in general, is determined to outdo in cynical savagery every person on earth, perhaps as a result of remaining unable to discern the essential psychic contradiction involved. If he were able to spot the flaw in his own fatal philosophy, resentful rage could make him twice as dangerous.

In my opinion, Carl Panzram was such a man. A killer fierce enough to send shivers of apprehension down even the spines of hardened criminals. A man perceived by others to be totally devoid of conscience or the least conception of compromise. A killing machine as lethal and remorseless as a shark. Someone either to be given as wide a berth as possible, or shot at point-blank range in the back of the head repeatedly, without warning, with a heavy-calibre revolver until dead and beyond salvage. Lesser measures and precautions in dealing with Carl Panzram would certainly have put your own life at risk.

Carl Panzram was born on 28th June, 1891, the fourth child of German parents who emigrated to America in search of the good life. His father, a sullen man with a violent temper, ended up a farm labourer. Still ambitious in this land of opportunity, he eventually managed to save up enough money to buy a small farm in Minnesota. But an earlier, less famous version of the Dust Bowl Depression that hit farmers in the 1920 and '30s (immortalised in Steinbeck's novel, *The Grapes of Wrath*) wiped out his hard-earned investment. Dispirited and discouraged, Carl Panzram's father simply packed up and left his family without a backward glance, never to return.

Here we have the first part of the classic pattern in the lives of many criminals: the broken home and the children neglected by the remaining overworked parent, through force of circumstance rather than deliberate cruelty.

In Carl's case it was in his most formative, learning years. A time when some sense of parental care and love was essential. A time when he needed to know someone really cared about him.

Frustrated by lack of reciprocal response, he became disruptive and pre-cociously violent. A tendency perhaps partly compounded by inheritance of his father's similar characteristics, and partly an attempt to gain some kind of attention that would reinforce a significant sense of identity and uniqueness. He was not to know that he would become one of the most unique criminals ever to have lived.

Panzram's first efforts were modest. At eight years of age he was charged with being drunk and disorderly. At school, he was regularly chastised for disobedience, and thrived on it. He then burgled a neighbour's house and ran away from home — perhaps another sign of attention-seeking, or the first stirrings of the obsessive independence which was to characterise his whole life. Having reached the ripe age of eleven, he was sent to reform school by some fool judge who thought it would do him some good. It did, in a manner that society would live to regret.

They made the fatal mistake of trying to break his spirit by beating and whipping him for the least infraction of the petty rules. It was like trying to douse fire with petrol. The day was not far off when Carl would be making rules of his own. If the authorities believed cruelty was a virtue, he would give them a taste of their own improving and reforming remedy.

There was one form of mental arithmetic for which he had developed an avid passion: keeping account of every wrong done to him, along the resolution to pay it back with interest at the first opportunity.

He had by then conceptualised his real enemy. Mankind. 'I began to hate those who abused me. Then I began to think I would have my revenge as often as I could injure someone else. Anyone at all would do. If I couldn't injure those who had injured me, then I would injure someone else.' That statement by the adult Carl reflects the misanthropic rationale of possibly the majority of serial killers, consciously or subconsciously, and no deterrent will sway them slightly from their chosen mission. In this they possess the zeal of the converted, martyrs. Revenge becomes the *raison d'être*.

His one religious experience consisted of being sent to a Lutheran school, where again they tried to teach by beatings. In the course of one such lesson in violence from the preacher, Carl drew a stolen revolver and tried to shoot him but the hammer fell on a dud bullet. He knew that this attempted murder would mean his being sent back to reform school or worse.

His beliefs and lethal philosophy of life were now irreversible: 'The only way to reform people is to kill them.' The articulate birth of a highly intelligent, homicidal psychopath, icy and incisive, divulging the incipient cancer in his youthful soul. A La Rochefoucauld, Nietzsche or de Sade would have heartily applauded his sentiments.

Carl promptly hopped a freight train and headed out into the unsuspecting world to avenge himself on life.

Panzram is another prime example of multi-motivational, multi-attributable reprisal. When dealing with authorities of any description, individually petty-minded tyrants, you must never wait for anyone to accept responsibility, for it is against their cowardly nature to do so. You must, without hesitation or pointless consultation, confer responsibility on the obvious culprits and decide the price you will make them pay, *one way or another.*

In short, you must act as tyrannically as they do, but solely on your own authority. Panzram did not need to be taught this principle, of course, as you shall see.

We next observe the still youthful Carl imprisoned for robbery. He and another youth of similar violent disposition managed to escape and go on a spree of robbery and indiscriminate mayhem. An existential celebration of freedom, in which action for the sake of action was both a means and an end.

Totally out of character for a man who loathed discipline and authority, Carl joined the army. Certainly not from patriotism. The brevity of his formal stay suggests there was an ulterior motive involved — most probably to hide from the police and simultaneously gain expertise in the use of firearms and all forms of destruction. He quickly earned himself a court-martial for insubordination and received three years in an army prison, where he promptly destroyed the prison workshop by setting it ablaze.

Secretary of War then was Howard Taft. Characteristically, still keeping personal accounts and settling old scores, Carl profitably robbed Taft's home some years later! Taft must be considered fortunate that Carl didn't burn the house down as well.

Released from the army prison, his criminal career became rather aimless. For four or five years he was in and out of various prisons for robbery and other offences. Finally he received a somewhat excessive sentence of seven years for burgling the house of a bank president. In later years, Carl maintained that he had struck a deal with the police for a lenient sentence in exchange for telling them where the proceeds of the burglary were stashed away, but that the police had then double-crossed him.

He decided to settle that account by immediately burning down part of the prison, after which he was battered unconscious by guards and transferred to a stricter prison regime in Oregon. There he repeatedly attacked the brutal guards, who in turn savagely beat him and kept him shackled in windowless punishment cells. Next he started a riot and, again, set fire to and totally destroyed the prison workshop!

Despite progressively inhuman treatment, year after year, they could not break Panzram's spirit. He seemed to possess superhuman will and strength, which caused him to be feared by every guard and admired by every prisoner. Psychologically, a state of affairs the prison authorities regarded as a disaster.

Holding all the top cards, they had still lost the game, because unless attacking in packs, prison guards who pose as macho are innately spineless, and, equating their uniforms with intelligence, their already inferior brains slowly atrophy.

Although they know the public needs them, they are still regarded as social pariahs normal individuals would not wish to befriend. Which is why prison guards suffer from an inferiority complex. Many are actually certifiable psychopaths and psychotics, who can kill prisoners and get away with it because they are part of the law enforcement industry, testifying for one another for collective safety. They stick together to reinforce their mutual corruption and mendacity.

Decent people in their ranks, with ideas of reform and rehabilitation, soon depart when they see the negative reality of the penal system. Thus only the inadequates are left to run the prison, by collective violence. Sadly, as most of the prisoners are themselves inadequate, unsuccessful petty criminals, this caters to the delusional superiority of the illiterate guards, the majority of whom are 'uniform freaks,' i.e., people who can't manage to retain and function in any capacity unless they have a uniform, any uniform, to bolster their psyche and protect them from revealing their lack of intelligence.

As touched upon earlier, some serial killers suffer from a non-affective category of schizophrenia, as good and evil continue the eternal struggle for control of the psyche. If the next illustration, of how this polarised tension warred even within Panzram, were not fully documented and officially authenticated, you would tend to disbelieve it.

By a stroke of good fortune, the inhumane warden of the prison was shot dead during the pursuit of an escaped convict. In the incestuous manner in which penal establishments are run solely for the profit of the staff, his equally ruthless brother became warden. This man tried the same harsh treatment on Panzram, who reacted by smashing up everything in sight with a two-handed axe.

The warden persevered in his policy of benighted brutality until he overstepped even prison standards by using methods of punishing prisoners that had been forbidden by state law and was dismissed.

The new warden who took over from him was a man called Murphy. He was that remarkable exception, a Christian who actually practised what he preached. Hearing of Panzram's fierce reputation, Murphy decided to use kindness where brute force had obviously failed. He saw to it that Panzram was given back his privileges, such as books and access to canteen facilities.

Panzram was naturally suspicious of this new approach and remained hostile and uncommunicative towards the prison authorities, wondering what game they were up to.

One day Murphy took the bull by the horns — one might say literally, with a man such as Panzram — and managed to have a conversation with Carl, which led to an astonishing offer being made to him.

Murphy must have been a man of shrewd psychological insight. He saw that Panzram could stand up to any amount of punishment with contempt and was perfectly at ease on such familiar ground, so he hit on what he considered would be a real challenge, a real test of will for Panzram. Murphy offered to allow him to leave the prison on his own, so long as Panzram gave him his solemn word that he would come back to the prison by his own volition by evening.

Panzram probably thought he was talking to a madman or a fool and readily accepted the offer.

But deep in Panzram's psyche, there obviously remained a remnant of the integrity he had been born with, a quality he had long forgotten and probably, at a conscious level, would have regarded as a fault. His criminal integrity was, of course, never in question; he bore it proudly like shining, battered armour. But the subconscious rules every person, and Carl must have felt bemused as, having made no conscious decision, his footsteps led him inexorably back to the prison gate as evening fell.

From personal experience, I myself can vouch for how the subconscious can take over complete physical control of the body, but that's another story.

This episode could have proved a crucial change of course in Carl's nihilistic path through life, and many lives would have been saved as a result. But sometimes ostensibly small things, misdemeanours, can irreversibly sway the soul.

One night Carl got drunk with a woman and failed to return to the prison on time, so he decided to go on the run. Soon he was captured after badly injuring the arresting officers. For this he was sentenced to a further ten years. The die was cast. Panzram was now destined to evolve into one of the most prolific serial killers in early American history.

In the spring of 1918 he managed to escape.

To most people, 1918 meant the end of the first World War in Europe. But to Carl Panzram it signalled time to begin in earnest his own personal war against humanity. And, perhaps conscious of the ironic parallel, he took to sea as a sailor and ended up in war-scarred Europe, as though drawn to the sweet smell of destruction.

However, he wasn't infected by it. After a few minor scrapes with the law, he sailed back to America — this time obviously drawn to the country upon which all his psychic resentment and thirst for revenge was centred. Impatient to start settling accounts, he must have found that particular voyage very long indeed. One can imagine his great head poised like that of a natural predator, eagerly sniffing the air for approaching land and the human prey he hungered for.

For him, it was a modest beginning. He broke into the house of the Secretary of War, making a good haul, with which he bought a sailboat, but not for leisure activities — unless you count opportunistic murder.

He began to offer jobs to sailors, usually to two at a time, got them intoxicated on his boat, robbed them of all they had, raped them and then put a bullet through their heads. Binding the bodies in anchor chain, he tossed them into the sea far offshore. He killed a total of ten sailors by this method, before miscalculating one dark night, running the boat onto the rocks, thus fortuitously sparing the lives of his two latest prospective victims who were on board.

Back to square one, Panzram got work on another ship and headed for the Belgian Congo. Here and there, he — to use his phrase — 'practised a little sodomy,' caving in the head of one black youth after raping him. A time later, he shot 'six niggers' and fed them to the crocodiles, simply to steal their canoe, which someone else rashly, but just as promptly, then stole from him.

Seeing no future in hunting crocodiles, he returned to America and hunted males, sodomising and killing. Some obtuse man tried to steal a sailboat which Panzram had stolen from another man. Panzram killed him. His total of rapes and murders passed the twenty mark.

———•◦•———

Doing a bit of freight-train hopping in the company of two hoboes, Panzram was surprised by a young railroad cop who was checking the wagons. Panzram turned the tables on him by drawing a gun and ordering him to remove his trousers. He then 'practised a little sodomy on him,' and, just for the hell of it, ordered the other two hoboes to rape the cop as well, which they did. An apt act of revenge on authority from Panzram's point of view. Needless to say, after being used and tossed out of the freight car, the distressed and sorely-tried policeman wisely kept his silence and, presumably, his trousers.

Panzram was next caught burgling a rail office. He received a stiff sentence of five years and was sent to the notorious Dannemora Prison. There he was faced with the same old inhuman regime and reacted violently as usual.

He made an escape attempt but only managed to break his ankles when dropping from the wall. Doing punishment in 'the hole,' his compensatory visions of destruction and mayhem became progressively more feverish and grandiose, as did those of the Marquis de Sade when incarcerated in the Bastille.

Panzram's solitary dreams included the derailing of a passenger train, the burning down of fully occupied grand hotels, and putting drums of cyanide in reservoirs supplying cities with drinking water. No act of destruction was too great for his resentful, seething psyche. Had the globe been miraculously transformed to an orange in his massive fist, he would have crushed it till the last pip squeaked.

'The deeper the sorrow the less tongue it hath.' — The Talmud

Or, as Carl himself put it, 'I was so full of hate that there was no room in me for such feelings as love, pity, kindness or honour or decency. I hated everybody I saw.'

Penal fanatics please carefully note, for you are systematically fostering many more Panzrams in your human warehouses at this very moment and, when they are eventually set free, or set themselves free, some of your number won't have time to whistle 'Dixie' or even say 'Amen.'

———•◦•———

Panzram, now afflicted with a permanent limp, was unfettered from Dannemora Prison without a cent in his pocket, and nobody wants to employ ex-convicts. So was he expected to simply starve or eat out of garbage cans?

He immediately burgled a house in Washington, taking a radio to sell and buy some much-needed nourishment; the householder, a dentist, was most fortunate that he didn't surprise Panzram in the act, for it would have been his last act. At any rate, Panzram was eventually arrested when trying to sell the radio and thrown into Washington District Jail.

It was in this unlikely and uninspiring location that some arcane mixture of time, circumstance and chance acquaintance gradually led Carl Panzram to needlessly reveal his unknown career as a highly travelled, rapacious and intelligent serial killer. There is no doubt whatsoever that the unexpected catalyst, responsible for Panzram's out-of-character decision to finally explain himself to another human being, for the first and final time, took the incredible shape of all Panzram had hated and despised the whole of his life. A representative of the totalitarian authority Panzram reserved an incandescent rage for, namely, a prison guard.

The name of this remarkable confessor was Henry Lesser, and a less likely recipient of Panzram's confidences could not be imagined, you might think. But all was not as it seemed.

Henry Lesser was far from being your run-of-the-mill prison guard, i.e., ignorant, brutal and lazy. He was a bright young Jew with ideals; an avid reader but not an intellectual. Like Carl, his upbringing had been impoverished and underprivileged but, very unlike Carl, he had not grown up with a chip on his shoulder or a wealth of homicidal resentment to assuage.

And perhaps there lies the key to Panzram's puzzling affinity with this man, and his almost casual decision to consciously seal his own fate forever by totally confiding in him and imparting the details of his extraordinary acts of murder and devastation.

I believe Panzram saw in Henry Lesser the man he himself might have been. I don't mean Panzram would have become a prison guard, of course, but rather would have evolved as a highly intelligent man who had triumphed over the adversities of his childhood and come to terms with life.

Part of him probably envied Henry Lesser. It was as if Carl was confessing to a personification of his better self, the child who had withered and died so far in the past but had not been entirely forgotten. But let us not forget the almost demoniacal man Carl Panzram had actually become, one who possessed the scornful, resplendent individualism, pride and will for revenge, of Lucifer.

There can be no doubt that Panzram, in confessing, had resolved that the moment had at last arrived to embrace Death voluntarily, as an old friend and ally he had long awaited to rid him of the repugnant, tedious world he had battled with all his life. It was time for Panzram to straighten his scarred back, disregard his limp, and formally present the sum total of reckoning he had exacted from humanity.

Did they really believe that he, Carl Panzram, had let them off so lightly? That they had inflicted upon him more damage than he upon them? What fools! Now they would hear the price they had paid for crass insolence, the collective pile of worms, and know that he would have crushed a million-fold more had it been within his power! Now was the time for the insects to crowd together and kill him while he laughed and spat his venom at them.

> Samson hath quit himself
> Like Samson, and heroically hath finish'd
> A life heroic.
>
> — 'Samson Agonistes,' Milton

Panzram's self-destructive, personal Rubicon was crossed in characteristically contemptuous style, as casually as casting his life like a bone to a ravenous dog.

His trial for burgling the dentist's house and stealing a radio was set for 11 November. As earlier recounted, Panzram's personal general declaration of war upon humanity had commenced in parallel with the conclusion of the First World War in Europe, which ended on the *eleventh hour of the eleventh day of the eleventh month*, 1918. Again, a fascinating synchronicity of events in time had occurred.

Some unknown force had drawn Henry Lesser's attention and curiosity to Panzram, who was of striking, formidable appearance. With his leonine head, large black drooping moustache and 'agate-hard eyes' accenting his pugnacious features, he bore a remarkable resemblance to the Mexican guerrilla leader Emiliano Zapata, who was betrayed, ambushed and shot dead by the Mexican army in 1919.

The gradual friendship between Lesser and Panzram began when Lesser broke the icy reserve of the man by inquiring about the burglary charge and his scheduled trial. Lesser, in a social manner, casually asked Panzram what his line of criminal enterprise was, and Panzram made his famous blunt reply,

'I reform people.'

Puzzled, Lesser asked him to explain what he meant. Panzram slowly smiled, 'The only way to reform people is to kill them.'

The reply and the implacable expression in Panzram's eyes chilled Lesser. Was the prisoner insane? There was more than enough proof of Panzram's violent temperament in his prison records, but they also showed that he had never killed anyone inside or outside of prison. However, examining the account of Panzram's arrest by the police for stealing a radio, it quoted Panzram as having laughed at them and, when asked what was so funny, he had laconically replied, 'Because a charge of stealing a radio is a joke. I've killed too many people to worry about a charge like that.'

Naturally the police had regarded such an unasked-for and fatal confession as another more morbid joke by Panzram. But Henry Lesser, who had been impressed by Carl's open air of unconcerned sincerity, was far from certain that Panzram had simply been indulging in gallows humour. Why would a man with the obvious strength of character and will as Panzram intentionally make such a fatal admission? He had no history of mental illness that would explain away his outlandish conduct as mere fantasy or delusion.

During a routine cell search that same day, guards discovered that the window bars in Panzram's cell had been tampered with and slackened in their frame. Mob-handed, the guards returned to Panzram, beat him with long, lead-loaded riot-sticks, handcuffed his arms behind his back and frog-marched him down to the punishment block.

There they attached a rope to the handcuffs, slung it over a beam and hoisted Panzram up till only his toes touched the floor — an excruciating, ancient method of torture used by the Spanish Inquisition, designed to dislocate the shoulders.

Panzram was left like that for a total of twelve hours and he never cried out.

Typically, as is still done today, a prison 'doctor' occasionally put a stethoscope to Panzram's heart in case there was any danger of him actually dying, which would cause them to work late, filling in bothersome forms and getting their stories straight for anyone who might bother to investigate the death of a prisoner.

That, my 'respectable' friends, is what you pay taxes for, and I know that it won't worry you one bit — until you make a mistake some day and land in prison yourself, bleating for sympathy you won't get from the outside world, because you knew what was happening and did not intervene when you had the opportunity to do so.

I am not suggesting that Panzram was a sympathetic figure, merely that *any* prisoner, no matter what the offence, can end up receiving the very same treatment as Carl Panzram. You think not? Then let me remind you that Panzram was in prison simply for *stealing a radio*.

———•◆•———

The guards eventually unbound the battered and bleeding Panzram and threw him into a punishment cell, where he lay semi-conscious on the concrete. Occasionally the guards called in to the cell and beat him as he lay there spitting curses at them. They again strung him up on the beam in the same position as before. He lost consciousness. When he came to, he was back in his own cell, probably because the guards were scared that he might die in the punishment block.

Henry Lesser got to know about what had been happening to Panzram. It is against prison regulations for any guard to give a prisoner anything he is not entitled to. So, through another convict, Lesser covertly sent a dollar to Panzram so that he could buy some food and tobacco from the prison canteen.

When the prisoner gave him the dollar, Panzram was suspicious that he was being set up so the guards could give him another beating. But the prisoner eventually convinced him that the offer was genuine, and was amazed to see tears appear in Panzram's eyes.

This big man, who had stood up to all the beatings and tortures the guards could hand out, had been made to weep by one kind gesture.

Kindness can be an extremely vicious weapon, when someone has deliberately programmed himself to deal with anything but. It sneaks through the defences like a knife between the ribs.

On one occasion, in the punishment cells, the offer of a cigarette from a prisoner once had the same effect on me, especially as I had initially threatened the prisoner when he proffered the cigarette, thinking he was only taunting me in a dire situation.

Quite frankly, I'd rather do without such gestures of generosity in prison, as it isn't worth the candle, and you have the trauma of having to get back into a normal character for the next run-of-the-mill, illiterate, looking-for-trouble guard or prisoner who comes along. Kindness has no place within a penal institution. It is also a sensible practise not to read any books which might induce human or altruistic sentiment.

Turn soft in prison and the sharks will surely close in swiftly to finish you off. Once you pass through a prison gate for breaking the law, no law exists —

except that of the strong and ruthless. Which explains why most prisoners are impatient to be released and give people in the outside world a taste of the same amorality they have been made to endure.

The danger of moral ambivalence or weakness is exemplified by Panzram thanking Lesser and saying: 'That's the first time any screw has done me a favour.' If you are thinking this was an oblique plea for more humane treatment, forget it.

The usual type of people who become prison guards, social inadequates and illiterates, do so because they know they are innately substandard goods and therefore hate or are afraid of normal company. They are farther beyond salvage or reformation than most of the inmates, which is why prisoners laugh at the officially expressed ludicrous concept that prisoners are supposed to be reformed by such moral bankrupts. All is most certainly not for the best in this worst of all possible worlds.

> I cannot but conclude the bulk of your natives to be the most
> pernicious race of little odious vermin that nature ever suffered
> to crawl upon the surface of the earth.
>
> — Jonathan Swift (1667–1745)

As recounted, Panzram had reason enough to hate humanity from an early age. The obvious sado-masochism of his later years, his compulsive urge to inflict like indignities on others, originated from traumatic incidents he experienced as a hobo and rider of the rails.

When he was fourteen, a group of hoboes attacked and repeatedly raped him while he was travelling with them in a freight car. During that same period, another gang of tramps offered him food, plied him with whisky, and raped him while he was intoxicated.

As he grew older and wiser, he contracted a venereal disease from a prostitute and avoided women from that moment on.

That is not to say that Panzram was homosexual. Like John Wayne Gacy, Panzram chose to rape men and boys as a more sexually satisfying method of catering to his sado-masochistic compulsions, adding a more vicious dimension to the punishment he was intent upon inflicting on society as a whole, and mirroring the suffering he had himself experienced in the same manner. That is the major key to enter Panzram's psyche and methodology: his obsession with settling accounts made him believe in revenging wrongs done to him by paying back in precisely the same coin. This method of revenge reveals also that those particular wrongs suffered had traumatically hurt and damaged Panzram sufficiently for him to wish to duplicate them compulsively upon others. A logical and psychologically satisfying system of compensatory retaliation.

We shape the present and the future by examining the past. Revenge is sweeter when supped cold, as they say. And as I said of myself in Chapter One, Panzram echoed: Might is Right.

I reiterate, you will observe throughout world history that the rights or wrongs of ethics are dictated merely by strength. Everything is ethical if you are on the winning side. The rest is window dressing for armchair moralists to fiddle around with.

Meanwhile, in the Washington District Jail, Panzram had been informed that newspaper reporters had heard of the remarks he had made about having murdered many people. Panzram refused to entertain their offers of interviews. But, amazingly, he told Henry Lesser that, if he could get him some paper and a pencil, he would write his own life story.

There is not the least doubt in my mind that, to some extent, Panzram was being cleverly manipulated by Lesser and the prison authorities.

Lesser must surely have felt it his duty to pass on Panzram's confessions to the authorities — as subsequent leaks to newspapers confirm — who would have then encouraged Lesser to gain Panzram's confidence further and report to them any incriminating facts Panzram divulged to him in trust. A man of Panzram's experience and intelligence must have known about this collusion right from the beginning, but it had not affected his liking for Lesser as an individual.

There is no question that Lesser must be given full credit for the astonishing revelations Panzram was about to commit to paper. Had Panzram hated him as much as he did the other prison guards, he would not have given Lesser the time of day, let alone the privilege of being the first person to be told the homicidal details of his life.

This extraordinary relationship between Panzram and Lesser can be more readily comprehended in the context of my earlier analysis, namely, that the dismal future which remained to Panzram was not worth the effort and that the time had come for him to depart this life, but not before experiencing the primal satisfaction, the resentful and triumphant joy, of telling all the world the horrific price he had inflicted upon humanity for the wretched life they had inflicted upon him since childhood.

It would also have appealed to Panzram's ironic sense of justice that he should force them to murder him for murder — thus, in one stroke, making a mockery of their claims to moral superiority and, simultaneously, impelling them to perform the only favour he now wished from the pathetic hypocrites: that of ending his miserable life and letting him escape from their loathsome company for eternity.

The vengeful, unholy litany of almost his entire existence had been anticipating this glorious moment of presenting his final judgmental invoice to wan faces, before scathingly bidding farewell, that in heartfelt sorrow he had not killed more of them! Death had been his one constant reason for living. His solitary love. Yet perhaps even Panzram, in his final hour, would happily smile at some long-forgotten childhood memory, a Kane 'Rosebud,' as it suddenly surfaced from the depths, reminding him of the innocence he once briefly owned.

Lesser secured pencil and paper for Panzram. This act then being against prison rules is further evidence that the prison authorities were manipulating the situation. As Panzram penned his brief autobiography over the weeks, he gave it to Lesser in sections and chapters.

The time for Panzram's trial arrived.

In accordance with his suicidal intent, he refused to be represented by an advocate and chose to speak for himself in court. As soon as he entered the witness box it became clear why.

He swiped trivialities out of the way by immediately admitting he had stolen the radio and then directed a cold, malignant statement at the jury:

'While you were trying me here, I was trying all of you too. I've found you guilty. Some of you I've executed. If I live I'll execute some more of you. I believe the whole human race should be exterminated. I'll do my best to do it every chance I get. Now, I've done my duty, you do yours.'

They did.

The judge, obviously taking the threats seriously, sentenced him to twenty-five years. Panzram was returned to Washington District Jail, where he continued to write his life story for Lesser.

The time for Panzram's transfer came. The authorities had wisely arranged that Lesser would be one of the escorts to accompany him, to exert a calming influence. Panzram was manacled to other convicts and transported by train to Leavenworth Penitentiary, Kansas.

Penitentiary?

> Sinning is the best part of repentance.
>
> — Arabic proverb

On the train to Leavenworth, Panzram intended to make an attempt to destroy the train by pulling the emergency cord when the train was on a dangerous bend, in a tunnel, or steaming at maximum speed. A convict informed on him to one of the prison guards escorting the train. Panzram attacked him and was pulled off by the guards, who then wisely disconnected the emergency cord.

From personal experience, I can assure you that, if you are without hope, it is surprisingly easy to face death when consoled by the certainty that you will take some of the enemy with you.

Having finished his written life story and given it all to Henry Lesser, it is safe to conclude that, in a sequestered region deep in Panzram's psychopathic personality, some psychic tremor decided it was now time for him to speed up the process of contemptuously closing the door upon life. He had begun to ease himself into a compensatory death-wish syndrome, a state of expedient dissociative reaction, an irresistible, self-destructive impulse which, in more meagre design and spite, had hounded him practically the whole of his waking existence.

The cold embrace of steel manacles, the sweaty rankness of crowded prisoners, the arrogant indifference of ignorant guards, the bleak prospect of another brutal prison, all now travelling inexorably towards him along the desolate, monotonous rails — what better than to end it all in a final cataclysmic act of mayhem and destruction, dashing himself and the whole contemptible mess of them into a crashing, craggy grave! And him the sole one glad to go! The Nietzschean sense of dancing delight when rushing eagerly to meet the singing void. Oh, yes, the void indeed croons sweetly at such times. You may hear it yourself one day, and remember.

Panzram's deathly disposition would have been added to by the glacial *gestalt* Leavenworth presented as the train drew to a halt.

Shrouded in snow grimy from the smoke from the boiler house stacks, it looked like a stale, mouldy wedding cake made of granite, the five storeys of small cell windows like black currants. An unappetising offering to a starving spirit.

Panzram started his stretch in the manner he intended to continue.

When the warden gave the assembled new arrivals his standard pompous catechism of do's and don'ts, designed to impress upon them their lowly status, Carl deigned to make only one laconic comment, 'I'll kill the first man that bothers me.'

The warden was not amused. Haughtiness of office made him blind to the obvious sincerity of the threat. He had presumably been less than diligent in the examination of Panzram's recorded history — particularly his astonishing devotion to the art of demolishing prison establishments single-handed.

Carl was put to work in the prison laundry. A location almost custom-made to exacerbate his volatile temperament. Add to this the fact that the prison was grossly overcrowded, prisoners unavoidably invading the spatial territory of one another, becoming as aggressive as rats in a cage, and you can predict Panzram's reaction.

To get moved from the laundry detail, the overseer being an illiterate thug and a member of the Ku Klux Klan, Panzram deliberately and overtly broke the rules, ending up in the punishment block.

He and the overseer of the laundry had taken an immediate dislike to one another, which perhaps explains why the overseer, instead of being grateful to get rid of Panzram, suicidally requested that Panzram be returned to work in the laundry after his punishment was over. It appeared that the man was out to humiliate or break Panzram. An unwise ambition, to say the very least, and a fatal misjudgment of character. He would have perhaps been safer had he slapped a grizzly bear across the nose.

Panzram was furious at being sent back to the laundry and the venom of his hated enemy. The place was worse than ever in the prevailing hot weather. He came to a pragmatic decision and bided his time patiently. Panzram already psychically and electively preparing for his own immolation, the overseer was as good as a 'dead man walking' — a term usually reserved for prisoners under sentence of death.

In the short interval before he took action against the overseer, Panzram received a letter from Henry Lesser, informing him that he had shown Panzram's written account of his life to a very well-known writer and literary critic named H.L. Mencken.

This, at first glance, suggests that Lesser had not been in collusion with the prison authorities or the police to obtain Panzram's confessions, but I still believe that he had been, and had probably written a second copy of Panzram's story for himself.

The laundry overseer's last day on earth arrived.

A good day to die weatherwise, an irritating one for a prisoner working in the humid laundry, scorching sun making temperatures and tempers rise to boiling point. Warnke, the fat overseer, waddled down between the steaming vats in the laundry to inspect the arrival of some machine parts just unpacked from crates — unaware that Panzram had done it with a crowbar.

As Warnke examined the new components, he heard a characteristic limping tread behind him. It was the last thing he would ever hear.

With a cathartic yell of hate and triumph, Panzram swung the heavy crowbar down onto his skull, and kept frenziedly swinging it until Warnke's head resembled a crushed watermelon oozing red and grey jelly. The white supremacist was as dead as Abraham Lincoln. Panzram, now raging with bloodlust and purgative nihilism, swung the dripping crowbar at anyone foolish enough to block his chosen path. He limped inexorably out of the laundry and into the prison proper like a latter-day wounded Attila the Hun without his horde, his Rome the warden's office.

Panzram smashed his way into the general offices, glass and splintered wood flying everywhere, the puny clerks fleeing at his colossal approach. The warden was not there. Panzram, as though by homing instinct, altered his course towards the punishment block and ordered the guards to open the gate, which they, eyeing the gory crowbar hanging from Panzram's great fist, wisely declined to do.

Prison guards rule in a climate of collective fear, without which they shrivel. Panzram contemptuously tossed the crowbar aside like a match-stick and stood there waiting empty-handed.

The guards opened the gate and parted before him as he strolled majestically into the block, selected and entered an empty cell and banged the door shut. Prometheus self-bound, the fiery rage contained. Victory in defeat.

In Nietzsche's *Also Sprach Zarathustra*, the pivotal factor is, in my opinion, the Great Contempt or, more precisely, the Great Self-Contempt. Once a man has achieved, in a praiseworthy sense, contempt for himself, he simultaneously achieves contempt for all man-made laws and moralities, and becomes truly free to do as he wills. Plunging into the very depths, he consequently rises above all. Panzram was in the grip of that exhilarating psychic experience.

Panzram stoically waited for the prison guards to enter in force and club him to death, but to his probable astonishment no one came. Indeed, when the guards finally opened the cell door it was to escort him politely to much better accommodation next to another famous prisoner, Robert Stroud, who had also killed a taunting guard. Stroud was later to become known to the world as 'The Bird Man of Alcatraz,' portrayed with great dignity by Burt Lancaster in the film of the same title.

Panzram, writing from this more humane accommodation, made a significant comment which *should* be of some interest to prison reformers.

'If, in the beginning I had been treated as I am now, then there wouldn't have been quite so many people in this world that have been robbed, raped and killed.'

Lesser was to reply that he was lobbying for support to gain a reprieve for Panzram, but Panzram would have none of that nonsense.

'Wake up, kid. The real truth of the matter is that I haven't the least desire to reform. It took me thirty-six years to be like I am now; then how do you figure that I could, if I wanted to, change from black to white in the twinkling of an eye?'

An example that even some of the worst of criminals can still retain integrity. And, conversely, we know that some of the most respectable of men cannot, and it's certainly a luxury no successful modern politician can afford.

> It is dangerous to be virtuous in a corrupt century.
>
> — Marquis de Sade

Panzram thoroughly enjoyed the falls of the high and mighty, as I do. He commented upon a particular case in a letter to Lesser, involving the warden of Deer Lodge Prison, who also happened to be the local mayor:

'He wound up his career by blowing out his own brains because he was due for a bit of his own cells for charges of stealing the state funds and a host of other crimes.'

Lesser continued to try to help Panzran, commissioning an eminent psychiatrist to interview him to see if he was certifiably insane. In the patronising manner most psychiatrists adopt towards prisoners, the psychiatrist, a man named Menninger, foolishly suggested to Panzram that he did not believe he was capable of hurting anyone who had not done him personal harm or injury.

Panzram, in lieu of a spoken reply, lunged at Menninger, only the length of his chains preventing him from getting his hands round the man's neck and strangling him right there and then. Menninger beat a hasty retreat.

The Sanity Commission eventually certified Panzram as insane, but the federal authorities still put him on trial in Topeka, Kansas, for a medically unqualified jury to decide whether he was insane or not — just as, as already recounted, an English judge did in the case of Peter Sutcliffe. Such grotesque decisions are made for political reasons, and not from any sense of justice.

Upon the judge's directions the jury naturally found Panzram guilty — they being simple props used to endorse a political manoeuvre for votes, an appearance of fairness and impartiality.

Panzram cynically laughed when the judge sentenced him to death, and told his defence lawyer not to appeal against the sentence. Panzram was not a man who would ask for mercy from anyone, especially the legal authorities.

However, a legal snag arose of its own accord.

At that particular period, the death penalty was forbidden by law in Kansas. The absurdity and hypocrisy of all this legal and political conniving enraged Panzram. He was eager for death and, probably to show his contempt for the authorities haggling over him, made several attempts to commit suicide. When a delegation of do-gooders was allowed to speak to him from outside the cell bars, attempting to persuade him to sign a petition to the state governor asking for clemency, Panzram shook the bars furiously and spat red rage at them, longing to wring their necks for interfering in what he regarded as his personal affairs. In his eyes they presented an affront to his dignity and the will to die.

He then wrote a lengthy letter to President Hoover, informing him he wanted no mercy or reprieve.

<hr>

The official reported descriptions of how Panzram walked to his execution were, unintentionally, a fitting tribute to the resentful and vengeful philosophy which had guided his whole existence.

> The tigers of wrath are wiser than the horses of instruction.
> — William Blake (1757–1827)

As the first frosty approach of Fall withered the leaves, Panzram, at approximately 6 am, on September 5th, 1930, strolled jauntily along the corridor between the escorting guards singing an obscene limerick, probably composed by him lovingly for his final farewell appearance.

Unfortunately, none of the spectators had the presence of mind or enterprise to note down the words of the composition for posterity, as Panzram would no doubt have wished.

As he approached the scaffold his twinkling dark eyes fell on an assembly of clergy waiting to add piety to the occasion. He turned to the warden and roared, 'Get those Bible-backed cocksuckers out of here! Now let's get going. What are we hanging around for?!'

Panzram had successfully disrupted the organized, sham dignity of the authorities and turned their absurd threads of morality into an hilariously farcical and embarrassing charade. The last man to feel the cutting edge of Panzram's tongue was the hangman. When this public servant solicitously asked Panzram if he had any last words or requests, Panzram swung on him.

'Yes, hurry it up, you Hoosier bastard! I could hang a dozen men while you're fooling around!'

I laugh with delight even now at Panzram's magnificent final performance on earth, full of such tremendous insolence and spirit. Those were Panzram's final words, his contemptuous goodbye to a world he loathed having to breathe in. The lever was pulled, the trapdoor opened. With that fall the world became a duller place. A great spirit had flown. A star had been extinguished. The air seemed subdued.

> The value of life lies not in the length of days but in the use you make of them; he has lived for a long time who has lived little. Whether you have lived enough depends not on the number of your years but on your will.
>
> — Montaigne

Chapter Eighteen
The Hillside Stranglers

My soul, do not seek immortal life, but
exhaust the real of the possible.

Pindar (518–438 B.C.)

In the previous chapter on Dean Corll, I alluded briefly to the psychiatric mechanism known as *folie à deux*, by which, in a close relationship, a mental illness or abnormal pattern of behaviour in a dominant individual is simultaneously contracted by a second subordinate individual. The two individuals become, as it were, two minds with but a single psyche.

Pragmatically, leaving aside the abnormal or criminal element in this process, it could reasonably be argued that *folie à deux* occurs in most normal love affairs, where two individuals unconsciously begin to share and combine their tastes and beliefs and gradually behave as one entity, an almost telepathic communion of minds taking place between them.

Logical extension therefore indicates that criminality, like any other form of behaviour, is a learning process which can occur through: (a) a close relationship with a person whose drives and motivations are not considered by others to be the norm; (b) the aptitude of an individual to analyse, reject or accept the definitions of another as to what is lawful or unlawful, their ultimate conclusions depending largely upon personal experience and observation as to who benefits most by this or that law — a rudimentary methodology of moral relativism which, unfortunately, most people are not fully conscious of and, therefore, fail to extend and develop into an active philosophy.

Just as it is my already expressed opinion that an individual can only be corrupted if the seeds of corruption are are already within and predisposed to flower, it is also my contention that most people have no real natural respect for laws made by the arbitrary for their own benefit, and only refrain from ignoring or breaking said laws from fear of penalty, not fear of the 'crime' itself.

Lack of will and power are weaknesses, not virtues, no matter how much one tries to rationalise.

If one accepts that hypothesis, the *folie à deux* principle, or intellectual/emotional form of persuasion and conversion, can only convince if the person subjected to it is already fertile soil in which such proposals will readily take root. In short, the criminal desires, of one sort or another, are already there in every individual, simply lying dormant and awaiting the catalyst, the person who can teach the fastest and most pragmatic method of *safely* achieving those desires, whether by legal or illegal means.

It is human nature that, if caught, the pupil will blame the master for his criminal conduct. But, should the criminal enterprises succeed, I can assure you, from wide personal experience, the pupil's zeal and devotion to criminal activities can *outdo* that of the master like that of a convert.

Nothing succeeds like success. It is also axiomatic that *the quickest way to gain a confidence is to give one.* In which case, the pupil having integrated the master's knowledge into personal innate reserves, it is possible that role reversal can occur, the surpassed master, consciously or subconsciously, becoming the apt pupil/victim of *folie à deux.* Therefore, the determinants of criminal behaviour can be demonstrated to be a fluctuating compound of both internal and external multi-motivations and multi-attributes. We should perhaps rather more fully comprehend and treasure our 'flaws' or 'criminal' aspirations, as their often effortless practice and tenacious durability possibly argue them to be the most natural and genuinely hereditary or predatory qualities a person possesses. Enlightened or pragmatic atavism, as it were.

Many writers fear more being understood than misunderstood; I am not one.

The members of an Eastern monastic order literally walk through the secular world with eyes tightly closed so as not to see the wickedness that abounds there, thus, theoretically, remaining pure in mind and spirit. How much more illuminating were they to keep their eyes and minds widely open, appreciating and guarding against the guileful ways of the world.

The wise are less easily fooled than the innocent. The longer one delays confronting an unpleasant reality the more unpleasant it becomes. Basically you must know how to construct defences but also when to shift into attack mode.

> When they see an advantage but do not advance on it, they are weary.
>
> — *The Art of War*, Sun Tzu

On 17 October 1977, as the usual tail-to-tail columns of morning traffic made sluggish progress along the freeways into the working heart of Los

Angeles, drivers either baking in the heat or choking on the blue smog of exhaust fumes, the Los Angeles County Sheriff's Department received a call reporting a woman's body having been found near the expensive slopes of Forest Lawn Cemetery, final gateway to the stars.

The body of the black girl was nude, sprawled as though doing a spot of risqué sunbathing.

From preliminary on-the-spot rectal temperature of the body, the forensic scientists estimated she had probably been murdered the evening before.

A winding swath of flattened grass, from the road at the top of the slope to where she rested, indicated the body had probably been transported to the location by vehicle and then rolled down from the road to its final resting place. Untrampled grass in the immediate vicinity of the body confirmed this.

The methodology of psychological profiling was not yet fully appreciated at that period, otherwise the killing would have been tentatively evaluated as the work of an organised psychopath, the only psychotic factor being the lack of effort expended to conceal the body. An autopsy at police headquarters revealed significant aspects.

Semen from *two men* was found in the victim's vagina and rectum, and showed that one of the men was a non-secretor, that is to say someone whose blood group could not be deduced from his sperm or saliva. The girl's prints were on record, identifying her as Yolanda Washington, a convicted prostitute whose normal beat was Hollywood Boulevard. She had been strangled with a length of fibrous material, minute traces of which still adhered to her throat. Her profession altered the police's perception of the physical evidence.

She might have (a) entertained two clients together and been killed by them; (b) entertained two separate clients in a short space of time, the second being her murderer; (c) after entertaining the two clients, either together or separately, she might subsequently have met a third who had not bothered to use her for sex (or had used a condom) and had simply strangled her. So whether there was one killer or a duo involved could not yet be properly deduced by the Los Angeles Police Department.

This indecisive situation soon changed.

In the early hours of November 1st, the naked body of another girl was discovered, this time casually discarded on the pavement in Alta Terrace Drive in La Crescenta. She had been strangled in the same way as Yolanda Washington. The autopsy revealed that the girl had undergone vaginal and anal intercourse prior to death. Again, one of the men was a non-secretor.

So now the police were certain they were dealing with a killing duo — a fact which, unfortunately, was deliberately withheld from the media and public for absurd tactical and strategic reasons. Hence the use of a singular title arose, attributing the murders to 'The Hillside Strangler.'

However, this time there were marks on the wrists and ankles of the victim indicating restraints had been used. Second, traces of adhesive tape residue were found in the region of the mouth, and there were indications that a fibrous blindfold had been used, which possibly suggested that the killers had initially not planned to murder the victim.

All the organised signs again indicated the work of a psychopath. The additional use of restraints ostensibly evidenced lack of confidence or extreme caution, perhaps to prevent repetition of some dangerous incident which had occurred during the abduction and slaying of Yolanda Washington. But again, paradoxically, the dumping of the body in a public thoroughfare was a psychotic characteristic. This contradictory evidence could perhaps best be attributed to the fact that two minds were at work, or possibly that the more dominant of the two killers, the one who did the planning and made the decisions, had a secondary form of affective schizophrenia, with probable delusions of grandeur accounting for his callousness in publicly tossing bodies aside like litter. If that deduction were valid, this killer would most likely have a criminal record or a verifiable history of mental illness.

The prints of the second victim were not on file. But the investigating detective, Sergeant Frank Salerno, instinctively, rather than according to correct psychological profiling methods, did the right thing by having his squad show morgue portraits of the girl to residents in the area of the first victim's beat on Hollywood Boulevard.

This resulted in her being speedily identified as Judy Miller, a young inexperienced part-time hooker. It was a promising sign, indicating that the killers were still confident and careless enough to continue operating in an area familiar to them.

In less than a week another girl was murdered and dumped naked in the vicinity of the Chevy Chase Golf Course. She too had been raped and strangled. When her face was flashed on television screens, she was quickly identified as twenty-year-old Lissa Kastin, a dancer and part-time waitress.

The body bore signs of restraints having been used on her wrists and ankles. Obviously the killers were sticking to the cautious method which had evolved, thus leaving a helpful crime-scene signature.

Had the Los Angeles County Sheriff's Department been applying psychological profiling techniques, the basic conclusions they should have been able to reach, founded upon the mature and successful planning the killers were adopting up until careless disposal of the corpses: (a) both killers were probably in their early thirties or forties (younger men do not usually have to buy sex or own experience of picking up prostitutes); (b) the dominant partner would most likely be the older of the two; (c) a strong bonding relationship of some sort existed between them, indicating that they were either neighbours, work colleagues or shared some other intimate attachment contributing to an abnormal degree of mutual trust; (d) one or both of them owned a presentable car to cruise for victims; (e) one of them, probably the dominant party, most likely had a criminal record or mental history involving crimes of violence, possibly of a non-affective schizophrenic nature; (f) being the eldest of the two, the most mature, the dominant partner had probably been married, divorced or separated — the latter distancing process possibly depriving him of a necessary psycho-sexual safety valve, and a means of cross-referencing or cross-validating his delusional pattern of thought and behaviour with someone he loved or trusted; (g) this spiritual/emotional lack could have eventually led him to compensate by seeking out a partner who would actively support and reinforce his violent delusions and sexual fantasies; (h) having killed twice (or possibly more) in a short space of time, confidence in the active partnership had increased and so therefore had the rate of homicides. This had further cemented the relationship and stimulated increasingly rampant psychic cravings which, by this stage, would have infected both parties, creating a destructive unity, a twin-headed, homicidal Hydra, or perhaps even a metaphysical third entity influencing their dual microcosm. A perfect example of *folie à deux*.

———·•·•———

One may believe in the existence of ultimate truth along with the conviction that no human being will ever discover it. In which case, I believe our lives are better governed by moral relativism, a system of comparative truths and ethical agnosticism.

My personal concept or definition of intelligence is dexterity; eclectic versatility. The polymathic ability to juggle multiple concepts, and the associations or synapses existing between them.

I've known academics who were intellectually constipated with knowledge. A concept is simply a string of words, the bare bones, a hypothesis, which, if believed in, should then be taken under personal ownership and expanded into whatever avenues of action the belief indicates. In short, you must breathe life into the idea or philosophy, creating an organic structure.

My personal image of the being or 'soul' is that of a kaleidoscopic sphere at our centre, its periphery forever changing and adapting to additional knowledge and experience, but held together by a core or gravitation of central beliefs by which all else is influenced and governed. It is essentially an elitist principle. Those who have neither the will nor desire to become 'unconditional,' must perforce continue to function only on the periphery of the kaleidoscope of those who do possess such qualities. There will always be people to take care of them, one way or another.

A priest who goes to work in a leper colony enjoys a personal sense and reputation of self-sacrifice. But the fact that he chose to go, that it satisfies him to go, that he knows he will be *admired* for going, demonstrates that his decision is not really self-sacrificial.

We all, consciously or subconsciously, choose whatever satisfies us, therefore the good or bad that develops from the choice is secondary, part of the give and take of life, its pretences and realities. We are what we believe; we live what we believe. All else is marginal and neither to our debit or credit — though it is human nature to always claim credit for altruistic spin-offs which were not consciously intended in the first instance.

The elasticity of morality can be further advanced by the use of auto-hypnosis, the aim of which is, by a process of self-analysis and systematic conditioning, to detect our weaknesses and strengths, culling the former and reinforcing the latter. In a civilised situation, our strengths may be seen as our weaknesses; in a 'law of the jungle' situation, the reverse may apply. We adapt to suit our circumstances and aims. Therefore it is essentially a technique of self-survival.

The ability to change psychic gears fast reflects a superiority beyond transient moral codes.

———•◆•———

From a personal viewpoint, it seems quite palpable that most people are prone to believe that, as they have never been in prison, they are not 'criminals'; never been in a mental institution, they are therefore 'sane.' This illustrates a form of mass *folie à deux* cultivated and encouraged by social control. In which case, the majority of you have scant reason to feel morally or intellectually superior to the 'criminal' in any way. Quite the reverse.

Barring inadequates, as already intimated, those who have had first-hand experience at the hands of the law possess a more empirical intelligence, coupled with an instinctive grasp of moral relativism, than the majority of the population, who for the most part stroll through life in a deliberately structured haze of complacency. There are some secrets we intentionally conceal even from ourselves, not least the ones enjoyed in darkness, the domain where we most naturally become ourselves and feel vitally alive.

In some people, guilt may primarily spring not from committing an illegal or immoral act but from conscious or subconscious enjoyment of others committing it. In much the same manner as you are enjoying reading about acts of lust and murder at this very moment, drawn irresistibly to it despite, and in some cases because of, the artificial respectability and morality you are constrained to observe and subconsciously despise and resent. And why not?

You crave to be fully alive, taste the reality of experience — reading of crime being the most popular of all modern recreations. The mass media know only too well how such key words as 'scandalous,' 'horrific,' 'shocking,' 'appalling,' 'chilling,' 'perverted,' 'revolting,' etc., attract the 'law-abiding' like bees to honey. Appetite for forbidden pleasures is understandably voracious, though few will formally admit it and have myriad ready excuses to rationalise their attraction to the morbid.

> God give me chastity and continency — but not yet!
> — St. Augustine

The mere fact that, for the moment, you have been able to maintain a moral façade longer than those who languish in captivity, can hardly be proclaimed as moral superiority. Simply because someone possesses a stronger propensity for self-delusion, a heightened sense of self-survival, a need for social approbation, a lack of nerve and fear of penalty, a difference in taste, etc., is hardly a basis for moral self-aggrandizement.

Therefore, it would be wise to master the humble art of qualification; it will soften the blow when you slip, as so many eventually and gratifyingly do.

> The sky is darkening like a stain;
> Something is going to fall like rain,
> And it won't be flowers.
> — W.H. Auden (1907–1973)

The anonymous Hillside killers began to slide into a predictable trap of their own devising, comprised of a pincer movement: over-confidence and lust. Their psycho-sexual needs were increasing in direct ratio to degree of success. This was an encouraging development from the point of view of their pursuers, although it would entail immediate temporary drawbacks prestige-wise as the victims mounted.

Seven more victims, six bearing the unmistakable MO of the Hillside Stranglers, were claimed in rapid succession in the month of November, 1977.

However, there were reasonable doubts in the minds of the Los Angeles police that one of the seven additional victims, seventeen-year-old Kathleen Robinson, having been found fully clothed, unlike all the other previous victims, had perhaps not been murdered by the Hillside Stranglers but by a copy-cat, helping himself to an ego-trip slice of the hysterical publicity generated by the media. In tandem with this possible intrusive entry of a third opportunistic serial killer, the Hillside Stranglers themselves were about to undergo a change in appetite, indicating their palates had eventually become jaded with prostitute fare and craved a more tender form of prey.

On Sunday 20th November, another three naked victims were found discarded in one of the city's several garbage disposal sites. But this time two of the victims were missing schoolgirls, fourteen-year-old Sonja Johnson, and twelve-year-old Dollie Cepeda.

The fact that both girls had disappeared on the evening of the previous Sunday was also further alarming indication of the escalating psycho-sexual demands of the two killers. As with all previous victims, both of the schoolgirls had been raped and sodomised.

The third victim found on the rubbish dump was eventually identified by police as twenty-year-old Kristina Weckler, an art student who had been reported missing in the Glendale district of the city — the same area where earlier victim Lissa Kastin had been dumped on the slopes of the Chevy Chase Country Club.

Presumably the police would by then have been treating Glendale as a secondary target for special surveillance; their prime target should already have been the area where the very first two victims of the Hillside Stranglers were found, not far from Glendale.

Careful examination of a map indicating the disposal pattern of the corpses would, accurately interpreted, strongly suggest the probable base from which the killers were setting forth on their hunting expeditions.

After the all-important subconscious errors forced upon the killers by the novelty of their hazardous recreation, it was likely that they would belatedly adopt diversionary tactics designed to camouflage the position of their base. But if the police possessed the art to read such strategy in reverse, like an ill-conceived ploy in an elaborate game of chess, that too could betray the location the killers were trying to conceal. In this particular aspect of the game the killers were disadvantaged, being under the pressure of knowing that one mistake could lead to capture.

Conversely, if the killers were cool and intelligent enough to double-guess the police, cover up their initial errors and successfully disguise their ploys, they could retain the initiative and lead the police in a merry dance. The location chosen by the killers to dump their next victim, in some shrubbery by the side of the Golden State Freeway, could well have been just such a ploy.

The police discovered the body on 23rd November and identified it as being that of a twenty-eight-year-old student named Jane King who had been reported missing on 9th November. But the killers then reverted to their normal pattern, discarding the body of their tenth and final November victim, eighteen-year-old student Lauren Wagner, in shrubbery on Cliff Drive, Glendale.

She was discovered on 29th November, her parents having reported her missing only the night before. This time the autopsy examination revealed curious burn marks on the palms of the victim's hands, signifying that she had been tortured prior to being killed. The nature of the burns puzzled the police pathologists, the skin having retained no trace of ash or other residue to indicate how they had been inflicted.

The killers, or perhaps one of them, had now graduated to the realm of sophisticated, overt sadism, the run-of-the-mill variety inflicted by vaginal and anal rape having obviously palled by repetition. The police would have to wait until the next victim was discovered to determine whether this baffling new method of torture had found favour with the killers, thus leaving another helpful crime-signature.

The police used the media in a negative, counter-productive sense, obtaining their agreement not to tell the public that the so-called 'Hillside Strangler' murders were in fact being committed by two men, not one. What the LAPD expected to gain from this feeble strategy — apart from making it simpler for them to weed out cranks falsely confessing to the murders for instant fame — is difficult to discern.

It is always more sensible to over-estimate your opponent, thus retaining the initiative, keeping sophisticated ploys in reserve until sufficient information is gathered to estimate the intelligence of the protagonist, whose observed behaviour, conscious or subconscious, eventually reflects his personality. Only then will you be in a position to estimate his strengths and, more important, weaknesses, enabling you to employ affective proactive methods to best effect.

Axiomatically, the roles of hunter and prey are reversible; the killer may also be observing and estimating the police chiefs in the same manner, perhaps even researching their backgrounds, and using proactive ploys to which their history makes them readily susceptible.

Theoretically, in the context of covert manipulation and applied stress/distraction, anything the police chiefs can do, the killer can do better: he, after all, has the potentially major advantage of knowing the identity of his enemy, their degree of intelligence, methods previously used, and their background, including family and friends.

> Even though you are competent, appear to be incompetent. Though effective, appear to be ineffective . . . When you are going to attack nearby, make it look as if you are going to go a long way; when you are going to attack far away, make it look as if you are going just a short distance . . . Draw them in with the prospect of gain, take them by confusion.
>
> — *The Art of War*, Sun Tzu

Fear and panic were by now spreading throughout Los Angeles, fanned not least by media sensationalism, murder being the most valuable commodity of all to newspapers and television companies; the bloodier the mayhem, the better. One might almost conclude that, if murderers did not exist, the enterprising media would rush to incite or invent some at the behest of their shareholders.

The Los Angeles Police Department, going through the usual high-profile motions to reassure the public, set up a Special Task Force which included the investigating officers from the Glendale Police Department and the Los Angeles Sheriff's office. Not that they had anything new to go on, but all the busy commotion and news conferences looked good on television and attracted the usual spate of witnesses or cranks who claimed to have seen the mythical 'Hillside Strangler.'

Again, by keeping the public unaware that two killers were involved, what good were witnesses who were looking for and thought they had seen only one suspicious individual who might be the 'Hillside Strangler?' Perhaps witnesses who had seen two suspicious men in a car, conceivably the actual two killers themselves, would not regard the matter as being of any significance or worth reporting to the police.

As luck would have it, the police did get a crucial lead — by courtesy of the killers themselves, whose apparent immunity had imperceptively fostered arrogance and sloppiness, as predicted. But, against all reason, the police failed to realise the importance of the eyewitness account.

In the early hours of the morning when Lauren Wagner had disappeared, it transpired that one witness had actually seen her abducted.

By a stroke of misfortune, the killers had unknowingly chosen to strike directly outside her home and had brought her car to a halt in front of a house across from hers. The elderly occupant of the house, Beulah Stofer, roused by her dog barking, looked out of the window to see what was amiss. She immediately noticed that Lauren Wagner's car had for some reason parked outside her house rather than the Wagner household, and that the car door was open with the interior light shining. Close beside Lauren Wagner's car was another vehicle, a large dark-coloured sedan sporting a white top, and two men were arguing with Lauren Wagner.

Beulah Stofer maintained that she had not been near enough to hear what was being said or furnish a detailed description of the two men involved, but she did admit seeing Lauren Wagner reluctantly enter the dark sedan with the two men and being driven off.

The incident should have galvanised the police into action immediately, as it was the sort of lucky break they had been hoping for: a witness who had seen two men, not one. But, amazing as it seems, they did nothing at all.

The police inactivity was soon to become even more incredible.

A few hours after seeing Beulah Stofer, the detectives received a telephone call from her, in an obvious state of distress, urgently asking to see them again. When they arrived back at her house, she told them she had just received a call from a man who had first asked her if she was the lady with the dog. When she answered that she was, the man warned her that she had better keep quiet and tell the police nothing or he would kill her.

To the astonishment of the detectives, she was now able to furnish them with descriptions of the two men she had seen take Lauren Wagner away.

She described the older of the two men as being of Latin appearance with dark curly hair. The younger man had been taller, with pockmarks on his face and neck. When the detectives wondered why she had not been able to tell them all this earlier, she became evasive and flustered.

Quite obviously she had been ashamed to admit that she had been much nearer to the two men than she had at first admitted. In fact, considering the length of her driveway and the quality of light, to observe the descriptive details she now recounted she must have left the house and gone down her driveway to investigate what was taking place. This was confirmed when the detectives belatedly checked that she could not have seen anything from her front window as originally claimed.

The second major error the killers made was the telephone threat because (a) deadly fear makes people unpredictable; (b) they were as good as signalling to both her and the police that they were the killers, and that she could identify them in a line-up. It would have been more astute of them to remain silent, or kill her. They should also have calculated that, if she had already given detectives their detailed descriptions, the police could be guarding her house and tapping her phone.

In the actual event, the killers would have been profoundly relieved and jubilant had they known that the police had totally missed the significance of the witness' testimony and were doing nothing at all other than floundering around as baffled as ever.

＊＊＊

The uncertainty of the potentially catastrophic incident had obviously worried the killers.

In contrast to their former speedy rate of kills, they waited two whole weeks before gathering sufficient confidence to strike again. And this time they also changed their methodology to what they thought was a safer approach. But their enforced, *ad hoc* change of tactics for increased security had precisely the opposite effect, as such knee-jerk responses invariably do. It resulted in them furnishing the police with further important clues.

On 14th December, a call-girl agency, 'Climax,' received a telephone call from a man requesting that they send one of their girls to him at the Tamarind Apartments in Hollywood. He particularly specified that he wanted a blonde in black underwear. For this service he was prepared to pay in cash the sum of $150.

Background noises made the Climax telephonist suspect he was calling from a public telephone booth and she asked for the telephone number of his apartment. The caller glibly convinced her that he was calling from the pay-phone area of the apartment building to obviate the call being intercepted at the switchboard as he was a married man.

Subsequent police investigations discovered that the call had in fact been made from a telephone booth in the Hollywood public library.

The Climax agency sent a seventeen-year-old prostitute, Kimberley Diane Martin, to the Tamarind Apartments. On 14th December, her naked body was found discarded in a disused lot near the City Hall. Police forensics confirmed she was another 'Hillside Strangler' victim.

Detectives immediately interviewed of all occupants at the Tamarind Apartments. One helpful apartment holder, Kenneth Bianchi, a personable young Latino, helpfully volunteered that he had heard screams coming from somewhere within the apartment building but had assumed it was a domestic dispute of some sort.

The police, having traced the killer's call, next interviewed people at the Hollywood public library. One attractive young woman related that a wild-eyed man of Italian complexion had surreptitiously followed her as she wandered through the library browsing the bookshelves. None of the interviews were considered significant by the police.

A rather curious development occurred, one which the investigating police dismissed as 'screwy.' A German citizen from Berlin who claimed to possess psychic powers, flew all the way to Los Angeles to inform the Los Angeles Police Department that he believed the Hillside Strangler murders were being committed by two Italian brothers. During practically every highly publicised, baffling series of murders, people claiming to have occult capabilities invariably turn up. The interesting aspect of this particular incident was that the psychic either knew or had guessed that two men were involved in the killings, something which the Los Angeles police were still unwisely concealing from the general public. As for the truth or validity of the 'Italian brothers' part of the prediction, that only the future would reveal.

I can also speak from experience. The police used a psychic in my case. She, on two occasions, accurately described certain loci. Newspapers published her predictions and visions. After the first prediction I, always overestimating the police on principle — far too generously, as later discovered — put it down to inspired guesswork, or the police applying proactive methodology to force a wrong move. After the second accurate prediction, I began to think in terms of having the psychic source neutralised by a third reliable party from another city. There was no known connection between myself and the third party, but I insisted that he should try to make the killing look like an accident.

I still regarded the predictions as guesswork, but was pragmatic enough to take into consideration the possible psychological and random consequences of such visions and predictions. As they were public knowledge, either the police might start searching for the loci described, or, possibly the greater threat, some member of the public might recognise the loci. Conversely, if none of these possible scenarios was valid and the psychic source was neutralised in a manner eventually discovered to be non-accidental, this might validate the visions and predictions in the eyes of the police, and possibly channel their activities in directions I was trying to deflect them from. There was also the possibility that, if the police were using proactive methods, they might be expecting an attempt on the psychic's life and be waiting in readiness. So it was Catch-22. I did however suspend a final decision on the proviso that no further accurate predictions surfaced. None did.

In short, at all times I treated the matter from a purely psychological viewpoint, cautioned by personal empirical knowledge of 'criss-crosses' — the chance synchronisation of events in time — arguably, in some extraordinary circumstances, a factor of serendipity almost bordering upon the supernatural. After all, if psychic intervention were a reality, it would not only deter most criminals but also lead to widespread chaos and destruction — the mind, with its freedom of thought and action, being the final frontier that man would not tolerate being breached. At least not at the present, relatively primitive stage of human evolution.

There is perhaps a lesson in this for those progressive detectives and FBI agents interested in the art of proactive methodology — and an obvious note of discretion and prudence for 'psychics' who make lucky guesses, unaware of the very real potential dangers they could conjure upon their own heads.

———•◆•———

No further Hillside Strangler murders took place as celebrations ushered in the New Year of 1978. Then January also passed by with no new victims being added to the list. This unusually long cooling-off period encouraged police to hope that the killers had perhaps exhausted the novelty of their lethal hobby and progressed to some less harmful field of sexual stimulation. They also selfishly speculated that the Stranglers had possibly decided to give Los Angeles a rest and pursue their homicidal recreation elsewhere.

Consequently, the Task Force was beginning to slow down and relax, in relative terms, as their best efforts had produced nothing anyway.

An incident which *should* have dispelled such wishful thinking — but did not — occurred in early February. An elderly woman schoolteacher reported to the Los Angeles police that she had witnessed two men struggling with a protesting girl, attempting to force her into their car. This scene had taken place in broad daylight.

The elderly lady had possessed the gumption to stop her own car, get out, and demand that the two men desist from attacking the girl. She then described how one of the two men, curly-haired with glaring eyes, had spun round and spat an outlandish warning at her, 'God will get you for this!'

The two men had then released the struggling girl and driven off at high speed, the indignant man still cursing and glaring back ferociously at the feisty little schoolteacher. Unruffled, the elderly woman had then tried to persuade the girl to go with her to report the matter to the police. The girl was too distressed and just wanted to go home. Again, with what was now appearing to be consummate stupidity, the police casually dismissed the brave schoolteacher as some sort of religious crank and did nothing.

The so-called Special Task Force, obsessed with retaining a 'secret' which was not only self-evidently worthless but also counter-productive, had still not even bothered to inform the rank and file of the force that they were hunting two prowling abductors, not one. It must also be assumed that the Special Task Force had not issued general instructions to their foot-soldiers to report to them all attempted or actual abductions within the city.

Such a general instruction would not have compromised their precious, ineffectual secrecy, and possibly would have resulted in the two killers being captured much sooner and several lives being saved.

Including that of the next victim, found shortly after the witnessed incident, on 17th February 1978. At first it was taken to be an accident.

An orange Datsun was spotted lodged in the rocks halfway down a cliff below a lay-by on the Angeles Crest Highway near Glendale. When the empty car was hoisted back up to the road and the boot prised open, crammed into it they found the naked body of a twenty-year-old girl later identified as Cindy Hudspeth, a waitress who had worked at the Robin Hood Inn.

The deep marks of restraints that had cut into her wrists provisionally indicated she was another victim of the Stranglers. This was shortly confirmed. Forensic examination revealed that she had been raped and sodomised by two men, one a non-secretor.

———————

Considering the ineptitude and complete lack of progress of the Special Task Force, it came as something of a surprise that months passed without the Stranglers claiming another victim. Apparently the wishes of the Los Angeles Police Department had been granted and the two serial killers had left the city to hunt elsewhere.

Had the Los Angeles Police Department perhaps adopted a revolutionary new policy? That of actually boring the criminals out of the city by offering no competition?

Drop shrewdness, abandon sharpness,
And the robbers and thieves will cease to be.

— The Tao Te Ching

As one door closed in blue-hazed Los Angeles, another opened in the nondescript, sleepy little town of Bellingham in the state of Washington.

Boasting only forty thousand inhabitants, Bellingham was almost a village by American standards, but placed in a strikingly scenic setting, facing forests of pines marching up the ridges of Vancouver Island and the Strait of Juan de Fuca. The sort of place to retire to and fish away the remainder of your days in peace. However, the sudden entry of a predatory fish of alien breed put an end to all that tranquility.

Terry Mangan, the police chief presiding over the town, was not unduly worried when one morning the boyfriend of a girl student, Karen Mandic, who was attending Western Washington University, reported that Karen and another girl student, Diane Wilder, had apparently disappeared without trace after telling him they had been offered a 'house-sitting' assignment for which they would receive payment of $100.

They were explained that the empty house they were being paid to occupy and guard for a few hours belonged to some married couple who had gone off to holiday in Europe. The security guard who offered them the paid assignment had told them that something had gone wrong with the alarm system protecting the empty house, and that he did not want to leave the place unguarded while he was checking and repairing the alarms at his workshop in town.

Karen had also told her boyfriend that the man had warned her to keep the house-sitting assignment a secret, as he wasn't officially authorised to employ people for such security work without first having them checked by head office. The girls would be doing him a personal favour.

Still confident that there was nothing seriously amiss, a few casual preliminary inquiries led police chief Terry Mangan to the Coastal Security Agency, where he spoke to the man who owned the firm, Mark Laurence. It took scant time to ascertain that the security guard employed to monitor the empty house in question was named Kenneth Bianchi, a reliable employee of Italian descent and good reputation.

Mark Laurence was adamant that Kenneth Bianchi did not have the authority to employ anyone at all, even on a part-time basis, and was also positive there was some mistake, as Bianchi was a conscientious individual who lived with a local respectable girl, Kelli Boyd, and had a baby son. Bianchi's work record was impeccable. He was diligent and hard-working with no history of absenteeism.

So much for respectability; anyone can adopt its intrinsically shallow veneer and structured artifice — indeed, everyone does, except those who are finished with life, or whom life has finished, leaving no advantage to gain from further vain posturing. Only the condemned and rejected experience this truth. The remainder hobble and stumble through life tightly bound by Infernal Circles: family, social, sexual, ethnic, work, educational, moral, legal, religious, etc., etc. — a subconscious hodge-podge of constrictive, confused convolutions from the day they are born till the day they die, their natural spirit and intellect stunted and extinguished by existential irrelevancies.

The inscription above the gate to 'Society' is not the honest warning carved in stone above Dante's vision of Hell: 'Abandon Hope All Ye Who Enter Here.' Rather it is the lethal lie, *'Arbeit Macht Frei'* (Work is Freedom), as wrought in iron scroll above the gate to Auschwitz.

Again, capture makes the criminal.

> Who is to doom, when the judge himself is dragged before the bar?
>
> — *Moby Dick*, Herman Melville (1819–1891)

Police chief Terry Mangan questioned the model employee, Kenneth Bianchi, who, with every outward sign of deep sincerity, categorically denied ever knowing Karen Mandic or having offered her a house-sitting job. Bianchi then proffered an apparently perfect alibi, namely that he had been attending a conference of the Sheriff's Reserve the evening the two girls disappeared. A nice touch of respectable finesse.

Meanwhile the police were conducting a thorough search of the empty house the two missing girls had apparently been paid to house-sit. Everything in the house was found to be perfectly in order. The police regarded this as reassuring, giving reason to hope that the two missing girls had simply planned to run off somewhere and had prepared a cover story for the escapade. The fact that Karen's car, a Mercury Bobcat, was nowhere to be found, appeared to confirm this theory. However the police routinely issued an All Points Bulletin and had the media broadcast a description of the two missing girls and the car.

That same afternoon, police headquarters received a phone call from a woman who had seen the televised broadcast and reported that she had spotted a Mercury Bobcat apparently abandoned in a nearby lane and, as no one in the immediate neighbourhood of the lane possessed such a car, thought it might be the one the police were searching for.

The abandoned vehicle confirmed the worst suspicions of the police. Detectives raced to the spot. A brief glimpse into the back of the Mercury Bobcat was sufficient. The bodies of the two girls lay entwined on the floor of the car in unmistakable lassitudes of death.

Forensic teams were called in to examine the crime scene and then gently remove the two pathetic corpses for autopsies to be performed. Examination by pathologists revealed that both girls had been sexually molested and brutally strangled.

The police now had no option but to take Karen Mandic's story about being paid to house-sit seriously. A warrant was immediately issued for the arrest of the prime suspect, Kenneth Bianchi. He was not at home, and when police sped to the offices of the security firm where he worked they learned from Bianchi's boss, Mark Laurence, that he was out in his truck on patrol.

In his capacity as a security guard Bianchi carried a gun, so the detectives wisely decided that they would have to take him by surprise.

They arranged for Mark Laurence to contact Bianchi by radio and instruct him to check an empty house in the deserted outskirts of town — if police suspicions were correct, they didn't want innocent civilians to be caught in any crossfire that might ensue. The police had already staked out the house and were waiting for Bianchi when he drove up. He offered no resistance and, in fact, was very amiable and apparently somewhat bemused and amused by the whole scenario.

The reactions of a perfectly innocent man anxious to cooperate and clear matters up, or that of a seasoned serial killer?

You see, it is sometimes difficult to distinguish between the two when image is all that counts. But Bianchi was about to out-act himself.

Under interrogation at police headquarters, Bianchi continued to insist that he had never met either of the two missing girls and had not offered them any house-sitting job. The good-looking suspect was perfectly at ease and composed, answering all questions courteously.

However, to the experienced eye of police chief Mangan, Bianchi was a little too relaxed; a really innocent man would have started to show concern and sweat a little as the determined interrogation by hostile detectives progressed.

The explanation is simple. Bianchi was playing a foreseen role and, paradoxically, his total immersion in projecting an image of innocence was actually protecting him from the very real mental and physical rigours of interrogation. In short, it wasn't Bianchi who was being interrogated but rather a simulated persona he had previously created for just such an occasion. Like any amateur actor, he was fairly detached and in control of the dialogue. Wooden.

But a method actor would have been more penetrating and adept, actually *feeling* the pressures of the dire situation he was supposed to be in, and thus visibly reflecting signs of physical and mental stress. Therefore, as a man, Bianchi was simply too good to be true; as an actor, too bad to be convincing. He had mastered the mind and neglected the emotions, mainly because a psychopathic personality possesses few or no genuine emotions in the first instance, other than purely selfish or manipulative. He could not truly experience guilt or innocence, only self, and this psychic vacuum inevitably flawed his whole performance.

Police formally asked Bianchi for permission to search his home. To their surprise he readily agreed. They should not have been taken aback. Bianchi may not have been the best of actors, but he was intelligent enough to know that, being a prime suspect, the police would search his house anyway, with or without his permission.

Tactically, Bianchi had obviously decided it would look better in court that he had readily agreed to the search; it would help to reinforce his projected courtroom assertion that any incriminating evidence found by the police had palpably been planted by them in his absence. Knowing what the police would find, he was already sensibly thinking in strategic terms of being charged and sent to trial, and every tactical point he gained would therefore assist his defence. He might even be lucky enough to entice the police into breaching some legal technicality to his advantage.

The initial police search turned up property Bianchi had purloined in the course of his security work. This gave the police grounds to retain Bianchi formally on a holding charge of grand theft, enabling them to continue questioning him and search for more important evidence in connection with the murders. This they eventually found, as Bianchi must have known they would.

First police discovered the keys to the empty Bayside house the two girls had been lured to. Next they found a scarf that had belonged to one of the girls, Diane Wilder. Forensic scientists were called in to conduct a more thorough search.

Meanwhile, forensic examination of the two corpses revealed more damning evidence proving that the girls had been sexually assaulted and murdered in the empty Bayside house. This included fibres from the carpet in the house found on their clothing. Blood stains on Bianchi's clothing matched that of Diane Wilder. Pubic hairs from the girls were also discovered in the house and on Bianchi.

Witnesses came forward to testify that both Bianchi's security truck and Karen Mandic's green Mercury Bobcat had been seen parked outside the empty house on the evening of the murders. So Bianchi had obviously been lying when he stated that he did not know and had never met either of the two girls.

Bianchi was formally charged with the murders.

He next promptly changed his story. He claimed he could not recall anything about the murders, obviously preparing the ground for a plea of insanity. Police began to dig deeply into Bianchi's past.

———— ❖ ————

When detectives found out that Bianchi had lived in Glendale not far from Los Angeles, they made a routine call to the Los Angles Police Department to inquire if Bianchi had a criminal record there, or if they possessed any relevant information about him.

When word of the telephone inquiry made by the Bellingham police reached Detective Sergeant Frank Salerno, of the Los Angeles County Sheriff's Department, he became immediately alert.

Although the so-called 'Hillside Strangler' murders abruptly came to an end a good time since, Salerno had never ceased his personal investigations. As soon as he learned that the Bellingham police were holding a former Los Angeles resident charged with the rape and strangulation of two girls, alarms began to ring. He made immediate arrangements to travel to Bellingham and check out the suspect.

There was something familiar about the name Kenneth Bianchi which kept nagging at his memory. Bianchi was an Italian name. Hadn't that German psychic insisted that two Italian brothers were responsible for the Hillside Strangler Murders? The very concept of divination was too far-fetched to reasonably contemplate, Salerno decided. No, the name Bianchi held particular significance, if only he could remember what it was. Perhaps sight of the suspect would trigger recollection.

Arriving at Bellingham police headquarters, Salerno sifted through objects collected from the suspect's house, some of which Bianchi had not been able to account for satisfactorily. Among these were several items of jewellery. Salerno almost immediately identified some of them as having once belonged to victims of the Hillside Stranglers.

There was now little remaining doubt that Bianchi was one of the killers he had been searching for. Relief flooded through Salerno, putting to sleep his apprehension that the Stranglers would recommence their murderous mayhem in Los Angeles, and with it further ridicule of the Special Task Force. Capturing the second Strangler before he decided to do a bit of killing on his own became Salerno's sudden preoccupation.

The second Strangler would probably stick to proven methodology and was perhaps now looking for or, worse still, had already met and collaborated with a homicidal soulmate who took Bianchi's place. Or if Strangler two had learned of Bianchi's capture, he might now be racing for deep cover and permanent safety.

There should have been no real doubt in the minds of the police that, no matter where he chose to go, this dominant partner would kill again when he thought it safe to do so. All factors considered, speed of detection and capture were paramount.

Urgent investigations of the Los Angeles police quickly uncovered that Bianchi's apparent constant companion had been his cousin, Angelo Buono.

From the pattern of the killings and sites where bodies were dumped, the police should already have been working on the hypothesis that Glendale was probably the Stranglers' base of operations. Therefore it should have come as no surprise that Angelo Buono owned a house in that district.

Buono's work consisted of upholstering automobiles. Covert police surveillance and investigations established that Buono, having greying curly hair and an Italian complexion, fit physical descriptions given by witnesses who had seen or narrowly escaped abduction. He also conformed to the projected psychological profile of the dominant partner.

He was seventeen years older and wiser than his twenty-seven-year-old killing companion, had been married four times and sired eight children. He had a wide variety of girlfriends, who testified that he was sexually insatiable and violently sadistic, frequently subjecting them to fellatio and sodomy.

In-depth police investigations revealed that both Bianchi and Buono terrorized a number of young girls into working as prostitutes on their behalf, beat them if they resisted, and apparently enjoyed sexually humiliating them by inflicting enforced sodomy and fellatio. A perfect psychological training ground for two killers whose hallmarks consisted of all these preliminary administrations prior to murdering their victims.

Further, there was also positive evidence that Buono had known one of the murder victims, black prostitute Yolanda Washington.

There was now no doubt in the minds of detectives that Buono and Bianchi were the Hillside Stranglers.

The police were now faced with the problem of how best to persuade Bianchi into confessing to the 'Hillside Strangler' murders and testify against his cousin Angelo Buono.

They were cynically certain that moral persuasion would hold no sway, so they relied upon the application of fear and extortion to achieve their end. Bianchi had been charged in the state of Washington for the two Bellingham murders. Washington had a death penalty for murder; California did not. If Bianchi confessed to the murders committed in the Los Angeles area, they would take legal precedence, meaning that if he was tried for those murders instead, he would receive a life sentence.

Bianchi had already devised a more advantageous alternative plan of his own. To be charged only to the two Bellingham killings, for which he would escape death and imprisonment by having himself declared legally insane.

At that point, police were unaware that the personable Bianchi had, at one time in his past, bought some spurious diplomas and set himself up in an office as a psychotherapist as a means of obtaining power over girl patients, then seducing and recruiting them to prostitution. To lend credence to the role of psychotherapist, Bianchi had read enough books to acquire a smattering of psychoanalytic language. In the process he also assimilated symptomatic knowledge of mental illnesses, which would now stand him in good stead in feigning them to save his life.

Bianchi had even been arrogant or foolish enough to use this academic front/effrontery on the Los Angeles Police Department on one occasion. He had smoothly convinced them that he was working on a psychological research project, and obtained official permission to accompany officers on a cruise through the city in a patrol car; and he had helpfully been shown some of the sites where the 'Hillside Strangler' had dumped victims.

This element of frivolous risk-taking suggests a secondary, non-affective psychotic side to Bianchi's psychopathic nature.

Had the more pragmatic and coldly calculating Angelo Buono learned of this dangerous indulgence of ego on the part of Bianchi, it might have cautioned him to kill Bianchi before his idiosyncratic japes attracted unwanted attention and led to their capture.

———•◆•———

The mental illness Bianchi had expediently chosen to simulate in his bid to escape execution was that of multiple personality. Meaning his personality was comprised of two or more distinctly contrasting personae, each functioning independently and unconscious of the other.

Bianchi was entering into an area of psychic contention and deception open to all manner of perilous psychological entrapments. In brief, he could have hardly chosen a more treacherous and ominous battleground.

It is not easy pretending to be two-faced whilst pretending you don't know it. Politicians excluded. Or pretending to possess no memory of unpleasant actions which are perfectly clear in the mind, causing the subjective to constantly play tag with the objective.

If Bianchi did not succeed to some extent in fooling himself, then he would not prevail in hoodwinking others. One little slip and the whole house of cards would collapse. If Bianchi had gathered some knowledge of the psychobiological and psychogenic symptoms he would have to simulate in the case of multiple personality — delusional fugues, sudden headaches, erratic behaviour, conflicting dreams, uncommonly frequent episodes of *déjà vu*, etc. — this could have made his role harder to orchestrate, especially if he sunk into the part so deeply as to lose sight of the overall multiple image he was trying to create.

In effect, Bianchi was setting out to be the playwright, producer, director, prompter, stagehand and sole performer of diverse, discordant characters who would have to interact with a live, questioning audience. Not even the genius of Orson Welles aspired to such exalted heights of theatre.

On top of this, Bianchi agreed to undergo examination under hypnosis. An expert from the University of Montana, Professor John G. Watkins, was enlisted to perform the task of putting Bianchi into a trance — but not of the drug-induced variety (injection of sodium pentothal, the so-called *truth drug*), which might have eroded Bianchi's will-power and endangered his conscious control of the scenario.

———•◆•———

Meanwhile, Angelo Buono, though alarmed by Bianchi's arrest due to his own stupidity, remained contemptuous of the police.

He calculated that they had no substantial evidence against him. He knew Bianchi was engaged in a damage limitation exercise, the choices being death or captivity in prison or a top-security mental institution, perhaps with some prospect of release at a distant date.

Personally, I'd prefer execution, and the satisfaction of illustrating that the authorities are no better than the criminal when it comes to cold, premeditated killing, no matter how they trick it out in official finery.

There was a very significant tactical and strategic spin-off from Bianchi's plan which was worthy of consideration from Angelo Buono's point of view.

If Bianchi's scheme to fool the psychiatrists met with success and he was committed to a mental institution, this would automatically mean that he could no longer appear as a witness against Buono, the testimony of a mental patient not being legally admissible in an American court of law. With Bianchi securely tucked away in a lunatic asylum, Buono would be able to breathe easy again, there being no other evidence of consequence at police disposal — not yet, at least.

Buono was therefore understandably confident that Bianchi was too intelligent not to see that, if he confessed to the Hillside Strangler murders, they would throw the key away.

Police were continuing a psychological campaign of overt surveillance against Buono, similar to that used against John Wayne Gacy, in an attempt to break his nerve, but it was not working. Buono remained the detached, scornful psychopath, too icy a specimen to be pressured into panic by such crude methods.

However, had Buono fully comprehended just how slim Bianchi's chances of deceiving the authorities were, and the concomitant psychic nihilism such defeat would probably engender in Bianchi, perhaps he would have more wisely packed fast and made a run for it, well armed to blow away all obstacles, or his own brains.

In my particular case, captured by surprise, all three guns were perversely in the wrong place at the wrong time, something I shall always regret.

Being too cool can also be a disadvantage, over-confidence blunting intelligent insight and foresight; wishful thinking stultifying an accurate reckoning of perceptible odds, and restraining the instinctive urge for positive remedial action while the initiative is still within grasp.

> The enemy increaseth every day;
> We, at the height, are ready to decline.
> There is a tide in the affairs of men,

Which, taken at the flood, leads on to fortune;
Omitted, all the voyage of their life
Is bound in shallows and in miseries.
On such a full sea are we now afloat,
And we must take the current when it serves,
Or lose our ventures.

— *Julius Caesar*, Shakespeare

There comes a point in most instances of *folie à deux* when, rightly or wrongly, the tables are turned. As already stated, the pupil has learned much from the master, the master has learned little or nothing from the pupil. Therefore the pupil, combining his own knowledge with that which he has been taught, almost inevitably concludes at some juncture that the synthesis of knowledge has made him superior to his teacher, and this conviction usually erases any former obligation he felt towards the latter.

Yet again, this exemplifies that 'bloody instruction,' having been taught, 'returns to plague the inventor.' Buono, the teacher of ruthless principles, was now being repaid in the same coin by Bianchi, his former pupil.

The police evidence against Angelo Buono was mounting relentlessly as he waited indecisively in the wings trying to bluff it out.

Beulah Stofer, the elderly neighbour of Lauren Wagner who had witnessed two men bundling her into their car, was now able to identify them as having been Buono and Bianchi. Further, the boyfriend of the prostitute victim Judy Miller was also able to identify Buono as being the final client who had picked Judy up the evening she vanished.

The feisty schoolteacher, who had intervened when she witnessed two men trying to drag a girl into their car in broad daylight, did not hesitate in identifying them as Buono and Bianchi. But, in strictly legal terms, apparently there was still not sufficient evidence for the police to arrest Buono and charge him with the Hillside Strangler murders.

At face value, it is puzzling that the LAPD did not at least take Buono into custody on a holding charge of technical assault and attempted abduction. Doubtless there were obscure legal reasons of some sort which may have jeopardised their main case against him. Perhaps by leaving him free they were still trying to pressure him into making an incriminating dash for cover. For Buono must have been acutely aware that detectives were assiduously digging into every aspect of his background, interviewing practically everyone he had ever had contact with.

Think of the things you yourself wish to hide or are ashamed of, the number of enemies you have accumulated through life who would be only too willing to do you down, and you will perhaps fully appreciate the psychological pressures Buono was having to cope with in addition to guilty fears connected with the murders.

Anonymity is a luxury much undervalued until you lose it.

As predicated by his psychological profile, Angelo Buono did indeed have a criminal record and history of violence. In his mid-teens, shortly after completion of his schooling, he had been in and out of police custody frequently, culminating in a term at a reformatory — which usually 'reforms' amateur criminals into professionals.

In a broader sense, Buono's psyche began to conform to a classic pattern. Deep hatred for his mother been transformed into a hatred and contempt for the female species in general. He viewed them only as sex objects, violently abusing and sexually humiliating them to assuage his pathological resentment at being weak enough to need them at all. He partly compensated for this by spurning normal sexual intercourse in favour of sodomy and forcing them to perform fellatio.

Each of Buono's four wives, all of whom had divorced him, in separate interviews testified to Buono's sexual preferences and violent tendencies. It was also revealed that Buono had seduced one of his fourteen-year-old stepdaughters and one of his teenage natural sons, performing sodomy on them both. The overall developing portrait of Buono was that of a violent paranoid-psychopath with satyric sexual appetites. The murders themselves had already postulated as much, adding stylized homicide and designer sadism to the comprehensive profile.

However, something for citizens to ponder:

> Today, over half the world's governments continue to use torture against their own citizens.
> — Amnesty International Report, 1990

As previously suggested, Bianchi may have eventually deluded himself into believing he was superior to his master, Buono, but in reality he was still the weaker and less cunning of the two; some things either can't be easily learned or naturally assimilated without the subconscious first being reprogrammed by auto-hypnosis.

Bianchi was a natural born follower, superior to Buono in only one fatal area: that of making mistakes. And he was in the process of making his biggest.

His original plan to have himself declared insane, be tried only for the two Bellingham murders, escape the death penalty and be committed to a mental institution, from which he would some day be released, at least held some sense, though a minimal chance of success. However, when police evidence against himself and Angelo Buono reached alarming proportions, Bianchi decided to change his strategy a third time.

He would expediently confess to the Hillside murders through his other personality, his evil alter-ego, which he named 'Steve.' He would also use 'Steve' to place most of the blame for the Hillside murders on Angelo Buono, and the remainder of the blame would be generously accepted by 'Steve.' In effect, Kenneth Bianchi himself would be innocent of all but insanity!

It could cynically be posited that Kenneth Bianchi really was insane if he thought such a crazy scheme would succeed. It was one thing to have 'Steve' take the blame for 'Ken,' but when 'Steve' also shielded himself by putting all the blame on Angelo Buono, 'Steve' was actually revealing himself not to be the evil alter-ego of 'Ken,' but Kenneth Bianchi himself. In Jamaica they have a saying: 'Play fool to catch wise.' Bianchi was attempting the opposite.

And thus it was through the courtesy of 'Steve' that detectives at last heard factual details of the Hillside Stranglers' murders.

Bianchi, by sacrificing Buono on the altar of his multiple personality scheme, was meeting with some significant degree of success.

Two eminent clinical psychiatrists were truly convinced that Bianchi was a genuine case of multiple personality.

The police were more sceptical, and had good reason to be, considering that their case against Buono largely depended upon Kenneth Bianchi being judged sane and concomitantly being able to testify against Buono. So they decided to call in a clinical expert of their own choosing, Dr Martin Orne, from the University of Pennsylvania, an acknowledged specialist on hypnosis, who was to decide whether Bianchi was faking or not. (Without wishing to impugn Dr Orne's professional integrity at any level, clinical experts are by and large in roughly a similar position to that of lawyers, in that they are tacitly obliged to represent the best interests of whoever commissions them, be it the defence or prosecution.)

In my own case, for instance, much of the testimony by 'experts' on behalf of the prosecution was so blatantly absurd, contrived and, more to the point, absolutely inaccurate, that, for me, the term 'expert' holds no connotation other than hilarity.

In my view, a preliminary but adequately comprehensive analytical study of Bianchi should have resulted in the following psychodiagnostics. There was little doubt that he was of above-average intelligence, but primarily of a reproductive rather than an inspired nature. His ambitions exceeded his intellectual endowments and, perhaps spasmodically cognitive of this affective/effective gap between comprehension and self-attainment, he tended to vault over his inadequacies by ad lib reliance on rationalisations and compulsive self-deception. This alternated with defensive patterns of studied indifference whenever he became conscious that his mechanistic efforts to create a favourable impression were faltering.

He exhibited an almost complete lack of emotional depth and self-insight and, on the whole, could be likened to a poorly baked layer-cake, retaining surface attraction but lacking essential quality. Paradoxically, these deficiencies did not prevent him from holding an over-high estimation of himself and his potential capacities. He was, as it were, quite convinced greatness lay somewhere within him — it was just that he was encountering a little difficulty locating it.

Therefore Bianchi, because he was a natural subordinate, subconsciously compensated for this by deceiving himself into believing he at least *latently* possessed all the innovative and unorthodox qualities required of a cohesive leader. Eventually seduced by his own self-fulfilling prophecy, he unwisely decided to attempt the role. Even his speedy arrest, and the disastrous predicament to which his one significant attempt at independent action had guided him, still failed to disabuse him of this grand delusion, or persuade him to abandon the obsessive urge to pursue it to forlorn fruition. He should have taken the considered advice of W.C. Fields:

'If at first you don't succeed — give up, and stop making a darn fool of yourself!'

But that course of empirical inaction does not enter the mind of the obsessive-compulsive personality, destined to defy failure against all predictable odds, like a gambler who knows the dice are loaded against him, yet senselessly expects some *deus ex machina* to pluck victory from certain defeat, then glibly attributes his losses to 'bad luck.'

This and other symptoms of affective dissociation suggest latent suicidal tendencies in Bianchi, probably rooted in emotional deprivation as a child.

Bianchi's hypercritical antipathy towards all figures of authority indicates that he most likely ascribed this emotional neglect, either directly or indirectly, primarily to the influence of his father. It may also be the case that, incongruously as a result of this, Bianchi had subconsciously striven to emulate or better his father's qualities of leadership and had fallen victim to the law of reversed effort.

In effect, Bianchi was a brooding resentful weakling in need of a more forceful, active mentor to bring his ambitions into being, and Buono proved to be the necessary catalyst.

Interactionally, each man took advantage of the other to achieve his own obsessive aims. Had the two men never met, shared their beliefs and sexual fantasies and forged a homicidal partnership, it is more than probable, in my estimation, that neither of them, separately, would ever have committed murder.

> When I play with my cat, who knows whether she isn't amusing
> herself with me more than I am with her?
> — Montaigne (1533–1592)

The time had come for Bianchi to overplay his part and be caught in the snares that his own rashly-conceived ambition had set.

Prior to interviewing Bianchi or putting him under hypnosis, Dr Martin T. Orme made a close study of the previous videotaped sessions of Bianchi acting out the role of his alter ego, 'Steve.'

The first potential flaw Dr Orme detected was that 'Steve's' performances were becoming more rounded, expansive and accomplished with each progressive session. This suggested that rather than bursting forth from his bonds as a fully-fledged, dominant and separate personality in no need of prompting, 'Steve' was, in fact, being fleshed out in the course of each successive appearance on stage.

In the course of ostensibly casual preliminary interviews with Bianchi, Dr Orme obliquely implanted the suggestion in Bianchi's conscious mind that, in the majority of instances of multiple personality, the patient normally has more than one alter ego and often several, each one independent of another. Consequently, after Dr Orme had apparently put Bianchi under hypnotic trance, Bianchi obligingly created for the first time an additional alter ego named 'Billy,' proof positive that Bianchi was in fact simply feigning a trance and consciously attempting to manipulate the situation to legal advantage.

As predicted, he overplayed his hand and would now have to face the full consequence of having confessed to the Hillside Strangler murders to enhance the odds of his multiple personality gambit paying off.

> I have heard of your paintings too, well enough. God hath
> given you one face and you make yourselves another.
> — *Hamlet*, Shakespeare

Dr Orme and his associate for the prosecution, Dr Saul Faerstein, were now of the joint opinion that Bianchi should go to trial, and their medical opinion was accepted.

At the subsequent sanity hearing on 19th October '79, Bianchi pleaded guilty to the two murders he committed in Bellingham and to five others committed in Los Angeles. The judge sentenced him to life imprisonment without the legal need for a trial, according to the law of Washington state.

———————

The Los Angeles Police Department still had five additional murder charges outstanding against Bianchi. In other circumstances the LAPD probably would have waived these further five charges as being superfluous in view of Bianchi's sentence of life imprisonment, but they still needed Bianchi's evidence to nail Buono for sure. Therefore the Los Angeles District Attorney broached a deal to Bianchi, namely, that if Bianchi pleaded guilty to the five additional murder charges and agreed to testify against Angelo Buono, instead of being sentenced to death under California law, Bianchi would be given another sentence of life imprisonment but with the possibility of parole.

This deal was more than generous, the priority of the LAPD being the successful conviction of Buono. Bianchi wisely accepted the deal without hesitation, and simultaneously dropped his multiple-personality charade in his haste to supply the LAPD with a detailed account of the Hillside Strangler murders.

The Los Angeles police consequently arrested Buono on 22nd October '79 and charged him with the Hillside Strangler killings. But the legal merry-go-round was just beginning.

———————

The close proximity of Buono, now being held in the same county jail-house as Bianchi, was bad psychology on the part of the police, especially considering the vacillating weakness of the chief witness for the prosecution. Bianchi almost immediately changed his mind and nullified the deal with the Los Angeles District Attorney, claiming that he had made it under duress, that the DA had threatened him with death to extort a confession. The DA had naïvely placed too much trust in Bianchi and, as part of the original deal, made the mistake of publicly proclaiming that, in view of Bianchi's initial co-opera-tion, he had agreed to drop the additional five murder charges against him. The DA obviously underestimated Bianchi's tenacity and psychopathic survival skills.

Police forensic teams were now faced with having to work overtime in amassing as much concrete evidence as possible before the trial. As this went on, Buono's lawyers, with incredible audacity and panache, sought to free their client on bail. The presiding judge, Ronald M. George, ruled against the motion.

The next legal tactic by Buono's lawyers met with more success — namely, a motion to drop the lesser charges of rape, sodomy, kidnapping, etc, against Buono as a waste of public funds, in view of the fact that Buono was already facing ten cases of murder. The advantage to Buono's defence, if this proposal was agreed to, was that the jury would then not be informed of his unsavoury past during the trial for murder.

Judge George granted this motion chiefly not to provide grounds for a possible appeal.

In tandem with these events, Kenneth Bianchi was working on less propitious criminal schemes of his own without consulting his lawyers. During his incarceration he received letters from a fascinated girl, Veronica Lynn Compton, who was engaged in writing a play about a female serial killer who injects sperm into her victims to convince police a man was committing the murders.

Bianchi conceived the grotesque stratagem of having Veronica Lynn Compton, who by now was madly in love with him, turn her fictional plot into reality. By reasoning that if another girl was strangled in Bellingham, his defence could argue that the police had charged the wrong man. This absurd wishful thinking totally ignored the fact that Bianchi had not only already confessed to the Bellingham murders but had also supplied the police with details of their execution which only the killer would have known that he had also confessed to the Los Angeles Hillside Strangler murders, again relating details only the genuine killer was privy to. His Bellingham scheme, even in the unlikely event of success, would not improve his situation one jot.

Bianchi had fallen prone to the most common form of psychodynamic caused by imprisonment: escape into fantasy. Some inmates find it in religion, others in the secular world. In whichever field it manifests itself, the shared subconscious drive is self-survival, either by retention of the individual psyche, or at least some sense of self-determination in its altered formation.

Many prisoners actually end up half-believing the fictitious past, present and future they ingeniously invent to escape the tedium of sensory deprivation that all incarceration inflicts. In short-term prisoners, it is a temporary expedient to ward off spiritual destruction. In others, faced with decades of oppressive uniformity, the condition may graduate to permanency. There are those who will start playing an adopted role in response to the moral blackmail that constitutes the parole system and, after years of daily dissembling, may actually become the fiction they created.

In light of these observations, it is perhaps easier to comprehend why Bianchi was apparently reduced to pinning his hopes on the illogical and absurd murder scheme concocted with Veronica Lynn Compton. Yet again we have an example of *folie à deux* in action, this time with Bianchi as the dominating partner.

Veronica Lynn Compton, similarly blind to reality, infected by Bianchi's delusive vision, took a room at the Shangri-La motel and went out to hunt for a victim. She found her in a bar, a girl by the name of Kim Breed, and after a couple of drinks inveigled her into riding back to the motel with her. Once in her room, she plied Kim Breed with more alcohol and convivial conversation before attempting to strangle her from behind with a length of rope. Veronica soon discovered she had underestimated her prospective victim, who promptly sent her flying over her shoulder into a corner of the room, and then ran out of the motel.

Kim Breed reported the matter to the police but Veronica had already skipped from the motel. The police eventually managed to track her down to the airport and took her into custody.

Veronica Lynn Compton gradually broke down and confessed to the wild plot with Bianchi. Rather harshly, considering the mitigating circumstances, she was sentenced to life imprisonment.

Bianchi was now worse off than before, if such were possible, while matters were progressing at a miraculous momentum in Buono's favour.

Roger Kelly, the assistant District Attorney, had actually moved that, because of the increasingly unreliable nature of Bianchi's evidence against Buono, discredited by the highly publicised murder plot hatched with

Veronica Lynn Compton, the ten counts of murder against Buono should be dismissed entirely.

Kelly further moved that the lesser counts of rape and sodomy against Buono be reinstated and that he should be released on bail of $50,000. In effect, this would mean that Buono, if found guilty on the lesser charges, could end up serving as little as five to ten years in prison.

The police were flabbergasted by the turn of events. In court Buono was now openly swaggering with self-assurance and cocky contempt at this unexpected reversal of fortune. The judge wisely decided to postpone for a week his ruling on the startling motion by the prosecution.

On 21st July 1981, all parties assembled in court to hear Judge George scrupulously review the evidence the prosecution had formerly presented against Buono with such confidence. Gradually it became obvious that the judge retained the confidence and nerve that the prosecution lacked. He ruled that the forensic evidence, witness testimonies and circumstantial evidence against Buono was sufficiently substantial for the prosecution to continue. And he cautioned the DA that, should he not proceed with sufficient vigour in prosecuting Buono, he would officially bring the matter to the attention of the Attorney General.

The DA promptly escaped his embarrassing dilemma by withdrawing from the case. The Attorney General subsequently appointed two of his personal assistants, Michael Nash and Roger Boren, to proceed with the prosecution of Buono.

This dramatic reversal of fortune left Buono shaken and dispirited throughout the duration of the trial, which was to lumber on for another two years, becoming the longest murder trial in American jurisprudence.

Bianchi was eventually to stand in the witness box a total of five months, far less confident under Buono's glaring, hate-filled eyes. Under cross-examination, not only by Buono's lawyers but also by the prosecution and the judge, Bianchi became progressively more entangled in his own intricate web of deceit and was now not only trying to save himself but also attempting to squirm out of helping the prosecution convict Buono.

Faced with this backsliding, Judge George had to caution Bianchi that his prevarication and the ambiguity of his evidence against Buono was endangering the benefits he had received under his deal.

This word of warning caused Bianchi to be much clearer in his damning testimony against Buono, whose defence lawyers were employing every legal trick in the book to discredit and make the informant appear solely responsible for all the murders.

On 4th January 1984, the judge sentenced Kenneth Bianchi to serve his life sentence in Washington, as he had breached the terms of his plea-bargaining. He then sentenced Angelo Buono to life imprisonment without possibility of parole.

Asked afterwards whether the murders committed by the Hillside Stranglers did not, by definition, prove they were insane, the judge replied:

'Why should we call someone insane simply because he or she chooses not to conform to our standards of civilised behaviour?'

My answer, already inferred, is that if a person truly does not believe in any given standards of 'civilised behaviour,' laws or morality — whether they be those of the USA or the Third Reich — he owes no innate responsibility to them and therefore his or her contrary acts cannot be considered sane within the context and terms of that society.

Society will exact its pound of flesh from the transgressor one way or another. So why quibble? Only society is concerned for its own sake about the dressing of it. It matters naught to the prisoner.

Epilogue

> Man's capacity for justice makes democracy
> possible, but man's inclination to injustice
> makes democracy necessary.
>
> *The Children of Light and*
> *the Children of Darkness,*
> **Reinhold Niebuhr (1892–1971)**

All matters turn not on reality but on perception of reality. A virtue or an evil is only as significant as one believes it to be. There is no cosmic influence or categorical imperative involved, merely an assortment of particular, transient tribal laws, morals and customs set up expediently to protect and sustain a particular community and its leaders, whether they be considered by others for the general good or bad.

The weaker members in every society have the fewest rights and privileges, their magnitude decided solely by the extent to which they benefit the rulers.

The reason why acts of kindness and compassion bring a lump to the throat is their rarity, their taking one by surprise, as it were. By selective, atypical acts of generosity, the powerful seek to manipulate the good opinion of others to reinforce that of themselves.

Naturally if an individual believes he is superior to others, any hurt he inflicts upon a person he considers inferior concomitantly has lesser moral and psychic impact upon him. So what others may regard as monstrous acts in fact seem quite natural to him and of little account.

Similarly, $20 given by a rich man to a poor may seem generous to the receiver but be considered less than nothing to the giver. But if a poor man gives a beggar a few cents, both will have a genuine sense of generosity and human sympathy.

In this book I have offered a few modest methods which may assist in tracking down the serial killer. Some of you may regard that as generous coming from me, some may not. Both arguments hold water.

For I could write several more chapters, or even another book, on how to foil police forensics and confound the methodology of psychological profilers.

In not doing so, am I displaying a sense of morality, exhibiting praise-worthy altruism? Or am I simply bowing to the fact that no publisher would dare print such subversive information?

Or do I care at all either way?

> The rest is silence.
> — Shakespeare

Afterword by Peter Sotos

It is a much uglier level than this.

In 1975, *The Trial Of Ian Brady And Myra Hindley* was published in the UK by David and Charles. And inside one could find the complete transcription of the infamous tape recording made while Ian Brady and Myra Hindley — argued — with little ten-year-old Lesley Ann Downey:

Man: Just put it in now, love. Put it in now.
        (Retching noise)
Child: *(Muffled)* What's this in for?
Man: Put it in.
Child: Can I just tell you summat? I must tell you summat. Please take your hands off me a minute, please. Please — mummy — please.
Child: I can't tell you.
        (Grunting)
Child: *(In quick sequence)* I can't tell you. I can't breathe. Oh.
Child: I can't — dad — will you take your hands off me?
        (Man whispering)
Man: No. Tell me.
Child: Please god.
Man: Tell me.
Child: I can't while you've got your hands on me.
        (Mumbling sound)
Man: Why don't you keep it in?
Child: Why? What are you going to do with me?
Man: I want to take some photographs, that's all.
Man: Put it in.
Child: Don't undress me, will you?

In October 1999, the BBC broadcast a three-part documentary on the crimes of Ian Brady and Myra Hindley. The first episode featured a shot of one of the seven photographs of little ten-year-old Lesley Ann Downey taken by Ian and Myra shortly after that tape recording was made. And just before the little naked child was murdered. The photos themselves and the act of photographing her and the tape recording of her pleas and tiny protestations and confused child's desperation can all be considered, in contemporary humanist terms, rape. And it is an ugly thing indeed to have to speculate on how or when the child was actually physically raped. Penetrated. Made.

Little ten-year-old Lesley Ann Downey is seen in the photograph, lying naked on top of a bed, on her stomach. Her head in a pillow with her gentle face turned toward her photographer. Her dark eyes open. A scarf is wrapped around her mouth and tied behind her tousled black lovely hair. There is no genitalia or graphic nudity in this carefully broadcast and cropped picture. Her naked shoulder. She does seem small.

It is the only photograph shown. However, in a talking head interview, retired detective sergeant Roy Jarvis was allowed to describe another from the small collection before he trailed off into police techniques and procedure:

> When we found the photographs of Lesley Ann Downey stand-
> ing on a bed, naked, legs apart, hands outstretched, clothed in
> nothing but a pair of socks and wearing a gag, with a terrified look
> in her eyes, we realized that if we could link the bedhead . . .

There is a much more precise level than this.

Devil's Disciples was the first of two books on the case written by Robert Wilson. Published in 1986 by Express Newspapers and based on the author's contemporaneous coverage of the trial for "an evening newspaper," Robert Wilson seemed to agree — slightly — with the defense's argument when it came to the legally required deconstruction of the pornographic evidence:

> Yes, the tape recording was a "harrowing experience", but on
> the photographs taken of Lesley Ann, she appeared to be "calm
> and reasonably" composed.

Over ten years earlier and just six years after the crime itself, *The Trial Of Ian Brady And Myra Hindley* had recorded the argument for the defense without comment:

> It was one thing to say that the accused were so ruthless that
> they were prepared to photograph the little girl; it was quite
> another to say they killed her to dispose of her as a deadly
> witness against them. When one looked at the photographs,
> what perhaps was a little astonishing was how calm the little
> girl looked. The child appeared to be reasonably composed,

and that might give the jury some idea of what went on at the time of the tape recording.

And there are higher levels of honesty.

Little ten-year-old Lesley Ann Downey's mother published her personal account of seeing only two of the seven pornographic photographs of her naked daughter in *For The Love Of Lesley* in 1989. Published in hardback in 1989 by W. H. Allen and in an updated and revised paperback edition by Warner Books four years later:

> Lesley . . . naked, bound and gagged with a scarf that had been viciously forced into her mouth and tied tight at the back of her neck with a savage jerk. Lesley . . . pale and naked on a can-dlewick bedspread with her hands together in desperate prayer. Lesley . . . her hands tied together by sick people who revelled in her humiliation.
>
> The second image swam behind my tight shut eyes and superimposed itself over the first horror. Lesley . . . bent double over a chair. Lesley still naked, bound and gagged. I screamed louder and louder, trying to make the images go away. But the expression of terror in Lesley's bulging eyes remained in sharp focus, imprinted on my mind. Lesley . . . who had never experienced a hand raised in anger at any time in her short life.

A check through the index in the back of *Topping* — the autobiography of Peter Topping ("the police chief in the Moors murders case"), published by Angus and Robertson, UK, in 1989 — details a good many pages devoted to "Downey, Lesley Ann — tape recording." Among them page 72:

> (Myra) moved on to talk about the tape recording made of Lesley Ann Downey. Contrary to popular belief, she said, the tapes had not been made while photographs were being taken — not during the torture session. She denied that Lesley Ann had been subjected to any physical torture. Having assessed the evidence at the trial and having heard the tapes, I accepted that they had been made while photographs were being taken; but I told Hindley that to deprive a child of her mother, then strip and bind and gag her, was in my book a form of torture —

even if it was not the kind that had grown up in the public imagination.

And on page 148:

> I have also carefully studied the photographs of Lesley Ann, in which she is bound and gagged. I have looked at the expression on her face. As a father myself, I believe that the full horrors of what happened to that child have not been misunderstood. Although, as Hindley points out, no fingers were cut off, and what was being forced into the child's mouth was a gag — not, as some people have construed, Brady's penis — torture certainly took place. When you think of the effects of what they did to the defenceless child then you can only conclude that she was dreadfully tortured. My heart goes out to Mrs Ann West. Who will never and perhaps should never forgive them for their actions.
>
> If ordering the child to strip, binding and gagging her, photographing her and then subjecting her to sexual abuse is not torture, what is? I viewed Myra Hindley's attempts to put herself in a favorable light with great suspicion throughout: in the case of Lesley Ann Downey I do not believe that anything she could say would ameliorate her position. Her voice, clearly to be heard on the tape, is harsh and brutal: she blames her own fear for that. She never stopped to consider the fear on the face and in the voice of the young child she had in her power."

There are better things to do. First off, you don't ask a child molester to write a book on serial killing. A child rapist. A child pornographer. A child murderer.

Colin Wilson, from his introduction:

> Therefore I advised him to do the thing I would have done: to think about writing a book. Since he obviously knew about serial murder 'from the inside', this suggested itself as the obvious subject.

You don't ask him to do the obvious. You especially don't ask him to do what you would do.

Because the child rapist and murderer and pornographer will obviously lie. And, because he wants to believe you need to hear more and see more than you'll ever actually do, he'll even start to enjoy telling you he's lying. Because it's the easiest thing to do. It is the obvious choice. He can adopt the dime-a-dozen serial killer front of puffed-up superiority, all from his tiny cell, and serve the typical cold dish of chest-beating mental clarity over personal introspection. A wide view of painful dark humanity instead of tastes and salacious dives. Roots over themes. Brave actions rather than fearful words.

Ian Brady:

> Some authors invariably rationalize their prurient intrusion in the name of science and the furtherance of human illumination. I believe most serious students can discern when that line has been crossed and morbid sensationalism begins.

And

> The common individual craves prohibited sensation minus responsibility and risk. And perhaps the most psychologically intolerable aspect of all, such people resent inner knowledge that they will spend all of their life as timid spectators, never players.

And

> As previously stated, it is invariably the case that actions bright and exciting in the imagination are, unfortunately, often disappointing or farcical in practice, more so when it has not been thought through thoroughly. Deep thinking gives people a headache.
>
> They think they are thinking when in fact they are merely day-dreaming. For instance, if you were to ask them what they thought of 'adventure,' they would express a vague, undefined pro-adventure attitude, as practically everyone does, albeit from the comfort of an easy-chair. They equate, or confuse, their liking for the idea of adventure with an ability to possibly participate in the real thing. Whereas, in practice, they might immediately discover that real adventure — of the neck-on-the-line variety — is unsettling, like entering a fourth dimen-

sion where the comfortable laws and rules they take for granted in normal life no longer apply; adrenaline speeds the pumping blood and distorts the faculties; immersion in the immediacy of action obviates wider appreciation. Riding the whirlwind is an acquired taste. The psyche aspires to accommodate the new perspective of both inner and external vision. The more times you act as supreme architect, *the more you become one*.

The reader, the student — if you will, the voyeur — if you must, is left with exactly what he came in with. The only option is to pick apart the text and combine it with what few details have been sifted and mined through the press and court transcripts and paint the ugly picture again and again as ugly as anyone wants it to be.

So the painting has to be made special. The truth will lie. Excellent. The only worthwhile honesty has to be found in probing the desperate nervous system through the veils and the obvious and the hideous other's need to impress.

Ian Brady knew enough about transference to get a young girl — close enough in age to little ten-year-old Lesley Ann Downey — to read a newsclipping on Lesley's disappearance into his tape recorder. But, here, he doesn't come close to admitting it:

> The audience is the value and quality of the act. During the process of artistic creation, in the killer's psychic dimension beyond good and evil, the audience is merely a possible off-stage threat. If his "play" is a success, at home he will read the critical reviews with interest, not least as a technician in search of dangerous, structural flaws.

But, here, without discussing how fantasy bleeds inside an overactive yearning mind, he nonetheless might be edging closer to the point:

> Being in the position of having tasted both fantasy and deed, I can candidly testify that fantasy is invariably more hedonistically superior, its creator having the advantage of omnipotence. The safer one feels from interruption or capture, the more intense and rounded the act.

There are more boys than girls on Ian Brady's known victim list. Keith Bennett, John Kilbride and Edward Evans. The oldest victim was Evans at seventeen. And poor Edward's death has never seemed to capture the public imagination as intensely as little ten-year-old Lesley's has. Brady was questioned in court over his homosexual tendencies and over what it was — exactly — he was putting into little ten-year-old Lesley's mouth as heard on the tape recording. But it is usually the little girl's mouth that keeps the tongues wagging. Stupid questions all around. The children found with their pants down in both sexes. And the availability of young Edward having as much to do with rolling a queer as in fucking one. But when one searches for crumbs, one has to crawl up to assholes:

From *Topping* again:

> It is part of the paradox of Brady that he cares a lot what people think of him, and he is ashamed about certain aspects of his life. I questioned him once about the trips he made into Manchester without Myra Hindley, and asked him if he was picking up men. He did not reply, so I asked him straight out if he was bisexual. He nodded, but kept his head down and his eyes averted as though he was deeply ashamed to admit it.

From *The Trial Of Ian Brady And Myra Hindley*:

> I think you told the court that you had met Evans before. I am interested in the club which you claimed on Friday was frequented by homosexuals. You were a visitor there?
> Brady: I have been there about three times.
> What were you doing in that hive of homosexuals?
> Brady: Watching the antics of them.

And Brady, forever connected to his partner in crime Myra Hindley, has never seemed particularly forthcoming over the subject. He pores over the information on John Gacy:

> Gradually Gacy discovered that this form of sadistic sex was far more satisfying, making normal heterosexual sex tame and boring by comparison. So, when he abruptly informed his second wife that he would no longer be sleeping with her, Gacy was not abandoning her because he had become a homosexual,

but rather that he had evolved into the enthusiastic, sadistic scourge of homosexuals.

Peter Topping explains what he was told by Myra about the death of little ten-year-old Lesley Ann Downey for the BBC documentary:

> She sees that the child was bleeding. And . . . there's ligature around the child's neck. And um . . . that . . . Brady carries the child and puts it in the bathroom, washes the blood off the child. And — and then they . . . wrap the body in a sheet, with the clothing, because the child is naked. And then they put the body in the back of the mini-traveller with a view to going up to Saddleworth moor to bury it.
>
> She didn't go like a lamb to the slaughter. As Hindley said the others did. She fought very violently until eventually, she was quite horribly murdered.

And Brady delves into the mind of a Mad Butcher whose victims were cleaned:

> If any victim, male or female, politely declined the offer of a bath, what would the killer do then? Cut their throat and flood his house with blood? Or knock them unconscious (which, in practice, can be a protracted, bloody business in itself), then carry them into the bathroom, undress them and put them into the bath to kill them?

Brady smashed Evans' head in with an axe before finally strangling him to death. Lesley's head was caved in. How do you deconstruct Brady's choice of characters? How did he come across his books and how carefully did he sift through the incredible trash heap of serial killer lore? How much is expansion — an honest desire to see himself in the mistakes and traumas and struggles of others like him — and how much is lonely rutting and rummaging:

> The plain and, perhaps, regrettable fact is that it is part of the eternal human psyche and cycle for the normal individual to derive cathartic satisfaction and enjoyment from savouring the crimes of others, and from luxuriously dreaming of personally committing them.

And who can you trust when you play both ends against the middle? How desperate are you for perfect context?

It is worth mentioning that *The Gates Of Janus* was written under the telling pseudonym François Villon. And that explains Brady's brief mentions of himself in the third person, altered to first person. It may also be worth mentioning that, contrary to Colin Wilson's claim that it was he who sought out a publisher for this book, it was actually Adam Parfrey of Feral House who first contacted Wilson about the book after being alerted to its existence by a notorious child pornographer in the US. This child pornographer shares a chapter with Brady in Tim Tate's exploitative exposé *Child Pornography — An Investigation* (Methuen, 1990, UK).

It is a much uglier level than this.

This gross monster, this fucking gross pig takes his newspaper clippings of Ian Brady and Myra Hindley — the boxes of them he's saved and searched for for years — and picks out all his little favorite ones. Especially the ones that have photos. Especially of the little victims, the little children who weren't quite young enough but perfect nonetheless. And he, this prick, this greasy fucking slime, takes these clippings and puts them in between the pages of this book called *Show Me*. And there's nothing graphic in these pictures cut out so precisely from the British newspapers from nearly thirty-five years ago and still counting. Some of the headlines proclaim the garish horror that is the media's selling point on the case, but there is no nudity. No autopsy shots. No blood or skeletons uncovered from the peat and ground and wrapped in the clothes the children were raped in. Just snaps the children's parents and maybe their teachers handed out to the press. To, fuck knows, maybe help in the search or to help the idiot public remember the real point in such horrible affairs or however these pictures usually make it into the hands of paid journalists and greedy or well -intentioned friends and family and acquaintances. And this cocksucker takes these highly suspect black and white and mostly yellowing paper-thin shots of these smiling little rats and places them in between these pages of this book that was taken off the bookshelves years ago, back in the '70s, because after obscenity cases and major shifts in public taste, St. Martin's Press looked like they were publishing kiddie porn. From *Child Pornography — An Investigation:*

> The book *Show Me* for example, purports to be a sex education text for children and depicts children in various sex acts, including masturbation, oral copulation and vaginal intercourse.

And

> Not surprisingly, *Show Me* is found with regularity during
> searches of exploiters' homes and victims often report that
> exposure to this book preceded the initial act of molestation.

And

> If manuals like *Show Me* pose a dilemma — how to sex-
> educate our children and at the same time not validate or
> encourage paedophilia — they also highlight the essential and
> consuming power of this aberrant sexuality.

You see, this will drag this book down into the gutter now. The people
involved in its creation will not appreciate this. They have better things to do
than be dirtied in the disgusting snail's trail of this fat beast pervert fuck trying
to ruin their best efforts. Their chances to help. Their chances to do the
obvious. And what they would do. To get something better out of such a terrible situation. With all the hurt and pain on one side. And all that tragic humanity and confused existentialism on the other. And all of it surrounded by the
braying angry masses in the coliseum hoarding their own desperate fears
soaked in lust and safety and outraged inequity.

Show Me! A Picture Book Of Sex For Children and Parents. Photography,
captions and design by Will McBride, Explanatory text by Dr. Helga
Fleischhauer-Hardt. St. Martin's Press, 1975, New York:

> We are of the opinion that only an explicit and realistic presen-
> tation of sex can spare children fear and guilt feelings related
> to sexuality. For this reason we chose photography as a
> medium. With much care and under great difficulty we suc-
> ceeded in photographing the children in such a way that their
> natural behavior came through.

This prick-yanking lonely degenerate isn't doing his pathetic little mas-
turbating tricks to make a point. It doesn't even want anyone to know. It isn't
here to help you understand the insides of frightened child peering insects like
its lonely sweating self. Itself. It just needs the connection. The children —
naked — in the pages of the book. And the children — smiling, mother and
father coveted family snaps, clothed, face shots mostly — stuck up against

them. Washed in fucked murder. Bathed of blood in strangers' bathtubs and dumped headfirst into holes in the freshly dug Moors.

The little smiling boy with his cheeky grin pasted over a fresh hard-on sold as an ostensive sex-manual. The best caring intentions seen clearly as thin lies to avoid tasteless questions, brutal answers and unending searches. A repeated image on a TV screen recorded over and over again so as to not wear down the much prized and coveted videotape. An excuse for knowledge and plight empathy, of greater and more human understanding, seen as empty and ironic as the desire to actually just fucking figure it out and be fucking done with it.

Inside the pages of the big black book:

"But I've got a penis and you don't."
"So what? I've got a vagina instead."

A full-on close-up of the little girl — about seven, one would be forced to guess — with her legs in the air and her slit crotch looking as much like a fatty white pig's hoof as a sex organ. Blonde bob cuts and page-boys and a slight dis-cussion about circumsicion to accompany the numerous little penis black and whites.

"When my penis is stiff, it feels great."

There is a much more precise level than this.
Pauline Reade. Sixteen.
From the *Manchester Evening News*, April 12, 1988, under the frontpage headline "THROAT-CUT HORROR OF MOORS GIRL":

Mr Topping said the body was very well preserved and was dressed in a woolen coat. Pauline's dress was pulled up above the waist, exposing the buttocks and her stockings and sus-penders were visible. Her knickers were missing.

The *Daily Mirror* of August 8, 1987 gave its first three pages to Pauline Reade's funeral, held just after the sixteen-year-old's body had finally been found:

Patrick Kilbride, father of twelve-year-old victim John Kilbride sat in the back of the black limousine, shook her hand and said:

"I'm sorry you have had such a hard time, Joan."

Joan had been allowed out from her psychiatric ward on the understanding that three nurses did not leave her side throughout yesterday's ordeal.

Keith Bennett. Twelve.
From *Topping*:

> When (Myra) asked him how he had killed the boy, he said he had strangled him with a piece of string. He never volunteered any information, she said, never bragged about what he had done. Brady told her he had taken a photograph and that he had sexually assaulted the boy, but added "Why, does it matter?"
>
> I asked her about the photograph. She said there was blood on the boy's body, and because of that she had not looked at it closely. But she had seen that the boy was lying on his back with his trousers down; she could not tell whether he was alive or dead.

From *The Manchester Evening News*, April 12, 1988:

> Mrs. Johnson (Keith's mother), a kitchen porter at Christie Hospital, still has the wire-framed spectacles with pebble lenses that Keith used to wear. Now, all she longs for is to bury his body in Southern Cemetary near her home. She lives in a world of her own, hardly able to sleep and praying daily that the police will get new information to resume the dig.
>
> 'I live for the day I can visit his grave. Please God, don't let them give up the search for good,' she said.

John Kilbride. Twelve.
From *Topping*:

> I asked her if Brady talked about the killing. He told her he had taken out a small knife about six inches long with a serrated blade, and said it was so blunt that he had been unable to use it, so he had strangled the boy with a thin piece of string."

And

> Brady told her that he had pulled the boy's trousers and under-
> pants down and given him a slap on the bottom before cover-
> ing him over in the grave. She asked him what else he had done
> and he told her: "It doesn't matter."

From *Myra Hindley: Inside The Mind Of A Murderess* by Jean Ritchie,
Angus & Robertson, 1988, UK:

> Mrs. Kilbride's ordeal was not over. She, a quiet, shy woman,
> would be forced to give evidence twice against her son's killers:
> at their committal and again at their trial. Hers was some of the
> most touching evidence in the case.
>
> John's body was unidentifiable. But his clothes were intact
> enough for her to recognise. There was a grey check jacket,
> given to John's grandmother by a friend whose son had out-
> grown it, and carefully hemmed to make it shorter by Sheila
> Kilbride. She'd also sewn on new buttons, plastic ones in the
> shape of footballs. She had one left over, which she'd given to
> the police, to match with the ones on the jacket.

Edward Evans. Seventeen.
From *On Iniquity*, Pamela Hansford Johnson, Macmillan, 1967, UK:

> When he went in, he found, in Hindley's upstairs bedroom, the
> body of Edward Evans, aged seventeen, bundled up and pack-
> aged in a dark-coloured blanket. He had been battered to
> death by fourteen blows with an axe. To make assurance doubly
> sure, Brady had put an electric-light cable round his neck and
> pulled it tight.

And

> The Attorney General (to Brady): "What were your feel-
> ings when striking the boy with this axe? What were your
> emotions?"
> Answer: "I didn't have any. I can't remember what my
> emotions were. I was just hitting him."

It was David Smith, Myra Hindley's brother-in-law, who had called the police after seeing Brady kill Edward. His testimony at Ian and Myra's trial is considered by many to be highly suspect. But. From *The Trial Of Ian Brady And Myra Hindley:*

> 'We have seen how eventually the body was found with the knees up and head down, almost done up into a ball. Who worked out the method of tying him up?'
>
> Smith: 'Brady.'
>
> Did you notice anything about Edward Evans's clothing?
>
> Smith: 'Yes, sir. His jeans' zip was down.'
>
> 'Was it partly down or fully down?'
>
> Smith: 'It was all the way down.'

And there are higher levels of honesty.

Lesley Ann Downey. Ten.

In *For The Love Of Lesley,* mother Ann remembers having to identify Lesley in only two of the pornographic photographs of her daughter taken by Brady:

> Lesley was the shyest and most modest girl alive. PE at school was a nightmare to her. She hated to do handstands, in case her knickers showed. At bathtime the bathroom door was firmly locked; her innate modesty would not allow her to be seen undressing or in the bath by her brothers. They would tease her about her shyness, and especially about a photograph of her taken at the seaside when she was a toddler. It showed her standing at the edge of the sea with bucket and spade in hand, her dress tucked into her knickers. The innocence of that scene and the cruel attempt at pornographic humiliation I had just witnessed were in stark and terrible contrast. I tried to imagine what it must have been like for Lesley having to undress while two weird strangers stood by sneering and laughing. It is impossible to imagine. In twenty-five years I have never been able to feel what she must have felt. Maybe my inability is a protection from the madness that would surely follow if I were to have to undergo, even mentally, what she had to.

She suffers through having to listen to the tape recording of her daughter being — tortured. She suffers again to tell her readers:

> There was bewilderment and terror in her voice.
>
> 'What is your name?'
>
> This time the question was shouted. It was the bullying shout of an interrogator.
>
> 'Lesley Ann Weston.'
>
> The voice was small and desperate.
>
> 'Please don't make me get undressed again. Let me go home to mummy.'
>
> 'Shut your mouth! If you don't shut your mouth and stop crying I'll give you another good hiding.'
>
> The voice, low and venomous, was that of a woman. It was obscene.
>
> 'I won't tell nobody what you've done to me. Just let me go home to mummy. She'll be so angry with me for not going right home. Let me go. I won't tell anyone, honest.'

Ann gets the details wrong like a mother should. Lesley's mother could not be expected to check the transcripts for her already painful enough book. For her painful enough life. Plus, it was long ago and she was fed massive amounts of painkillers. If anything, her personalizing and paraphrasing only increases her veracity.

> Seventeen minutes of tape and I had heard only a minute or less. What unimaginable monstrosities remain hidden from me? They do not remain unimagined. Through the sleeping tablets and the tranquillisers the images insist on smearing themselves across my brain. Maybe the imagined horrors are worse than Lesley had to suffer . . . but what if they are not? What if Brady and Hindley's sick imaginations dreamed up more than I could to fuel their foul, deadly games?

It's only wrong around the edges and her disgust is sympathetically understood. Her pain must be incomprehensible. She convinces her audience by standing as straight as only can be expected, slightly teetering as is human, but determined to face the hideous truth as is extraordinary. One short minute sunk beneath emotional shale as hard as red raw cancer. For the rest of her life.

Ann confesses and evinces a serious drug problem. Or reliance — if you will. Addiction — if you must. In her painful book, she all but vomits onto herself:

> I thrashed around in the confines of the bed and prayed for the pills to take me away from such grotesque reality. When I slipped for brief periods into unconsciousness the photographs came alive. Lesley was abused, humiliated and degraded before my eyes and I screamed helplessly while it went on and on.

Ann West, interviewed by the BBC, sniffs and breaks down her slow slur into tears:

> I'm on eleven tablets a day. Sleeping tablets. And I've been on them for thirty odd years. And I can't go to sleep without them. She's always in my mind and in my thoughts.

And.

> I think everybody loved Lesley. She never gave cheek. I never had to smack her. She always done as she's told. She came in from school every night. She'd go up. Change out of her uniform. Make her bed. Come down. Do her homework. She's . . . well, every mother says she's perfect. But she was perfect.

In an article about claims compensation titled THE FINAL ANGUISH — MOORS FAMILIES TO LOSE OUT? from the January 29, 1988 *Manchester Metro* news, Ann West was interviewed:

> Sitting in her Whalley Range home below a portrait of Lesley Ann, she said 'No one has suffered more than I have. It's not the dying. I'd have sooner have seen her run under a bus. It was the torture, the screams on that tape. No one really knows what she went through. I still hear her now. She could have married and had children. *That's a whole generation lost.*'

Brady steers almost clear of the relation of criminal to victim:

Other authors most often do use such victim biographical material, but in many instances simply as humanistic or artistic padding. In this particular case it would only serve to distract from the prime purpose.

And

It is human nature to derive comfort from the misery of others, and it is the nature of those in the media to derive maximum profit from it. Some serial killers are obviously intent upon a more equal distribution of misery.

This, then, can't be a book on serial killing.

Kenneth V. Lanning defines the difference between child pornography (*'More simply stated, child pornography is photographs or films of children being sexually molested.'*) and child erotica in his chapter on collectors in *Child Pornography And Sex Rings* (edited by Ann Wolbert Burgess, D.C. Heath & Company, 1985, USA):

CHILD EROTICA, on the other hand, is a broader and more encompassing term. It can be defined as any material, relating to children, that is sexually arousing to a given individual. It is in a sense a subjective term, as almost anything potentially could be sexually arousing. However, some of the more common types of child erotica include photographs that are not sexually explicit, drawings, sketches, fantasy writings, diaries, and sexual aids.

And, again, in *Child Pornography: An Investigation,* lazy investigative journalist Tim Tate works a little harder:

Child erotica is not illegal — how could it be? It is only the association in the pedophile's mind that invests it with a sexual content.

This, then, is child pornography.